Researching Intimacy in Families

Palgrave Macmillan Studies in Family and Intimate Life

Titles include:

Harriet Becher
FAMILY PRACTICES IN SOUTH ASIAN MUSLIM FAMILIES
Parenting in a Multi-Faith Britain

Elisa Rose Birch, Anh T. Le and Paul W. Miller
HOUSEHOLD DIVISIONS OF LABOUR
Teamwork, Gender and Time

Jacqui Gabb
RESEARCHING INTIMACY IN FAMILIES

Peter Jackson (*editor*)
CHANGING FAMILIES, CHANGING FOOD

David Morgan
RETHINKING FAMILY PRACTICES

Eriikka Oinonen
FAMILIES IN CONVERGING EUROPE
A Comparison of Forms, Structures and Ideals

Róisín Ryan-Flood
LESBIAN MOTHERHOOD
Gender, Families and Sexual Citizenship

Palgrave Macmillan Studies in Family and Intimate Life
Series Standing Order ISBN 978–0–230–51748–6 hardback 978–0–230–24924–0
paperback (*outside North America only*)

You can receive future titles in this series as they are published by placing a standing order. Please contact your bookseller or, in case of difficulty, write to us at the address below with your name and address, the title of the series and the ISBN quoted above.

Customer Services Department, Macmillan Distribution Ltd, Houndmills, Basingstoke, Hampshire RG21 6XS, England

Researching Intimacy in Families

Jacqui Gabb
The Open University, UK

palgrave
macmillan

First published 2008
This paperback edition published 2010 by
PALGRAVE MACMILLAN

Palgrave Macmillan in the UK is an imprint of Macmillan Publishers Limited, registered in England, company number 785998, of Houndmills, Basingstoke, Hampshire RG21 6XS.

Palgrave Macmillan in the US is a division of St Martin's Press LLC, 175 Fifth Avenue, New York, NY 10010.

Palgrave Macmillan is the global academic imprint of the above companies and has companies and representatives throughout the world.

Palgrave® and Macmillan® are registered trademarks in the United States, the United Kingdom, Europe and other countries

ISBN 978–0–230–52722–5   hardback
ISBN 978–0–230–24809–0   paperback

This book is printed on paper suitable for recycling and made from fully managed and sustained forest sources. Logging, pulping and manufacturing processes are expected to conform to the environmental regulations of the country of origin.

A catalogue record for this book is available from the British Library.

Library of Congress Cataloging-in-Publication Data

Gabb, Jacqui, 1963–
    Researching intimacy in families / Jacqui Gabb.
        p. cm. (Palgrave Macmillan studies in family and intimate life)
    Includes bibliographical references and index.
    ISBN 978–0–230–52722–5 (alk. paper) ISBN 978–0–230–24809–0 paperback
    1. Intimacy (Psychology)   2. Family Psychological aspects.   I. Title.
    HQ728.G17 2008
    155.9'240942—dc22

                                                                        2008015929

10   9   8   7   6   5   4   3   2   1
19   18   17   16   15   14   13   12   11   10

Printed and bound in Great Britain by
CPI Antony Rowe, Chippenham and Eastbourne

To my family, one and all – especially Jocelyn and Liam, whose love and support I hold most dear; and to the memory of my mother, who will remain forever in my heart.

Contents

List of Figures

Acknowledgements

Thanks to the research fellows Anne Fairbank, Joan Heggie and Melissa Dearey who worked with me on the *Behind Closed Doors* project, and to the families who welcomed the researchers into their homes and gave us their account of family relationships. Thanks also to everyone in the advisory group whose guidance and support helped to shape the project, and to colleagues and friends who shared with me their time and creativity in discussions of ideas and draft chapters, notably Rachel Thomson, Jane Ribbens-McCarthy, Sasha Roseneil, Brid Featherstone and Stevi Jackson. Biggest thanks are due to Elizabeth Silva and Wendy Hollway whose belief in me and the merits of this project helped to realise this book. Thanks to the Open University for my research leave and to the many colleagues in the institution who, in so many different ways, supported this project.

Foreword

I have been somewhat taken aback with the reception of *Researching Intimacy in Families*. In many ways writing this book was for me a rite of passage. It is the culmination of empirical research and a longstanding personal interest in the fields of family and sexuality studies. The aims were ambitious, bringing together methodological, theoretical and empirical interdisciplinary inquiry. Feedback on the book however suggests that my aims were achieved and readers have said that they have found it both useful and thought-provoking. In 2009, at the annual conference of the British Sociological Association, I was delighted and honoured to receive the Philip Abrams Memorial prize for the best sole-authored first book in Sociology published in the UK. When Palgrave Macmillan said that they wanted to produce a second edition – including revisions – I thought this would provide an excellent opportunity to add new material and to advance my analysis utilising the post-writing period of reflection, taking full advantage of the power of hindsight.

One of my original objectives was to interrogate the conceptual frameworks that have advanced understandings of intimacy in families; as such this book could only ever hope to present a partial and time-limited account. New work being published moves forward the debates and as friends and colleagues have read this book they have pointed me in the direction of other work that extends and enriches my own understanding and knowledge base. Needless to say my desire to append and rework sections of this book was an ambition too far! New work may add another dimension but it does not change the overall scope of the field and/or my analysis of empirical data. In this second edition I have therefore made only a few notable and substantive additions which are included in this foreword. These additions are clustered together around two key themes: intimacy and class; personal lives and psycho-social approaches. I have selected these two areas in particular because they so effectively demonstrate the synergy of methodological and conceptual enterprise – something that lies at the heart of this book. In the first edition I did account for work and data in these areas however I do not feel that I did them justice.

Intimacy and class

In my overview of debates on the detraditionalisation of intimacy, particularly around the ideas of Giddens (1992), I discuss materialist feminist critiques which point to the absence of power relations in his work. It is argued that Giddens' theoretical narrative obscures the class, gendered and ethnic dimensions that shape everyday practices and family relationships. In analysis of empirical data I discuss the ways that understandings of 'good parenthood' are steeped in class assumptions. For example good intentions and parenting practice are often designed to sustain class positions, passing sets of moral values between generations. I did not however focus on the intersections of class and intimacy.

There has been sustained attention on social class in UK sociology including its affect on parental practices, family forms and children's wellbeing (Vincent and Ball 2006). Work has demonstrated how determining ideas of 'bad mothering' are hard to dislodge from prevailing understandings of working-class parenthood. Working-class mothers remain marginalised, disrespected and the scapegoats for many social problems associated with unruly and/or unhealthy childhood and youth (Gillies 2007). Recent work on lesbian and gay parenting has extended the research gaze to examine how class simultaneously reproduces and ruptures understandings and experiences of sexuality (Taylor 2009). These and other analyses usefully account for the ways that class positioning, educational advantage and cultural capital shape perceptions and experiences of parenthood but these ideas do not tend to be fully developed in theorising on intimacy.

Extending her earlier ideas on bodily formations of social class and gender Bev Skeggs (1997) has advanced a class critique of the individualisation thesis, analysis that engages with theorising on the detraditionalization of intimacy. Skeggs (2003) claims that the theoretical emphasis on self-agency can be traced back to Thatcherite rhetoric on the consumer market which developed in the UK in the 1980s and which devalued communal investment, bringing to the foreground individual enterprise and endeavour. She argues that authors who now seek to portray a normative model of individualism and individuality are ignoring its derivation and are fostering a very specific middle-class formation of privilege and lifestyle. Echoing the voices of other feminist researchers (Gillies et al. 2001; Taylor 2009) she reminds us that 'the resources and techniques necessary to self-formation and self telling are not equally available' (Skeggs 2003: 134). In contrast and taking issue with the association of individualisation and middle-class values, Sasha Roseneil argues that class is not a *determining* feature of individualised forms of living. In her study of non-heteronormative and personalised patterns of intimacy she found that these forms were open to anyone: 'attention to self was not the luxury of privilege—whatever the socio-economic position and background of the interviewee—and it was not an exercise in self-indulgence; rather, it was psychic wellbeing, or its lack, and, sometimes, psychic survival which compelled it' (Roseneil 2007: 91). This shift in emphasis away from material context onto the psycho-social dimensions of personal experience represents a definable trend in contemporary UK studies, something that I shall address in more detail later on in this foreword.

Returning us to materialisations of class, UK sociologist Les Back (2007) explores the ways that class is ingrained in certain embodied practices of intimacy. Back is not concerned with mapping identifiable classed forms of attachment to various bodily practices but with finding sociological means to capture the subtle and typically ignored ways that different people connect with one another. To this end he explores how tattoos express particular signs of allegiance and devotion, meanings that tend to fall beneath the academic radar (Back 2007: 71–96). Notwithstanding the 'tattoo renaissance' that has taken place over the past decade and which has broadened their appeal, Back argues that tattoos remain a source of class stigma. Middle-class commentators and press reports collapse together deviancy and 'chav culture' epitomised by the tattoo, especially those personalised designs which display an individual's attachment to someone/something other.

In Back's reflective and personally moving account he traces the meanings of tattoos to the people whose bodies they adorn. Working-class lives have been largely written off as expressionless, lacking in both sensitivity and commitment. Back claims tattoos materialise working-class emotions. From the football fan who wears his club emblem with pride to the father whose children's names are etched into his skin, beloved names and symbols are literally carved into their 'fleshy canvas'. Back claims these 'inscriptions of love' are particular to white working-class tattooing using registers of feeling which typically go unspoken. 'Love is given a name: it is incarnate. But this commitment is not made in elaborated speeches. It is performed rather than described. It is a kind of illocutionary love, a love that is expressed without painstaking announcement' (ibid.: 82). The point which Back wants to make is that, as researchers, we need to find ways of being attuned to these silent and silenced voices; to develop the sociological imagination so that we can hear these verbal and non-verbal 'alternative modalities of love'.

In *The Art of Listening* Back implores us to 'pay attention to the frag-ments, the voices and the stories that are otherwise passed over or ignored' (ibid.: 1). His task is therefore methodological as much as it is conceptual. He advocates a sociological inquiry that heeds the realms of embodied social life that operate outside of talk, using a broader spec-trum of senses to listen and hear, to see and notice; to take account of the practices of intimacy that are in operation. In this book I have tried to be attentive to these wide-ranging registers of feeling, for example the way one young man demonstrates his gratitude and love for his father by spending a bit more money on him at Christmas. In another fam-ily, the ways that a cup of tea symbolises an emotional gift and form of affective currency that does away with spoken words. In these and other instances I have explored diverse registers of love but I did not examine these through class practices. The work of Back adds another dimension to my understanding and analysis and extends the conceptualisations of intimacy that are explicated in earlier theoretical sections of this book.

Personal lives and psycho-social approaches

In Chapter 4 I focus attention on conceptualisations of intimacy espe-cially as these pertain to family relationships, to some extent however this has excluded work that interrogates relational living using differ-ent analytical lenses and which leave the concept of intimacy to one side in favour of other conceptual foci. For example recent work by UK sociologist Carol Smart (2007) suggests that we need to define a new con-ceptual field known as personal life rather than fall back on unhelpful tropes that privilege certain ways of relating and/or grand theorising that obscures lived experience. She argues that we should move away from the 'flat world' of family sociology to incorporate all kinds of emotional and relational dimensions that are meaningful in everyday life; a strat-egy that would enable us to better understand the 'yearning, desires and inner emotions' that make us who we are (ibid.: 3–4).

Smart's focus is on connectedness, what holds us together and what pushes us apart. Her argument is that current thinking on individualisa-tion epitomised in debates around the detraditionalisation of intimacy, 'reflects a contemporary cultural Zeitgeist about individual agency and choice' which begins from the starting point of the self, the individ-ual as an ongoing reflexive project (ibid.: 22). Smart aims to shift this starting point, suggesting that lived experiences are characterised by con-nection, relationship and memory. She contends that the term 'personal life' better captures these multidimensional webs of relationality. It is more than a 'conceptual holdall' it stands in contradistinction to ideas of the individual and/or disconnected individualism, taking us on a different intellectual trajectory. The term does not aim to dissolve different forms of relating into a 'formless sludge' but to acknowledge the breadth of relationships that criss-cross people's lifecourse, providing a 'conceptual orientation' and analytical 'toolbox' that enables us to make sense of relational living. As such she does not dismiss the usefulness of intimacy as an analytical concept but frames intimate practices through biographical, socio-cultural and temporal contexts of personal experience. Her aim is to refocus the analytical gaze more than to set up another form of theorising on intimacy and personhood.

The ideas presented by Smart reflect a current trend in some quarters of sociological inquiry, focusing on the *interiority* of family relationships through exploration of the factors that constitute and shape the emotional and relational dimensions of everyday living; factors which are, as Smart says, crucial to understandings of personal life. Taking these ideas one step further, a number of researchers are now engaged in psychoanalytically informed analysis, looking at people's individual psycho-biographies. Coming together under the conceptual umbrella of 'psycho-social research', this work is becoming methodologically and theoretically influential in the field of family studies and the term is now part of the UK Social Sciences vocabulary. Current interest in the psycho-social may in part stem from the prevailing cultural investment in psychology more generally and it is certainly not an approach that is equally embraced by all parties across the disciplinary boards, but notwithstanding reservations it does represent an interesting shift in the theoretical, conceptual and methodological imagination.

In the empirical research which underpins this book I used open narrative interviews which drew on methodological frameworks developed in psycho-social studies, notably the works of Wendy Hollway and Tony Jefferson (2000) and Tom Wengraf (2001). I have accounted for sociological and psychological debate around this method but I did not engage with discussion on psycho-social approaches more broadly. There were many reasons for this omission, including time and scope, but I acknowledge that my decision to walk away from this debate was also partly motivated by my sense that different 'sides' of the argument were becoming polarised at points along the 'psycho' or 'social' narrative and that a battle for theoretical legitimacy was defining critical conceptual debate. Since completing this book these arguments have intensified (Layton 2008) primarily around how we, *as researchers*, make sense of the 'psychic reality' presented to us, *by research participants*. The defining characteristic (and source of contention) of current psycho-social studies is the transposing of methodological and analytic tools that originate in clinical settings into empirical research (Thomson 2009a). How social research may benefit from a 'psycho-analytic sensibility' without mis-reading the interview encounter as a form of therapeutic consultation (Frosh and Baraitser 2008). This foreword is not the place to develop a thorough evaluation of psycho-social research, but focusing on the socio-logical dimensions of ongoing debate I do want to outline why I believe the approach is useful in advancing understanding on family life and intimate relationships.

It has been suggested that the idea of psycho-social studies is notably British; developing out of post-war work completed by the Tavistock Institute into its current burgeoning, diverse and pluralist forms (Walk-erdine 2008). Most research in this vein makes use of interviews that are guided to a lesser or greater degree by psychoanalytic methods. The core issues that characterise this work are a desire to question what consti-tutes truth, knowledge and subjectivity. There are two interconnected aspects of psycho-social research which I find particularly helpful and that I want to focus on here: these are the re-conceptualisation of the researcher as a constitutive factor in research and the enriched use of field notes which often explore issues of 'counter-transference' (Hollway and Jefferson 2000) and/or the impact of the researcher on the subject of study.

Psycho-social approaches are designed to examine intersections between the psychic and the social, locating these in the cultural con-text and biography of the individual (Roseneil 2006: 851). Perhaps not surprisingly given the personal–social intersections that characterise experiences of families, motherhood and personal relationships, there is a growing body of work which is developing a 'psycho-social-analytic' (Roseneil 2009: 412) to explore the patterning of contemporary rela-tional living (Phoenix and Hollway 2008; Thomson et al. 2008). Much of this work is both conceptually and methodologically innovative. For example in a psychoanalytic exploration of maternal subjectivity Lisa Baraitser uses personal anecdotes to illustrate, contradict, inform and dislodge theoretical investigations of maternity. She advances what she terms 'an approximation of anecdotal theory', aiming to remain *with* the mother rather than stepping outside to inhabit a separate analytical position (Baraitser 2009). Using isolated moments of personal experi-ence she interrogates the physical viscosity and emotional range that comprise motherhood. She does not lay claim to comprehend maternal experience per se but instead looks for 'scraps that may help to articulate, understand or describe maternal moments of undoing' (ibid.: 18). In this way she seeks to capture the fragments of being a mother, illustrating how maternal subjectivity disrupts notions of the unitary and bounded self, creating a 'set of untotalizable multiplicities that make up the situation of motherhood' (ibid.: 159). The shifting facets of motherhood are thus extrapolated through attention to the psychic–biographical–social dimensions of maternal experience.

Autobiographical writing has been a feature of feminist writing for many years and the inclusion of personal experience in maternal scholarship is certainly nothing new. Recall the power of Adrienne Rich's writing on *personal* experience and the *political* institution of motherhood (Rich 1986). Where psycho-social research extends understanding is that it accounts for the individual's emotional–social worlds through psychoanalytically informed inquiry that interrogate the *interiority* of 'maternal encounters' (Baraitser 2009) as these emerge through lived experience – while never losing sight of *how* these accounts are brought into being.

It is this second dimension that I now want to consider, exploring the ways that psycho-social methods can enhance understandings of the research encounter and the quality of data collected. The point here is that psycho-social approaches are 'methodological practice, not theory' (Clarke 2006: 1154); they analyse and explore the emotional lives of both the researcher and respondent, the interviewer and the interviewee. Advocating a psycho-social method that is informed by psychoanalytic sociology, Simon Clarke argues that psycho-social methodology builds on good ethnographic practice' (ibid.: 1166), in many ways deploying 'the art of listening' that Les Back previously referred to: listening with humility and with ethical care. In several sections of this book, I discuss in some detail the rich and multidimensional data that can be collected using psycho-social methods of interviewing (notably in Chapter 3: 51–5 and Chapter 6: 150–4). I also demonstrate the usefulness of good field notes and the ways these enrich understanding, but I did not wholly account for the analytical gains offered through a psycho-social-analytic approach.

In a recent qualitative longitudinal project on changing experiences of motherhood, Rachel Thomson and colleagues situate field notes within a psycho-social framework. Using 'a day in the life' observations and repeat interviews, they have begun to explore how a reflexive psycho-social approach captures something of the researcher–participant dynamic. These researchers aim for 'full immersion' in the research process. In one extract of her field notes Thomson describes a trip to the park and café that she shared with a mother and toddler. She talks of being 'drawn into a three way dynamic' as the child plays off the mother and researcher. She feels awkward and finds the encounter 'tricky', at one point opting to go to the toilet to give the mother some time on her own with the child so that the two of them can resolve the situation. In the field notes and subsequent analysis the researcher's expectations, as a mother, are not left outside the scene but are acknowledged as a factor in how she perceives the child's particular likes, dislikes and behaviour around food. She feels 'drawn into' the relationship, complicit in the world of mothers by being involved in the child–food issue in the public scenario of the park.

Field notes produced in psycho-social research can in some ways be seen to follow on from infant observation techniques that characterise some child development studies. Where they diverge is that they do not aim to produce an objective record, in fact to the contrary, researcher–participant interaction and the researcher's (psycho-social) biography are recognised as playing a crucial role in shaping understandings of family dynamics. Thomson's contention is that by observing practices, taking note of the researcher's 'emotional responses' and locating these in the context of personal experience, normative ideals and wider popular understandings, it is possible to see how all parties 'begin to act out' in research, taking on particular roles in the 'family narratives' that are being performed (Thomson et al. 2009b: 7–8). The 'research relationship' is dynamic as roles and interactions shift between the various participants, in this case researcher–mother, mother–child, researcher–child and mother–researcher–child. The claim being made is more than previous feminist assertions on the significance of researcher subjectivity, it suggests that we should examine *reflective data*, analysing the emotional responses of researchers that are provoked through research participation, as part of the overall dataset. Rich and personally revealing field notes are not separated from analysis and/or restricted to research context, researcher subjectivity is interrogated as 'a rich source of evidence' (ibid.: 9).

The inclusion of researchers' thoughts and emotions *as data* may shift the analytical lens and they certainly can add new insight but this strategy does also raise important ethical issues. It can render individual researchers vulnerable because to anonymise their role would make it difficult to afford personal credit and status where it is due. Interpretations are laid open and the fine line between judgement and description is presented on show, for the reader and participants to see. Ethics in family research are becoming evermore fraught, a situation that is exacerbated by psycho-social approaches and the intensification of regulatory procedures (Gabb, 2010). The degree of personal involvement that is being advocated takes the researcher along an individually revealing and ethically precarious path. But in writing up findings we inevitably invest and divest much of ourselves, maybe psycho-social methods simply take us one further step away from scientific-objectivist traditions. Research on family lives and intimate relationships can surely be only enriched by this new dimension.

On reflection I am aware that the recent work which I find most engaging and that I have included in this foreword brings into play the personal life of the author/research in the development of analysis. It is therefore interesting, in hindsight, to note that I largely write myself out of this book. In contrast in previous work on lesbian parent families I have tended to foreground my insider status and at times to include personal experience. Both Back (2007) and Smart (2007) talk about the need to enliven sociological writing, to move beyond dry descriptions that erase the dynamic of lived lives. In similar ways, psycho-social approaches aim to situate the researcher within the analytical equation. It is probably true to say that methodology text books have tended to be at the 'drier' end of the sociological imagination, providing detailed information on the methods and analytical processes involved in research inquiry. As Back so eloquently puts it: 'The lacklustre prose of methodological textbooks often turns the life in the research encounter into a corpse fit only for autopsy' (Back 2007: 163). Back's intention and what I have similarly aimed to achieve in this book, is not to simply breathe life back into the methodological corpse but to retain the vitality of lived lives; to find ways of researching and writing about relational experience that capture the richness and multidimensionality of family living (Gabb 2009). I may not have written myself onto the pages of this book, but I hope that I have enlivened research methods and captured the dynamic of researching family relationships and people's everyday practices of intimacy.

References

Back, L. (2007) *The Art of Listening*. Oxford, New York: Berg.

Baraitser, L. (2009) *Maternal Encounters. The Ethics of Interruption*. Sussex: Routledge.

Clarke, S. (2006) 'Theory and Practice: Psychoanalytic Sociology as Psycho-Social Studies', *Sociology*, 40(6): 1153–69.

Frosh, S. and Baraitser, L. (2008) 'Psychoanalysis and Psychosocial studies', *Psychoanalysis, Culture and Society*, 13(4): 346–65.

Gabb, J. (2010) 'Home Truths: Ethical Issues in Family Research', *Qualitative Research*, 10(4).

Gabb, J. (2009) 'Researching Family Relationships: A Qualitative Mixed Methods Approach', *Methodological Innovations Online*, 4(2): http://www.methodological innovations.org/.

Gillies, V. (2007) *Marginalised Mothers: Exploring Working-Class Experiences of Parenting*. London, New York: Routledge.

Gillies, V. et al. (2001) *'Pulling Together, Pulling Apart': The Family Lives of Young People*. York: Family Policy Studies Centre, Joseph Rowntree Foundation.

Hollway, W. and Jefferson T. (2000) *Doing Qualitative Research Differently: Free Association, Narrative and Interview Methods*. London: Sage Publications.

Layton, L. (2008) 'Editor's Introduction', *Psychoanalysis, Culture and Society*, 13(4): 339–40.

Phoenix, A. and Hollway, W. (2008) *Becoming a Mother*. Modern Motherhood Conference, Family & Parenting Institute.

Rich, A. (1986) *Of Woman Born: Motherhood as Experience and Institution*. London: Virago Press.

Roseneil, S. (2006) 'The Ambivalences of Angel's "Arrangement": A Psychosocial Lens on the Contemporary Condition of Personal Life', *The Sociological Review*, 54(4): 847–69.

Roseneil, S. (2007) 'Queer Individualization: The Transformation of Personal Life in the Early 21st Century', *Nora, Nordic Journal of Women's Studies*, 15(2): 84–99.

Roseneil, S. (2009) 'Haunting in an Age of Individualization', *European Societies*, 11(3): 411–30.

Skeggs, B. (1997) *Formations of Class and Gender*. London: Sage.

Skeggs, B. (2003) *Class, Self, Culture*. London: Routledge.

Smart, C. (2007) *Personal Life*. London: Polity.

Thomson, R. (2009a) 'Creating Family Case Histories: Subjects, Selves and Family Dynamics', working paper: unpublished.

Thomson, R. et al. (2009b) 'Acting Up and Acting Out: Encountering Children in a Longitudinal Study of Mothering', seminar paper, European Sociological Association: Lisbon.

Thomson, R. et al. (2008) *The Making of Modern Motherhood. Memories, Representations, Practices*. Swindon, ESRC.

Taylor, Y. (2009) *Lesbian and Gay Parenting. Securing Social and Educational Capital*. Basingstoke: Palgrave Macmillan.

Walkerdine, V. (2008) 'Contextualizing Debates about Psychosocial Studies', *Psychoanalysis, Culture and Society*, 13(4): 341–5.

Wengraf, T. (2001) *Qualitative Research Interviewing: Biographic, Narrative and Semi-structured Method*. London: Sage Publications.

Vincent, C. and Ball S. J. (2006) *Childcare Choice and Class Practices*. London, New York: Routledge.

1
Introduction

Researching Intimacy in Families is an incisive engagement with the subject of intimacy and kin relationships and the methods used to research family life and childhood. Families have been the focus of sociologically informed research for some considerable time. Recently, the field of inquiry has broadened to include our intimate relationships with those within and without our familial circle. This draws attention to the processes by which families are made and remade through everyday family practices and intimate interactions. In this book I take stock of contemporary debate and trace the academic background of family studies and childhood research. I examine the methodological frameworks and conceptual approaches that characterise the study of relationships and everyday life. Through this analytical approach I aim to bridge the gap between methodology handbooks (which provide practical guidance) and monographs (which typically advocate a single conceptual model). As such, this book is both a useful resource for researchers working in the fields of families and relationships and a platform from which to develop new directions and/or methods of data collection in studies of relational life.

I examine the contribution of different approaches used in family and childhood studies, introducing the qualitative methods and innovatory techniques that are being developed. Through original data I bring to life debate on methods by situating methodology as a dynamic process, showing how different methods shape the findings of empirical research. Alongside this, I focus attention on the experiences of everyday relational life and interrogate the sociology of intimacy in contemporary Western society.

This is a timely review of the subject because since the landmark publications of Anthony Giddens' *The Transformation of* Intimacy (1992) and Lynn Jamieson's *Intimacy* (1998), intimacy has been a hot topic in the social sciences. Intimacy is about our everyday relationships and affective interactions, but the term has been asked to do a lot more in recent years. It now denotes an emergent intellectual framework around the detraditionalisation of interpersonal exchanges and kin formation. In this book I aim to provide an even-handed critical review of sociological research literature on intimacy, and, in particular, consider how this work has shaped family studies. I explore where and in what ways dominant conceptual frameworks are useful in understanding everyday experiences of intimacy and how prevailing discourses on risk have influenced non-abusive family practices. To this end, I refer to both the meta-theorisation of intimacy and (predominantly small-scale) qualitative research of interpersonal relationships, characterising key interventions and themes in sociological debate. Through analysis of empirical data I begin to tease out the scope and/or limitations of key conceptual paradigms to open up debate for further inquiry.

Structure and outline

This book is structured so that it can be used in several ways. Some chapters will be particularly useful for readers embarking on research as they provide a critical review of current work and/or the methods and approaches typically used. In other chapters I problematise the subject of intimacy and interpersonal family relationships in greater depth. Read as a whole, the book demonstrates the intersections between methods and conceptual frameworks and the utility of a mixed-methods approach in the analysis of personal lives. In my explication of the topics I cite many sources and as such the book is reference-heavy. This is so it can be used as a research resource, not just introducing qualitative approaches and studies of intimacy, but also providing a platform from which the reader may move on to more focused work, aligned with their own research.

In chapter 1 I foreground the ideas that run throughout this book and the original research through which I subsequently interrogate these ideas and arguments. In chapter 2 I contextualise the academic fields of families and childhood studies, including the ethical issues that often arise in sensitive topic research. In chapter 3 I extend this introduction to research and focus on key qualitative methodological approaches that have informed these fields. I discuss the different techniques typically used in research of childhood and family life and introduce innovative participatory approaches, including the move towards mixed-methods. In chapter 4 I review conceptualisations of intimacy and sexuality in family relationships and examine how sociological research has studied the interiority of everyday family experience. I map out the emergence of intimacy as an area of academic interest and, in particular, how this work has shaped family studies.

Chapters 5–7 draw on original empirical data to examine research on intimacy and family relationships. In chapter 5 I open out key theoretical debates on intimacy by asking questions of the conceptual frameworks. I explore how and in what ways theoretical models and empirical research speak to one another. The ideas that emerge illustrate and extend thinking about intimacy. I examine the materiality of parental roles and the parent–child relationship through critical engagement with the democratisation thesis, exploring the processes of intimacy in everyday family experience and the ways through which public–private discourses intersect around the management of sexuality boundaries and affective behaviour in families.

In chapter 6 I return to methodological debates around researching families, children and private lives. I explore the ways that sociological understandings of families are produced through the dynamic process of fieldwork and analysis and how experiences of family intimacy are rendered meaningful through different research strategies. First, I outline participatory approaches – notably, diaries and visual methods – and observational techniques which situate family experiences in their everyday context. I then interrogate psychosocial interview methods and the usefulness of this approach in researching relational life. Finally, I demonstrate the potential of third-party vignettes, photo interviews and focus group research in generating data on a social level. In the concluding chapter I review the preceding chapters and point to areas for future research. I pull together some of the key dimensions previously highlighted through case study analysis of mixed-methods data from one family. This demonstrates how multidimensional data capture the dynamic processes of family living and relationality.

Behind Closed Doors: the project and empirical data

The data that inform and underpin this book come from an Economic and Social Research Council (ESRC)-funded methodological pilot project: *Behind Closed Doors: Researching Intimacy and Sexuality in Families* (RES 000 220854). Most family studies scholarship focuses on experiences and understandings of family. In this project I honed in on the processes of everyday relationships – our relational practices, or what Lynn Jamieson terms our 'practices of intimacy'. In some ways writing a book around small-scale pilot data could be seen as academically pre-sumptive because of the tentativeness of the findings. If this book made substantive claims from the data I would probably agree. However, this has never been my intention. I use the empirical data and fieldwork experience from the pilot study to *illustrate* key points – to materialise theoretical and methodological analysis rather than to advance a par-ticular hypothesis or framework. I outline the research process because I believe this information may be useful to researchers starting in the fields of family and childhood studies, and/or research of intimacy and personal relationships. This information also contextualises the empiri-cal data through which I develop my analysis. To these ends, my candid account of the research process serves a purpose.

First and foremost, *Behind Closed Doors* was a methodological pilot project that aimed to interrogate the potential of different methods of researching intimacy and emotion in families. The project also aimed to problematise the concept of 'intimacy' and begin to develop understandings of how family members demonstrate love and affection non-abusively across generations in order to examine sense-making prac-tices of intimacy in families. In doing so it explored the boundaries that are set up around different kinds of feelings and how parents talk about managing these differences. It considered the ways that biography, cul-tural debates, social policy and legislation shape ideas of morality and propriety in families and how these affect the structuring of 'family intimacy'.

Research sample

Empirical data were collected from parents and children living in the North of England. In total 24 participants took part; 14 parents (nine mothers, five fathers) and ten children. Diversity among such a small sample is inevitably limited, but nevertheless the project achieved its aim of including different kinds of family form. This was important because I wanted to interrogate normative understandings of intimacy and sexuality and this would have been jeopardised had data derived from predominantly white, middle-class, two-parent households. Dif-ferences among families included: single-mother/father and dual-parent households, sexuality, disability, socio-economic background, age and generation, and religious belief (including Catholic, Church of England, Mormon, Buddhist and Hindu). Notwithstanding the small sample size the amount and richness of the data collected were significant, with participants completing a combination of different interdisciplinary methods, resulting in 102 units of data. In this book, I supplement these data with illustrations from my previous research on lesbian parent families (Gabb 2002). This material adds a further dimension to my exploration of different methods and experiences of sexuality.

All participants have been given pseudonyms to ensure confidentiality as far as possible. Where certain words or phrases might have disclosed their identity I have substituted more generic terms that convey the meaning while preserving anonymity. The age/maturity of children is a constitutive factor in shaping and understanding experiences of sexuality and intimacy in families and for this reason I have included the age of children with their pseudonym when citing from their data. Each family has been assigned a number (F1 to F10) so that it is easy to trace emergent narratives and methodological patterns within and across families and for the reader to pull together individual and family accounts across the chapters if they wish to do so.

The inclusion and frequency of participants' accounts have not been determined by their adeptness at self-expression, but by how thought-provoking and useful such accounts are in illustrating, developing and/or initiating points of interest. Thus quotation is used selectively both to substantiate conceptual arguments and, in some cases, challenge theoretical assumptions. When interviews are quoted, they are usually edited for the sake of clarity and brevity. I have used ellipses to denote this. In analysis of mixed-methods material, particularly in chapter 7, I have tended to summarise data rather than quote verbatim. This is in part due to good ethical practice, aiming to minimise the risk of identification, but it is also a pragmatic solution to the volume of mixed-methods data available. This can mean that there is a pull towards the narrativisation of data across the individual and/or family dataset. I try to resist the temptation to tie up loose ends in this way, but one of the strengths of a mixed-methods approach is that it provides multidimensional data. As such, refusing to pull together the picture that is produced from composite data defeats the object of using this approach.

Because *Behind Closed Doors* was a pilot project, funded for an initial period of 12 months, the target sample size was inevitably small and originally set at eight families. In the end ten families took part; this was necessary to increase diversity and, ironically, was a pragmatic response to the challenge of recruiting families to 'sensitive topic' research in such a short time. The original research design required all methods to be completed by all family members. This was both prohibitive in terms of recruitment and also disempowered parents and children in the research process. Therefore, quite early on in the project, I decided that it would be apposite to invite individuals rather than families to participate.

By being less prescriptive it was possible to include parents who were keen to take part in the research but whose partners and/or children were not. It accommodated individual preference about which methods appealed to them, with participants electing to opt in and out of different methods. This afforded them control over the research process. In six families all co-resident members of the family took part, in the other four there was participation from one or more family members. Children of all ages were invited to take part and the youngest participant was five years old. Observations included young children (aged two and upwards) but this cannot be seen as participation in the same sense.

Recruitment strategies

Families were contacted through a variety of means. In the first instance a leaflet was produced to publicise the project and accord legitimacy to research that was initially perceived by some people to be 'suspect' or an invasion of their privacy. The leaflet was distributed widely. It provided an overview of the research topic and the website address so that the credentials of the project and researchers could be confirmed. A small feature publicising the project was published in two regional newspapers with quite distinct catchments. A feature was also placed in a women's e-newsletter with a large national readership, primarily aimed at a lesbian audience. Four mothers contacted the project in response to this 'cold calling' publicity, although two subsequently withdrew. The remaining eight families were recruited via face-to-face contact.

The project researchers attended many local community groups, including different faith communities, parent-and-toddler groups, pre-school nurseries and women's groups. These meetings generated a lot of interest and in most instances one or more of the group said that they would like to participate in the project. Leaflets were handed out so that those who wanted to could take them home and talk through the ideas with family members. For families without ready access to the internet, the information on the website was made available in hard copy format. Liaison with parenting groups such as SureStart was a particularly productive method of recruitment. These groups were already talking through many of the issues that were to be addressed in the research so those involved had established interests in developing their understanding of parent–child relationships and how families operate. Working with SureStart also enabled the project to reach minority ethnic community groups and extend the diversity of the sample.

Notwithstanding the varying degrees of success of all these recruitment methods, the single factor that cannot be underestimated in any outreach work is the significance of researchers' local and/or 'insider' knowledge. It takes time to establish trust and in time-limited research it is imperative to capitalise on all available resources. In the end, the use of prior contacts, snowballing out from previously established community, research and extended-friendship networks, remained the most effective means to recruit participants.

Whatever recruitment strategies prove to be successful, participant attrition invariably occurs during fieldwork and *Behind Closed Doors* was no exception. The reasons for withdrawing varied, but several explanations recurred: objections from partner and/or children, unforeseen changes in personal circumstances, limitations of time. Fitting mixed-methods research into busy work and family schedules meant that taking part in the project was not easy. Most fieldwork was carried out in the evenings, at weekends or during school holidays. The limited time frame of the project meant that the researchers had to walk a fine line between 'encouraging' participants to complete certain tasks while not hounding them. The commitment needed was considerable. To collect the data from the different methods meant on average four to five visits per family. Timescales for this contact varied from one family to the next, but research was most productive when it spanned several months.

Not surprisingly, there was a direct correlation between the time the researchers spent with families and the quality of data that were produced. Spending time with families enabled the researcher to establish mutual trust and in some cases to develop friendships. Where children were involved this investment of time was particularly important. It was clear that the more children got used to a researcher being around the more inclined they were to complete different methods and to talk more openly about their family relationships. In some cases their participation was motivated by their natural curiosity about 'this woman' who kept turning up at their home and in others it was because they wanted to use the research context to have their say.

Research timetable

In the following section I outline the order and framing of the methods used in *Behind Closed Doors*. In this account of the research process I describe a schedule where all methods are being completed. Detailed information on the application and utility of particular methods can be found in chapter 3. After group meetings or in response to individual enquiries, the researcher would contact interested families either by telephone or by letter. A leaflet, an information sheet and a copy of the website text would then be posted to ensure that participants were fully cognisant of all aspects of the project and research process. An appointment was made for the researcher to visit parents and children in their home, at a time that was convenient to them. The first meeting provided an opportunity for the researcher and the family to get to know each other and to clarify what participation would involve. Individuals were asked to sign a consent form. This contained detailed information about the project and ethical protocols and asked participants to indicate which methods they wished to complete. Parents were also asked to complete a simple questionnaire providing background demographic information.

Towards the end of the first meeting, to build research momentum and capitalise on participants' initial enthusiasm, the research diary was explained and one book per participant was provided for this purpose. Similarly, the practicalities of the emotion map method were explained, likening the method to a 'feelings sticker chart'. A floor plan of the home was drawn up as one or more participant walked the researcher around the home. Children were often extremely keen to lead this 'guided tour' and this afforded a good opportunity for the researcher to start getting to know a bit more about them and their interests. The floor plan was graphically reproduced by the researcher and returned by post or in person, along with a selection of coloured stickers, a few days later. A draft schedule was drawn up for observation sessions. It was expected that diaries and emotion maps would be completed over a period of seven to ten days. An appointment was made to collect these data and this meeting provided another opportunity for the researcher to build up the research relationship.

After these initial meetings the researcher wrote up field notes, including descriptions of the family, to produce a 'pen portrait'. Once diary and emotion maps data had been returned, first stage analysis was completed and the researcher shaped the semi-structured interview around this information. This first round of interviews typically took place on the third encounter. The recursive format enabled the researcher to talk with the participants about the patterning of interactions in the family, situated around recent events and the discursive framing of these emotion exchanges. Participants were asked to reflect on their completion of the participatory methods and to elaborate on the material they had produced. This interview aimed to settle participants into the research topic and get them thinking about their experiences and understandings of intimacy in family life. The first observation session was often completed after one or more of the participants' semi-structured interviews. Further observations took place on consecutive occasions, arranged around the timing and location of the activity. At the end of the first round of inter-views, an appointment was made with parents for their biographical narrative interviews.

This second round of interviews was typically more intense and par-ticipation tended to be emotionally demanding. At the start of the biographical narrative interview participants were asked to recall a signif-icant family event and describe what had happened and what it meant to them. These interviews took on average two to three hours. The accounts spanned their lifecourse and were often deeply 'private', sometimes rais-ing difficult and/or painful memories. For this reason no further methods were scheduled for this day, although on several occasions the researcher remained with the family and incidental family activities were observed at their request. An appointment was made for the third and typically final round of interviews in which participants were asked to respond to various scenarios, presented in a series of vignettes and photographs. The aim of having these methods at the end of the research process was to take individuals away from their own experience and decrease their personal and/or emotional investment in the research. To similar ends, focus groups were completed among families, friends and sibling groups, either directly or soon after the final meeting. These aimed to round off the research project.

Troubling terminology

In any empirical study one should expect the unexpected. In this case a logistical issue which arose very early on was the project name. The study had been originally funded as *Behind Closed Doors: Researching Intimacy and Sexuality in Families*. The title aimed to describe the analytical scope of the research and to highlight the intersections between public–private spheres. 'Behind closed doors' alluded to the ways that experiences of private family life are mediated through particular sets of rules and normative understandings of appropriate affective behaviour and 'good parenting'. As such the closed doors remain potentially ever open to the flow of advice and cultural imperatives that affect parent–child rela-tionships and the contraflow of everyday family practices which shape understandings of family in the social world. What I had *not* consid-ered were the negative connotations of the phrase 'behind closed doors', which is associated with the concealment of parent–child interactions and domestic abuse. While the project did not aim to idealise family relationships, it was not designed to examine harmful and/or abusive practices.

Issues and concerns with the research title were vividly brought to light once construction of the project website began. 'Behind closed doors' was a previously used domain name of websites which distribute pornography. It was imperative to disassociate the project from any link to this area because not only did it misrepresent the research remit, but there was also the possibility that parents or children might do an online search and stumble across a pornography site rather than information on the project. This would not be a positive introduction to the research and certainly demonstrated neither its integrity nor its focus. Hence the project was renamed *Researching Families*. The need to change the project name served to refocus my attention to the sensitivities of the topic. It reminded me that representation of the project would require extremely delicate handling if misinterpretations were to be avoided – a consideration that I had become desensitised to because of my familiarity with and investment in the research.

From the outset it was clear that a balancing act had to be achieved between wanting to give accurate information about the study (an ethical necessity) and not wanting to scare people off (pragmatically, I needed families to want to take part). This meant that the terms intimacy and sexuality needed to be carefully used in descriptions of the project not to obscure what was being studied but to frame it in ways that did not raise anxieties. Descriptions in both the leaflet and website focused on relationships, affection and the exchange of emotions. I used terms that did not have sexual connotations but which accurately captured the areas of everyday affective experience that were of interest to the project.

At times in the empirical research when parents and children talked about their everyday relational experiences there was slippage between how the terms intimacy and sexuality were understood and experienced and at these points their meanings became blurred. At other times they were clearly differentiated as *the* marker between different forms of intimate experience, with sexuality being associated with 'the sexual' and intimacy with more diverse forms of affective experience. Through the research process I have endeavoured to be clear in my academic purpose and to utilise them as separate but nevertheless linked terms. There are evident parallels here with materialist feminist scholarship on the interrelationship of gender and sexuality, which suggests that while gender and sexuality may be separated in order to facilitate academic clarity, experientially they coexist: 'Sexual learning is part of gender learning, for we learn to be sexual as women or as men' (Jackson 1982: 83). Gender and sexuality are materially embedded in one another at the level of everyday experience; so too intimacy and sexuality.

At this point it may be useful to unpack some other, particularly tricky terms in order to clarify their meaning and my interpretation of them. Sexuality as a term is problematic insofar as it is frequently expected to perform a generic purpose, standing as shorthand for sexual identity, sexual desire and/or the practice of myriad forms of sex acts. While 'the sexual' may be to a lesser or greater extent part of everyday family life, this is not the focus of this study and I do not examine sex or sexual practice. I use the term sexuality in its broadest context to refer to the way we experience a sense of our sexual selves and/or to signify interactions which invoke 'the sexual'. Intimacy is thoroughly interrogated in later chapters and to summarise it here would do an injustice to the differences in conceptual and theoretical frameworks that are detailed in chapter 4 and problematised through empirical data in chapter 5. However, at a general descriptive level I draw on Lynn Jamieson's characterisation, which positions intimacy as practices of 'close association, familiarity and privileged knowledge' which involve 'strong positive emotional attachments'; 'a very particular form of "closeness" ... associated with high levels of trust' (Jamieson 2005: 189). Notwithstanding contestations about the different shapes, forms and structures which intimacy may take, this description captures the way the term is generally deployed in academic studies and reflects wider social understandings.

The term 'family intimacy' is used both to draw attention to the different dimensions of intimate experience within the context of this social–affective unit and to delimit the breadth of meanings pulled together under the rubric of intimacy – in this context, to separate intimacy from the inference of sex. I refer to the individuals who took part in the study as participants to draw attention to the process of co-construction through which lives and experiences are rendered public via the research process. I take families to be relational units that are constituted through various processes – social and personal – and which gain meaning through everyday practices of care, intimacy and emotional connection. *Researching Intimacy in Families* is concerned with the ways that these forms of relationality are experienced and understood and how they are rendered meaningful through sociological inquiry.

2
Researching Families and Childhood

In this chapter I set the scene by outlining the emergent fields of family studies and childhood research. I explore how these two interlinked areas have developed and identify some of the key constitutive issues which shape the respective fields. In just one chapter it is not possible to undertake an exhaustive review of all significant sociologically informed family and childhood studies research, let alone incorporate other perspectives, for example those that have shaped psychological understandings of parent–child relationships (see Hollway 2006) and cross-cultural kinship formations (see Carsten 2004). Thus my aim is more modest: to outline significant sociological approaches and interventions in family and childhood research inquiry. In the context of this book, this is important for two reasons. First, identifying who or what constitutes family shapes the scope for subsequent analysis of the patterning of family intimacy and the generational dynamic of parent–child relationships. Second, how families and childhood are characterised has affected the approaches that researchers adopt. For example, framed as a functional reproductive unit, the research lens tends not to look beyond the boundaries of 'the family'. If families are envisaged as relationships materialised through sets of practices rather than as a consequence of fixed social categories (mother, father, sibling, etc.), then research is likely to include analysis of the everyday.

I examine the ways that broadening understandings of family has initiated shifts in the research imagination, with extended and extending family networks requiring the development of more inclusive research designs. Similarly, shifts in the contemporary cultural agenda around children and childhood have destabilised traditional research models. In the UK, the introduction of the Children Act 1992 reflected and extended the framing of young people in childhood studies. Childhood is now understood through children's experiences rather than as a series of developmental phases interpreted by adults. This shift in perception has required the development of age-appropriate methods with which to capture these perspectives. The engagement of children as research participants has inevitably enlivened ethical debates around the collection and analysis of empirical data.

My intention in this chapter is not to provide a chronological mapping of developments in family and childhood studies, but to highlight how these changes have affected the scope and framing of research. I draw together some of the key issues in this area under the themes of 'sensitive topic research' and 'research ethics'. In particular, I consider how researchers manage sensitivities and ethical concerns which can arise in research of everyday family relationships and children's lives, and how disclosure and confidentiality are being handled and the debates around issues of informed consent and ethical research conduct. Overall, I acknowledge and build on the significant insights that have been provided by scholars working in the field. However, this overview is necessarily painted in broad brushstrokes and cannot hope to detail the nuances of individuals' research. As such it is intended as a useful starting point for those embarking in the area of family and childhood studies.

Family studies

Empirical research on families and family relationships did not become established until the first half of the twentieth century (Miller 1986). Early sociological studies tended to draw on functionalist logic, for example: What does the family 'need'? What 'need' does the family fulfil in society? (see Gittins 1993 for an overview). This functionalist model developed from the Enlightenment, a period when the family unit was represented as the sign of a 'natural' kinship bond, the (reproductive) outcome of the human species that was grounded in genetic and patrilineal inheritance. Scientific knowledge of biological function was used to consolidate *the* natural order, ascribing gender to familial roles and responsibilities. Early work, produced between the 1950s through to the end of the 1970s, established a sociology of 'the family' wherein family stood as a synonym for personal relationships. Some early studies did adopt a *network approach* which examined the patterning of relationships and roles in families (Bott 1971) and this work was pivotal in developing the field of community studies. But, over the course of time, in the UK it is the American sociologist Talcott Parsons who has become identified as the *paterfamilias* of family analysis.

Through Parsons' work (Parsons and Bales 1955; Parsons 1959) 'the family' was positioned as a bounded unit of intimates, characterised by mother–father and parent–child relations. Extended kin and friendships were seen as outside this family unit, primarily gaining emotional significance only when one or more of the family members were unavailable. In this framework friendships were included at only one stage of the life-course – during transition from childhood to young adulthood. It was assumed that these friendship associations would diminish in significance once an adult partner (mate) was secured and men and women, in heterosexual couples, formed families of their own (see Jamieson 2005). Parsons proposed that male and female roles were a consequence of biological compatibility. Men were 'designed' to provide sustenance, working away from the home as necessary, and women to stay at home to fulfil their biological role as the carer of children (Parsons and Bales 1955: 23). In this way Parsons not only fixed familial relations, he also constructed a theory of gender that was dependent on, and even determined by, the reproductive narrative. Women's role was not just to produce and subsequently nurture children; it was also to be a domestic support for the male worker – to *be* a 'wife'.

Not surprisingly, feminist commentators have taken great issue with this argument. For example, feminist work has demonstrated how institutionalised heterosexuality shores up gendered inequalities in familial relations (Jackson 1997) by shrouding the 'heterosexual imaginary' in naturalising discourses which consolidate the hegemonic ordering of social relations (Ingraham 1996). Women's secondary role in the labour force remains largely structured through their reproductive capacity. Their time and energy are a household resource that is available to support others (Seymour 1992). Many households may now depend on two incomes, but under the governance of familial ideology such as 'the family wage', women's earnings remain substantially lower than their male counterparts. In symbolic terms and in popular discourses their work is seen as less prestigious (Walby 1997). To counter claims that ascribe a natural order to the structuring of institutions such as 'the family', feminist analyses have highlighted how this social unit artificially perpetuates the oppression of women (Barrett and McIntosh 1982; Gittins 1993) and the powerlessness of children (Delphy and Leonard 1992). Feminist cross-cultural analyses of motherhood (Kitzinger 1978; Collins 1994) and 'the family' (Edholm 1982) have demonstrated differences among women engaged in a similar cognate activities. These studies evidence the unnaturalness or cultural specificity of maternal–familial practices. That is to say, they call into question the presumption that families are typically (and best) structured around 'blood lines' and in so doing disrupt the alignment of 'birth motherhood' with the role of mothering.

In a similar vein, historical feminist research has demonstrated how the ideal 'nuclear family' has never been a concrete reality for many people. Census records and research data illustrate that there has been, and by implication always will be, a *variety* of family forms. The family as a monolithic, biologically constituted institution is not an accurate representation of the diversity of family forms which exist in real life: 'There is no such thing as *the* family – only families' (Gittins 1993: 8). This focuses attention on the coexistence of a normative ideal family which resides in the cultural imaginary counterpoised with the lived realities of everyday familial experience. The work of John Gillis (1996) is particularly illuminating here in unpacking the historical coexistence of the family we live *by* (the ideal) and the families we live *with* – our relational connections with others.

Paradoxically, though families are experienced very differently, successive UK governments have tended to posit a standard model by assuming most families operate in particular ways (Finch 1997). Parenting is not seen as an individual and/or intimate relationship between parent and child but as 'an occupation' which requires 'knowledge and skills' (Gillies 2005: 77). This framing positions people in fixed categories which enable social groups to be identified as the passive beneficiaries of different policies (Williams 2004). Research in family studies has in some ways mirrored this categorisation, albeit that this work is often quite separate from the instrumentality of a policy-driven agenda. For example, analyses of families have examined the effect of class (Gillies 2006; Vincent and Ball 2006), ethnicity (Grant 1997; Beishon et al. 1998), social and cultural hybridity (Tizard and Phoenix 2003), sexuality (Weston 1997; Weeks et al. 2001), single parenthood (Silva 1996), divorce and separation (Dunn and Deater-Deckard 2001; Smart et al. 2001), the patterning of fatherhood (Smart 2004a; Doucet 2006) and step-parenting after divorce (Ferri and Smith 1998; McCarthy et al. 2003). However, rather than reifying families through a taxonomy of neatly defined family 'types', this work aims to demonstrate the particularities of experience – how context and circumstances affect family forms and practices.

In contemporary research 'the family' is now seen in different ways, as reflecting changing patterns of intimacy (Jamieson 1998; Silva and Smart 1999). This work suggests that our biological lineage no longer determines our intimate relations with others. Who we consider family to be and how we construct our kinship networks is now qualitatively oriented around self-fulfilment (Beck and Beck-Gersheim 1995). Research in this vein draws on claims around the individualisation of contemporary relationships and what has been termed 'transformations of intimacy' (Giddens 1992), ideas I unpack at length in chapter 4. In this model it is claimed that relationships are structured around 'elective ties', constituting 'the post-familial family' (Beck-Gernsheim 1999: 70). Once separated from a functional imperative, individuals are free to be creative in how they constitute kin networks (Stacey 2004); to generate their own 'relationship rules' (Holland et al. 2003). This sense of liberation – in Giddens' (1992) terms, the plasticity of sexuality – enables adults to construct intimate associations that meet their personal needs, structured around wider affinities such as friendship (Budgeon and Roseneil 2004). This does not ignore the need to care for dependants so much as displace obligation as the structural determinant of affective life.

For some family studies researchers this privileging of emotional choice above and beyond a more connected, relationally oriented paradigm misrepresents typical lived experience in contemporary society (McCarthy et al. 2003; Smart 2007). However, while this may be the logical extension of the 'transformations of intimacy' thesis, it is not the only way of reading this framework. The 'transformations' argument may indeed displace the centrality of family ties, but it does not diminish the significance of parent–child relationships *per se*. In fact, turned around, this framework can be read as increasing the significance of children, situating children as the means to counteract the transience of adult–sexual couple relationships. Families do not create lifelong adult relationships for everyone nor are they the affective bank where emotional connections to others may be stored; they are social and affective units that are created through the *processes of relationality*. Families do not contain emotional relationships, but are more aptly characterised as expansive 'networks of intimacy' (Jamieson 1998: 77). Framed in this way, it is the *quality* of personal relationships which is paramount rather than the structural familial parameters. This draws attention to the ways that different acts of care and intimacy serve to maintain relational ties (Williams 2004), a process which reflexively constitutes trust rather than take it for granted.

Contemporary research has effectively debunked any unitary basis of 'the family'. In the mid-1990s, the family sociologist David Morgan captured the shift in emphasis from a functional unit to relational connections in the phrase 'family practices' (Morgan 1996). This emblematic term has shaped the framing and character of UK family studies analysis ever since. 'Family practices' directs attention to the multifarious ways that families are created through sets of caring and intimate relationships. In this framework, roles and familial responsibilities are severed from biological parenthood (McCarthy et al. 2003; Williams 2004). The 'postmodern family' is a site of contestation, combining a mix of experiment, pastiche and nostalgia (Stacey 1996). However, notwithstanding this inclusive relationality and the acknowledgement of diversity among kinship formations, there is no corresponding demise of 'the family' as an institution. Families, as the structural framework of our private lives, remain 'the norm'. While singledom may be increasing, in a salutary reminder Stevi Jackson (1997) notes that over 80 per cent of the population continue to live in households constructed around an adult couple and/or parent–child relations. Divorce rates all but tally with rates for remarriage. Furthermore, rather than destabilising normative models, ideas of step-parenthood and extended families testify to the power of familial ideology in representing 'the family' as the best way to live our lives.

Framing families through research

Since the studies of Talcott Parsons (1955; 1959) researchers have been interested in the processes of family relationships, albeit that these early iterations tended to focus more narrowly on the purposes of familial roles and family structures than on the dynamic interactions of everyday interpersonal experience. Where there are clearly discernible shifts in the contemporary research agenda is in how family, kin and relationships with 'significant others' are defined – that is to say, *who affectively counts*. In part as a response to rising divorce rates and the growing number of multi-household living arrangements for many children, there has been a change in research scope. There is an evident move away from the family as defined through household and kin relatedness, towards one that acknowledges the different ways that families extend beyond these parameters. This 'extended family' requires an extended approach, a wide-angle research lens that can record the evolving matrix of intimacy. A focus that looks outward rather than inwards. Such an approach is designed both to capture and be responsive to the different spatial and temporal dimensions of family living arrangements. This goes beyond the charting of different stratifications of family and affective relationships. It places increasing importance on how these connections are constituted through everyday material interactions – the process of familial relationships. Change is in the foreground of this processual, lifecourse perspective and as such it is not surprising that the contemporary research agenda is steering towards a more longitudinal, intergenerational approach.

The in-depth qualitative interview, which has been the linchpin of relationships research for some 20 years, has not lost its centrality, indeed, this means of data collection remains pivotal to most studies of relationships and everyday living. However, the format of this interview is being adapted as researchers try to engage with participants' experiences across the lifecourse. For example, psychologically informed approaches (Hollway and Jefferson 2000; Wengraf 2001) are being used in sociological studies of parenthood and family lives as a means to elicit data on the narrative connections between the events and relationships that individuals experience. This relational perspective – the connections we have with others and the ways that experiential threads are woven together across the lifecourse – is a direct response to the conceptual interest in narratives and life stories.

Shifts of this kind in the theoretical and conceptual modelling of 'family' and intimacy indicate that it is through everyday *practices* that relationships are forged. This in turn has led researchers to search for more dynamic approaches which reflect how these everyday processes of care and affect are materialised. It is perhaps not surprising then that a mixed-methods approach is rising to the top of the family studies methodological agenda. Advocates of the approach argue that the combination of data produces a multilayered account of the times, places and forms of different interactions. The development of participatory methods means that children can be readily included as equal research participants, providing a cross-generational perspective that was often missing from earlier pictures of families and interpersonal relationships. There is no one method or methodological approach which can be singled out as characterising the field of twenty-first-century family studies. What is clear is that researchers are looking to a wide variety of means to access the diversity of everyday stories that constitute contemporary family relationships and these shape the forms and ideas of relationality that are being documented.

Childhood research

Research has illustrated how, prior to the 1970s, socialisation theories and sociological studies of childhood were framed by adults (James and Prout 1990). Children were viewed as products constituted through the environments in which they lived (Barter and Renold 2000). Childhood was seen as an interim period between birth and mature adulthood (Mayall 1994), a configuration which positioned children as adults-in-the-making rather than as agentic young people (Brannen and O'Brien 1995). Being positioned as 'objects of study' they were reliant on parents and carers to interpret what was in their best interest because, it was presumed, they lacked the cognitive skills necessary to express their feelings and emotions concerning events in their lives (Hill et al. 1996). As a consequence, scant attention was paid to what was important or meaningful to them (Woodhead et al. 1991). However, by the late 1980s childhood studies had developed into a distinctive research area in the social sciences, setting out a 'new sociology of childhood' (James and Prout 1990) in which children were seen as social subjects in their own right (James et al. 1998) and not just part of 'the family' (Qvortrup 1994).

Building on these ideas, recent studies have examined children's social worlds through studies of their intra-familial, sibling relationships (Mauthner et al. 2005) and friendship networks (Hey 1997; Frosh et al. 2001). This work highlights children's significant role in the relational matrix of families (Brannen and O'Brien 1996; Mayall 2002) and their involvement in the process of creating kin (O'Brien et al. 1996) and 'like-kin' relationships (Mason and Tipper 2006) through everyday experiences of family life (Morrow, 1998; Dunn and Eater-Deckard 2001). We may still live in a Western culture that does not particularly listen to children (Lansdown 1994), but, in the UK, reflecting and constituting rights enshrined in the Children Act 1992, young people are now listened to on issues which affect them (Clark 1996). Their participatory role in shaping families is recognised.

Accounting for children's age

The subject of children's age has been discussed at some length in sociological studies of children and childhood. Allison James and colleagues argue that while there are differences among children at different ages, age should be seen as a social rather than a natural variable in research (James et al. 1998: 175). Children may act and talk differently at different times of their lives, but we should be cautious before we read these (developmental) stages as 'natural' phenomena. Understandings of children's behaviour are refracted through cultural prisms which separate their experience into meaningful, age-appropriate vectors. For example, children's sexual knowledge differs widely across cultures and history. What is deemed 'precocious sexuality' in contemporary Western parlance has little meaning in an historical context. Similarly, there is little consistency between and within different cultures about the age at which children 'own' their sexuality and/or are capable of making judgements about sexual desire (Jackson 1982).

The contemporary significance that is afforded to children's age has fuelled corresponding interest in the age-appropriateness of methods, with renewed emphasis on the relationship between methods and underlying socio-cultural assumptions. Indeed empirical research on children's lives cannot sidestep the thorny issue of research methodology and the ways that methods signify broader social relations. It would be naïve to suggest that researchers and the data they collect stand outside the social world. Participants may or may not be cognisant of wider social relations, but the accounts they give are likely to be structured through their socio-cultural locations. As such researching children brings power relations into sharp relief and in many ways reinforces generational inequalities of status.

There has been a lot of attention paid to how researchers can minimise the adult–child power differential. It is advocated that researchers should be reflexive and continually question their role as a researcher. The cross-generational interview typically requires researchers to adopt the 'least adult role' (Mandell 1991), working to minimise their 'adultist' attitudes to children (Alderson 1995). Others suggest that the researcher–child participant encounter should be structured around 'friendship' (James et al. 1998), although this has been questioned as it could pose a serious ethical breach, portraying a false representation of the research interview 'relationship' (Harden et al. 2000; Mauthner et al. 2002).

The value of traditional interview techniques has been critically evaluated. It is now generally accepted that interviews and similar research methods provide a narrativised account of the individual (Miller and Glassner 1997) rather than accessing the experience of lived life. As such interviews illustrate 'the way people make sense of their own experiences and social worlds' (Harden et al. 2000: 5.4). Research with children is no different from that with adult participants in this sense. Their data are no more or less 'truthful' than those of adults. Like many adults, children may try to evade the truth because it is painful. They may say what they think the interviewer wants to hear or frame their answers within a socially acceptable framework (Punch 2002). This does not invalidate their data. Irrespective of whether their 'stories' are accurate or truthful, they are based in *their* real worlds (Holland et al. 1994) and so are legitimate.

The efficacy of exclusively child-focused participatory tasks and activities has also been questioned. It is argued that by creating a separate canon of methods we simply duplicate wider social attitudes which position children as distinct from adults, subjects which are non-adult and essentially different (Harden et al. 2000). There is undoubtedly some truth in this; however, similarities between adult and child participants do not mean that the research process should be uniform. The value of the wide-angle research lens is that it enables researchers to be responsive to the particularities of lived experience, which, in this instance, are shaped through age and generation.

Whichever approach is adopted, the adult researchers' knowledge of the cultural milieu and social capital of those whom they intend to research can be invaluable and far more useful than any formal interview technique. Knowing about the current trends and fashions of the study age group and being familiar with some of the chat that goes on among these children is important research preparation. This does not presuppose that researching children is a specialist activity; in fact the opposite: it suggests that adult–child communication skills are pervasive – learned and practised activities that are part of many people's everyday lives. For example, in the past my knowledge of *Pokémon* (a Nintendo videogame-based media franchise) was particularly useful when talking with young children in the 1990s. More recently, my familiarity with 'Brit-pop' and 'nu metal' music, and contemporary sci-fi cult TV series, has proved to be a boon. This cultural capital, gleaned through conversations with my son at various points in his life, has been worth its weight in research gold!

Researching sensitive topics

Irrespective of the ages of participants, studying relationships and private family life enters into the territory of what has been framed as 'sensitive topic' research. The term 'sensitive topic' is habitually used in social research as if the meaning was obvious, but as Claire Renzetti and Raymond Lee point out, 'it is used in a commonsensical way, with no attempt at definition' (1993: 3). Broadly speaking any research that has potential implications or consequences for individual participants or participant groups may be termed sensitive, likewise any topic that may be considered socially sensitive (Sieber and Stanley 1988). Judgements about what constitutes 'sensitive' are always subjective, but typically, in the area of family and relationship studies, this categorisation takes account of the vulnerability of the group (Elam and Fenton 2003), participants' age and how this may heighten the sensitivity of the topic (Caskey and Rosenthal 2005), and the degree to which research intrudes into participants' private life at home (Brannen 1988).

The issue of privacy is particularly pertinent to studies of families. In Western societies 'privacy of family life and couple relationships is something that retains an especially strong currency' (Edwards 1993: 181). It represents a notoriously difficult area to negotiate. Little is to be gained in repeating arguments about why studies of family life reside within (or for that matter outside) the conceptual framework of 'sensitive topic research' (for comprehensive overviews, see Lee 1993; Renzetti and Lee 1993; Caskey and Rosenthal 2005). What is far more useful is a consideration of the methodological issues that have arisen as a *consequence* of this categorisation process, in particular, how this affects the collection and dissemination of research data.

Renzetti and Lee (1993) suggest that sensitive methods need to be developed and adapted to suit the requirements of each situation. I have already outlined the scope and framing of research in family and childhood studies, and, later (in chapter 3) I extend this analysis and detail key methodological approaches. Here I want to focus on broader research concerns arising from sensitive topic work. For example, methods that are generally used in fieldwork without undue concern, such as in-depth interviews, become subjected to far closer scrutiny when researching 'sensitive' issues. Possible negative repercussions are considered in advance and in some cases detailed 'risk analysis' is undertaken, with steps being put in place to manage and/or ameliorate any distress that may arise through research participation. The most commonly cited example of research that requires this kind of close ethical attention is work on domestic abuse and sexual assault. Research in this area almost takes as read that interviews will recall painful memories of previous trauma, memories that participants may have tried to leave behind (Russell 1990; Bergen 1993).

However, rather than avoid research that can impinge on people's private lives and/or cause psychological distress, it has been argued that methodological approaches should be developed that mitigate negative effects on the participant. Research identified as 'sensitive' needs to make use of non-threatening environments, as participants, especially children, need time and space to be able to give a considered response to questions (Barter and Renold 2000). Thus it is not so much the method that needs to be tailored, but the conceptual framing and physical location of the research. In this sense the relationship between the researcher and the participant becomes crucial. The better the researcher understands and identifies with the interviewees' situation, the better the data are likely to be. For example, previous research has shown that women more readily talk to other women about private matters (Finch

1984; Graham 1984). It should be noted here that this claim must not be overstated as presumptions of sameness can also serve to obscure the differences that exist *among* women. As Rosalind Edwards suggests, 'there are structurally based divisions between women', notably race and class, which may lead them to have different interests and which may adversely affect the interview encounter (Edwards 1993: 183–4).

There are some general points of good practice. Gillian Elam and Kevin Fenton (2003) suggest that in order to reduce the sensitivity of the topic, the participant should be provided with enough information about the research to make an informed decision about their participation. The research process should include a warm-up period which enables potential participants to reflect on the topic and the level of their involvement. In an interview, questions should initially be general and non-threatening and gradually home in on the topic. This allows a rapport to be established between the researcher and the researched and puts the participant more at ease. Guidelines for 'sensitive topic' research do not differ significantly from those applying to mainstream sociological inquiry, but in practice the degree to which ethical protocols are adhered to may be more stringent.

In research on sensitive topics it is imperative that the participant is fully cognisant of how their material will be used and be reassured that, as far as is ethically possible, all material will be treated as confidential. Where there is a possibility of disclosure that might require further action to be taken, such as in cases of bullying or abuse, participants must be made aware at the outset of procedures that will be followed. It is recommended that participants be given the details of a named person who works outside the research project whom they can contact should they want to make a complaint about the conduct of the researcher and/or the research process. Equally, researchers should have resort to some form of support, preferably outside the project, so that they can discuss any concerns which may arise for them as the research progresses.

There are additional areas of caution in the analytical stage of sensitive topic research. For example, great care should be taken in handling and interpreting data in order to minimise the risk of misinterpretation. It is unlikely that this will be due to deliberate misreading of data, but it can result from over-claiming findings, making generalisations from a small sample or from superficial readings of research by the media who are ever-eager to create sensationalist headlines. One case which illustrates what can happen when things go wrong demonstrates why caution should be exercised in this respect. Drawing on data from only a few case studies, researchers formulated the 'cyclical hypothesis' in child abuse, concluding that parents who were abused as children are more likely to abuse their own children (Curtis 1963; Spinetta and Ringler 1972). Once this was published it not surprisingly attracted significant media attention and soon became accepted as fact. It is now known that this explanation is too simplistic, but at the time the revelation caused a lot of psychological harm to parents who had been abused; they feared that it was only a matter of time before they too became child abusers (Herzberger 1993). This may be an extreme case, but it demonstrates the need for careful handling of 'sensitive topic' data and to keep at the forefront of the research agenda what effects the findings may have for participants directly involved in the research and for the wider social group of which they are members.

Ethical issues in families research

Irrespective of the degree of sensitivity of any research project, effective methodology and engagement with ethical concerns are synchronous, especially when carrying out research involving children (Thomas and O'Kane 1998). There is consensus that researchers have a moral and professional responsibility to their participants; they must ensure that they avoid causing physical and/or psychological distress (Elam and Fenton 2003). To this end various professional bodies have produced guidelines to ensure that research practice is ethically sound. The main themes are informed consent, respect for privacy, subject integrity, avoidance of exploitation and betrayal, protection from harm and the possible negative effects of the research on participants.

The 'Statement of Ethical Practice' (2002) issued by the British Sociological Association (BSA) stresses that it is the responsibility of researchers to take seriously the possible negative repercussions of research on participants and to take extra care when working with vulnerable, disempowered adults and children (see http://www.britsoc.co.uk). These guidelines recognise that when a deep rapport is developed between interviewer and interviewee, then individuals are more likely to disclose information and feelings that they might have preferred to keep private or hidden – in some cases even from themselves (Duncombe and Jessop 2002). This has led some researchers to liken the interview exchange to a therapeutic encounter (Laslett and Rapport 1975). The increased use of biographical (Wengraf 2001) and/or free association (Hollway and Jefferson 2000) narrative interview methods has been identified as accentuating possible imitations of a therapeutic-type exchange.

The recourse to psycho-social methods in sociological research is relatively new and poses a particular challenge to the BSA ethical guidelines as this approach suggests that it can be 'reassuring and therapeutic to talk about an upsetting event in a safe context' (Hollway and Jefferson 2000: 86–7). However, the 'therapeutic imitation' only relates to the intensity of the encounter. If care is taken and the researcher is responsive to participants' ease and emotional comfort, then such methodological concerns are no more pertinent to this approach than to any other in-depth scenario. For example, when a participant appears to shut down a train of thought the researcher should respect this closure and not attempt to reopen it, however individually or academically tempting it may be. This said, silences occur naturally in any interview as participants think through their answers and it is legitimate for the researcher to nudge along an interview when such pauses become awkward, picking up threads presented by the participant. In the end it is common sense and respect which to a large degree shape the handling of such scenarios. Furthermore, it is important not to overstate the potential problems of psycho-social approaches. More than anything else it is the 'sensitivity' of the research topic that influences the interview dynamic and the intensity of the encounter, not the particularities of any method used. To suggest that sociological application of psycho-social methods will encourage interviewees to divest hitherto unknown 'stories' and memories after only a few hours of contact is arguably naïve and derives from a culture of risk assessment more than an ethical response to research practice.

Some of the concerns around disclosure and the researcher–participant relationship can be dealt with relatively easily through careful handling of the processes through which individuals 'sign up' to research. Debates around informed consent are longstanding and are germane to all research. But this area has been addressed with renewed rigour in recent years, in part channelled through the ESRC Research Methods Programme (Wiles et al. 2006). The various codes of ethical practice in circulation all place responsibility for this area, including the negotiation of informed consent, with the researcher (Edwards and Mauthner 2002). However, it remains all but impossible for any researcher to claim that a participant has given *fully* informed consent because, by definition, research and interviews are exploratory in nature. The process of research is necessarily dynamic and it is suggested that it may be more ethical and productive to engage in a moral conversation with participants rather than be over-reliant on formal informed consent procedures (Benhabib 1992). Consent should be negotiated on a *continual* basis, throughout the research process. This can create problems as well as ease them because repeatedly asking participants if they wish to continue may incline them to drop out (Duncombe and Jessop 2002). A fine line has to be walked between respecting participants' rights and the pragmatic need to keep people onboard the project.

The issues of informed consent do become slightly more tricky when researching children's lives, not as a result of any lack of understanding on their part but because their participation in any research is typically dependent on adult gatekeepers (Harden et al. 2000) and children's rights sometimes conflict with the parents' or carers' viewpoints. For example, children may be interested in a research topic and want to be involved but may be forbidden to do so by the adults who are (legally) responsible for them (Hughes and Huby 2001). In families research it is usually adults who are approached in the first instance and it is they who make the initial decision about whether to proceed; only then do they consult other family members to gauge their interest. Ethical considerations around researching children return us to conceptual standpoints on the status of children and the category of childhood, conjoining methodological and epistemological concerns (Morrow 1998b). What researchers in childhood studies have demonstrated is the need to balance the desire to avoid causing harm to children through clumsy or unethical research, with the harm caused by being too protective and silencing them by excluding them from research. Children are integral to families. To exclude them on the basis that uncomfortable issues and/or unforeseen consequences may arise from research participation would return us to previous configurations wherein adults talk for children.

Studies of families' private life and the interpersonal relationships of parents and children invariably raise concerns around issues of disclosure (Duncombe and Marsden 1996) and confidentiality (Mauthner 1997; Punch 2002). These issues remain particularly complex because participants are not simply revealing identity to the outside world but revealing secrets *among* family members (Larossa et al. 1981). For example, in group observation there is always a possibility, even a likelihood, of involuntary disclosure. Family members may reveal information about one another which an individual may have preferred to keep secret, or what is observed may be, on reflection, deemed too private by one or more of the participants. As a consequence in families research it may be more practical and ethical to frame ideas of consent as 'provisional' rather than 'informed' (Flewitt 2005).

Ethical concerns over disclosure, divergence among 'related' stories, confidentiality and the degree to which anonymity can be assured in families research often shape researchers' decisions on how to collect data (Mauthner 1998). For example, whether to interview couples separately or apart is not simply an organisational matter, but one that impacts on the content and quality of the data (Valentine 1999). In a portrait of newly-wed marriage Penny Mansfield and Jean Collard (1988) experimented with different interview designs, including interviewing spouses together, separately but simultaneously and separately on different occasions. They found that couple interviews typically produced 'consensus accounts', with one spouse taking the lead and seeking confirmation of their version of events from the other.

Interviews with couples or among wider family groupings can produce 'family stories' that gloss over individual differences, obscuring tensions between mothers–fathers, parents–children and siblings. In contrast, interviews with individual family members have produced comparative data on gendered experiences of relationships – 'his' and 'hers' marriages (Hochschild 1989; Pahl 1989) – and different generational perspectives on family processes (Gabb 2005a). However, advocates of collective interviews and focus groups point out that these methods produce *different layers of data* that are not easily captured in one-to-one encounters. As such this approach is particularly useful in families research (Smithson 2000). Focus group methodology by its nature exposes the interplay of gender and generation that structures family relations. It enables researchers to observe how subtle and blatant challenges to individual views reorient discussion, moving towards normative understandings of family and the creation of boundaries around kinds of intimacy.

Different methods and methodological approaches evidently create particular ethical concerns, but all share the need for integrity within research practice. Issues inevitably become more immediate as the perceived or actual levels of sensitivity in the research increase. In this light it is perhaps not surprising that the ethical clearance procedures for the *Behind Closed Doors* project were rigorous. In hindsight this undoubtedly benefited the research process, not so much in the development of structures and procedures for dealing with anticipated problems (these were already in place), but in focusing attention on the sensitivity of the topic – something to which I had become desensitised through my over-familiarity with the project.

In the chapters that follow I situate ethics as part of wider discussions of family and childhood research methods and do not single them out again for particular analysis. This is because they are so embedded in all aspects of the research process that to extrapolate them is counterintuitive. For example, issues of nudity and parent–child bodily intimacy may be perceived as ethically troublesome, but the point being made through-out both the project and this book is that ideas of risk, affective boundary management and experiences of intimacy and sexuality in families are shaped through normative understandings of what constitutes appropriate behaviour through which the parameters of risk assessment are mediated. As such the substance of the study and the underlying intentions of this book are to develop understandings of why and in what ways consensual, ordinary experiences of family intimacy are perceived as risky practices. Through this lens the research process and the topic of study are family ethics; to separate ethics from the mix contests its constitutive role at every level.

3
Methodological Approaches and Family Research Methods

In chapter 2 I touched on some of the debates in family and child-hood studies around methodology and the pragmatics of researching personal life and relationality. In this chapter I fill in some of the detail, focusing on research approaches that have informed and shaped these fields. In qualitative studies of family life a phenomenological or eth-nomethodological approach is typical, in which theorising emerges from the data. Social phenomenologists are concerned with the experien-tial underpinnings of knowledge and ethnomethodologists focus on everyday practices and mechanisms that constitute and maintain social formations such as the family (Holstein and Gubrium 2005). Most of the research detailed in this chapter, broadly speaking, falls within these grounded perspectives. However, I do not focus on the epistemological standpoint so much as the different methodological approaches used in the study of family life.

In the first section I examine survey research that draws on large-scale datasets to trace trends in family and kin formations across house-holds and the socio-historical patterning of parent–child relationships alongside changes in children's lives. However, the main focus of this chapter and the book generally is qualitative research because a qualita-tive approach lends itself more readily to the messiness and particularities of family relationships and everyday intimate life. This does not render structural and/or demographic trends in families mistaken, but looks for patterning in 'the processes by which families create, sustain, and discuss their own family realities' (Daly 1992: 4).

In the next section I focus on longitudinal research which has built on the long-established tradition of using national population datasets to examine social change in family life. I examine how qualitative longitudinal approaches are beginning to amass rich data on relational practices and multidimensional experiences of family and childhood across the lifecourse, placing temporality and change at the centre of qualitative data analysis. In the following section I explore the ways that narrative and biographical approaches have been more broadly utilised in the study of family life and interpersonal relationships. I examine how auto/biographical accounts construct a story of self that can be particularly useful in analysis of sense-making practices of intimacy. I then move on to consider qualitative research more widely. I examine how participatory techniques are being used to engage participants in the co-construction of data about experience and the meanings of family. These creative methods have proved to be particularly useful in research with children and in studies of sensitive topics.

Irrespective of the popularity of participatory approaches, there is no doubt that interviews remain the default method in qualitative research. I critically engage with different approaches to the interview format, including online research and the strategies that have been developed to enhance interviews with children. I examine the move towards psycho-social approaches in families and lifecourse research and the rich biographical data they produce. The approaches discussed so far have focused on personal experience, I next examine approaches that step back from the individual and use third-party scenarios to access information about the opinions, values and beliefs that shape family behaviour.

Third-party vignettes, photographs and focus group discussion encourage participants to talk more freely about sensitive issues by generating data on a social level – that is to say, once removed from personal experience. I examine research that demonstrates the utility of this approach and how these methods capture the individual and/or group sense-making processes. In the final section I outline some of the different analytical approaches that are typically used in family and childhood studies. I consider the efficacy of case studies analysis in interpreting biographical data, pulling together the threads of an individual story. I then address cross-sectional analysis, through which researchers can trace patterns among participants' data and make generalisations from material across datasets. Finally, I examine mixed-methods research, suggesting that these layers on layers of data are most fruitfully analysed using an integrative analytical paradigm.

In this chapter, my explication of qualitative methods and the different strategies available to analyse this material do not aim to provide a step-by-step guide. For this it is best to consult a methodology handbook of which there are many good examples – notably Jennifer Mason (1996) and, in the area of family studies, Kerry Daly (2007). Instead I introduce readers to research approaches in families and childhood studies and methodological frameworks that characterise and shape these fields.

National surveys and questionnaire research

The focus of this book is qualitative research, but quantitative methods that generate questionnaire or survey data remain useful resources in the study of family life. They can be employed as either stand-alone methods or provide statistical data that inform and/or complement qualitative analysis.

Survey research

Secondary analysis of national survey data are commonly used in much family research to evidence trends in behaviours, lifestyles and beliefs. Survey research has three basic elements: a large number of respondents are included to represent the population of interest; questions tend to be closed and/or offer multiple-choice answers; and responses are numerically coded and often analysed using computer software (Greenstein 2006). In the UK there are five national surveys that are commonly used in family research: the British Cohort Study; the National Child Development Survey; the British Household Panel Survey; the English Longitudinal Study of Ageing; and the Millennium Cohort Study. The British Cohort Study (BCS70) is a continuing, multidisciplinary, longitudinal study that follows a cohort of people all born in the same week in 1970. Data on the group have been collected at ages 5, 10, 16, 26 and 30 using a questionnaire. The National Child Development Survey (NCDS) aims to monitor the individuals' physical, educational and social development. It follows a cohort of people born in the same week in 1958. Data from the group have been collected via questionnaire at ages 7, 11, 16, 23, 33 and 42. The 1999–2000 iteration of the BCS70 and NCDS surveys were combined to make them more accessible to researchers and other users. The British Household Panel Survey (BHPS) aims to further understanding of social and economic change in Britain. Members of 5,500 households were first sampled in 1991 and this cohort has been interviewed every year since. The BHPS remains the major large-scale source of information on the dynamics of British households.

The first round of survey data from the English Longitudinal Study of Ageing (ELSA) was collected in 2002–3. The information focuses on the UK's ageing population and addresses people's economic, social, psychological and health circumstances and how these change across the lifecourse. The Millennium Cohort Study (MCS) is the most recent birth cohort study and follows approximately 19,000 children who were born in 2001–2. Information was collected from parents whose children were aged nine months and then at three years. It aims to survey continuity and change in the context of diversity across children's family and parenting life. Information from all these surveys is available from the Economic and Social Data Service (ECDS) (http://www.esds.ac.uk/longitudinal). Other longitudinal ESDS data are available on their website, including the Families and Children Survey (FACS). This originally focused on lone-parent families and low-income families, but it has been recently expanded to include higher-income families and now provides a complete sample. One of its primary roles is to provide data on standards of living and how these affect child development and well-being in families.

The accuracy of participants' answers in questionnaires has been called into question and it has been shown that errors in reporting can result in skewed understandings of social phenomena. For example, it is claimed that the number of children who have experienced life in non-intact (separated) families is overestimated in BHPS data by approximately 10 per cent (Francesconi 2004). Notwithstanding these margins of error, the re-analysis of secondary data generated through national surveys is now commonplace in research on family life and children's well-being. The sample detailed below gives a flavour of the work in this area but does not aim to be representative.

Using BHPS data, research has examined the changing social world and the challenges that this poses to children (Scott 2000). Census and survey data have been used to map trends in solo living (Chandler et al. 2004) across the adult lifecourse (Wasoff et al. 2005). BHPS data have been utilised to assess changing patterns of care in families, including the increasing role of grandparents in formal child care provision (Gray 2005). These data have also been used in analyses of work–family balance in relation to women's employment (Warren 2004), lone parenthood (Ermisch and Wright 1995), class (Warren 2003) and how changing patterns of employment affect the division of domestic labour (Gershuny et al. 2005). Survey and BHPS data have informed analysis of the changing role of men as fathers (Burghes et al. 1997; Kaufman 1997) and patterns of parenting for non-resident fathers (Sobolewski and King 2005). In the past, sexuality research has drawn heavily on survey data on sexual lifestyles and proclivities produced by Alfred Kinsey and his colleagues (1948; 1953). More recently survey data have been used to examine the effects of premarital sex on subsequent relationships

(Teachman 2003) and personal interview survey data have been used to study sexual lifestyles (Field et al. 1994).

The combining or extending of survey research with qualitative methods of data collection has been seen as highly advantageous by some researchers, who have used 'a subtle fusion of the two approaches' (Thompson 2004: 242). Janet Finch and Jennifer Mason have researched trends in family obligations (Finch 1990) and responsibilities (Finch and Mason 1993) through the interweaving of qualitative and quantitative survey methods. Quantitative data evinced the patterns of kin exchange – their frequency, recurrence and commonality. These data also provided information which shaped the sampling frame for subsequent qualitative interviews and allowed researchers to test emergent hypotheses in depth. In another study, Gill Gorell-Barnes and colleagues blended quantitative survey data with qualitative information from interviews to compare the effects on children of parents' different management strategies during the transition to 'step-family' life (Gorell-Barnes et al. 1997).

National longitudinal and panel surveys may include additional, targeted research that is positioned as an adjunct to or extension of these surveys. Participants from sub-panels are typically interviewed and these data often assist in the interpretation of large survey information. However, there are challenges in trying to 'piggy-back' more in-depth or targeted research on national surveys (see Sin 2006). Data from these smaller, sub-panel cohorts remain the intellectual property of discrete research projects and do not at this point supplement the national survey data archive. A growing number of these and other smaller-scale datasets can be found at the national collection of independent family research (http://www.data-archive.ac.uk/).

Research questionnaires

Surveys and research questionnaires typically use a series of 'closed' questions that are administered through a written form and completed by respondents (Bryman 2001). The benefits associated with this method are that they are more economical than interviews, and, because they can reach large samples, they can gather large amounts of data in a relatively short time. Ethically, it is easier to ensure participant anonymity, but return rates may be low, especially in research with young people (Fletcher 1993); furthermore, there is no way to verify the authenticity of responses to postal questionnaires. Perhaps the most significant restriction of self-complete questionnaires is that they presuppose a level of literacy. This makes the method inaccessible for certain populations, often those who are already without a 'voice' in the community – children, disenfranchised groups or hidden populations (Balen et al. 2001). These problems can only be overcome if a researcher is present to facilitate questionnaire completion.

Beyond basic levels of literacy, questionnaires also require that participants are able and/or want to document their true feelings in writing (Hill et al. 1996). This is a particular problem in sensitive topic research and research with young people. Thus it is not surprising that postal surveys involving children are rare and are often only used in conjunction with qualitative methods, because without guidance, children can find questionnaires irrelevant and/or difficult to complete (Buchanan 1995). The low response rate to postal questionnaires can be improved if they are used as a follow-up to interviews (Sinclair and Gibbs 1996) or when young people's involvement is mediated through adults, although, as previously discussed, this mediation does raise another set of issues. These concerns over questionnaire data do not invalidate the approach in studies of family life and childhood, but require researchers to think through the management of methodological limitations.

In this section I have demonstrated the richness of research in this area, work that has productively and, in many cases, creatively used the 'hard facts' of statistical datasets to good advantage.

Longitudinal research and studies of lifecourse

In the UK, longitudinal qualitative research has built on national population datasets such as those generated by the Office of National Statistics (ONS) and the rich portfolio of birth cohort study data. In family sociology, longitudinal qualitative studies developed out of researchers' engagement with lifecourse studies (e.g. Bryman et al. 1985). Lifecourse studies aimed to move away from ideas of the lifecycle, which implies that life is divided into a series of transitional phases which shape the emergent individual. Lifecourse is typically used to conceptualise experience beyond normatively constituted imaginings of the individual, developing a framework that includes wider social networks. This framework links questions of age and time – individual ageing and social time, socio-cultural understandings of ageing and experiences of relational time. This focus on the time and texture of everyday life and how temporal and cultural dimensions of social life intersect enables researchers to analyse social change through the *individual trajectories* of parents and children. To gain 'a better appreciation of how the personal and the social, agency and structure, the micro and the macro are inter-connected and how they come to be transformed' (Neale and Flowerdew 2003: 189–90).

Longitudinal data are said to offer 'a movie rather than a snapshot' (Berthoud 2000: 15). The approach can map social shifts in experience and behaviour among particular sections of the population – for example, intergenerational social mobility among minority ethnic groups (Platt 2005) – or focus on changing patterns of social behaviour, such as the increasing significance of friendships in people's lives (Pahl and Pevalin 2005). Other longitudinal qualitative studies have looked more broadly across generational experiences – for example, children's experience of growing up (Neale and Flowerdew 2003; Henderson et al. 2006); the experience of growing older (Walker 2004); and how motherhood is experienced across generations (Hadfield et al. 2007). What these studies share is a methodological perspective that positions the individual along the continuum of the lifecourse. Experience is not seen as individuated and/or as a series of discrete events, but as part of a larger, extended, generational narrative.

Quantitative longitudinal survey research has a longstanding tradition which informs the epistemological and practical decisions of researchers in this field. In contrast, with a few notable exceptions (e.g. the ESRC-funded 'Inventing Adulthoods' project, http://www.lsbu.ac.uk/inventingadulthoods/), longitudinal qualitative research is relatively new to sociology. In the UK, it was not until 2003, when the *International Journal of Social Research Methods* devoted a special issue to longitudinal qualitative methods, that critical debate began to emerge among scholars. In the editorial Rachel Thomson and her colleagues suggest that the incidence and interest in qualitative longitudinal studies is due to a variety of factors: a desire for a more holistic understanding of behaviour from funders and policy-makers; an increasing interest in temporal understandings of behaviour across changes in the lifecourse; and theoretical developments around detraditionalisation and individualisation, within which the self is characterised as a work in progress. They suggest that what distinguishes longitudinal qualitative research from other approaches that have previously utilised longitudinal components is that this approach deliberately foregrounds temporality, 'making change a central focus of analytical attention' (Thomson et al. 2003: 185).

This point is extended in other essays in the collection. For example, Bren Neale and Jennifer Flowerdew (2003) suggest that a longitudinal qualitative approach evinces time and texture in dynamic relation to one another, something that is crucial to developing understandings of everyday family life and childhood. This shapes the research process through the evolving relationship between the researcher and participants. It encourages a reflexive approach from participants and researchers alike, something that requires renewed critical engagement with debates around subjectivity (McLeod 2003). As such, it is claimed that longitudinal qualitative research represents something more than just another methodological approach. It suggests a new framework for making sense of the social world; something that requires creative ways to operationalise theorising so that the relationship between agency and structure can be interrogated (Neale and Flowerdew 2003; Plumridge and Thomson 2003). There is agreement among these authors that singular conceptual and/or theoretical approaches do not work: 'no one theoretical perspective is sufficient to grasp the breadth, depth and complexity of a longitudinal qualitative data set'. Instead, there is a call for theoretical pluralism and 'the acceptance of a more provisional or strategic relationship between empirical data and theory' (Thomson et al. 2003: 186).

The need for pluralism in longitudinal qualitative research follows through to subsequent analytical stages. The depth and breadth of the approach mean that the material can be read in several ways – as individual case studies or slicing across the data analysing one moment in time. It is suggested that the practicalities of managing longitudinal qualitative datasets make it advantageous to adopt a combined approach, exploring data cross-sectionally (synchronically) and longitudinally (diachronically) (Thomson et al. 2003). This allows the researcher to observe the evolution of data over time, including taking into account changes in the socio-historical and/or research context (Tomanovic 2003), focus on comparable data between cases and finally examine the intersections and variance among diachronic/synchronic readings (Smith 2003; Thomson and Holland 2003).

Another factor that influences the shape and structure of this approach is the longevity of longitudinal qualitative studies. Research management problems are exacerbated with particular research cohorts, such as young people and/or those formerly living in residential care (Ward and Henderson 2003). However, some researchers have capitalised on the passage of time to consolidate the researcher–participant relationship (Harocopos and Dennis 2003). Beyond these practical considerations, the time scales involved mean that the research process is ongoing and thus contingent. This can lead to an 'absence of analytic closure' (Thomson and Holland 2003: 243). With this in mind, it is suggested that the researcher should consider carefully the timing of any interpretation and resist the temptation to rush into hasty readings that may not stand the test of time. The 'paradigms of longitudinal qualitative work must be sufficiently robust to provide ways of analytically utilizing data which may change initial interpretations' (Thomson et al. 2003: 186–7). It is not so much that hurried readings may misinterpret data so much that a methodological and analytical framework is needed which can accommodate developments in research design and the changing relationship between the researcher and participants (Gordon and Lahelma 2003).

Longitudinal research is extremely expensive to complete and necessarily requires the long-term commitment of both researchers and funding agencies. One creative response to this has been the pooling of researcher capacity. The ESRC-funded *Timescapes* project (http://www. timescapes.leeds.ac.uk) brings together a consortium of universities and researchers not only to combine expertise and research, but also to create an extended longitudinal data archive on personal lives, relationships and identity. While the challenges that face longitudinal qualitative research should not be underestimated, advocates of this approach suggest that it represents many possibilities, enhancing overall understanding of the *dynamics* of everyday life and wider social change (Neale and Flowerdew 2003). As such it offers great potential and is certainly an exciting research approach for the study of families and childhood and the passage of interpersonal relationships across the lifecourse.

Narrative inquiry and auto/biographical approaches

I have shown how qualitative longitudinal research is concerned with the study of changing experience across the lifecourse. I now consider how narrative and biographical approaches are more broadly utilised in the study of personal life and relational experience. Narrative inquiry is 'an amalgam of interdisciplinary analytical lenses, diverse disciplinary approaches' which are drawn together through an interest in auto/biographical 'life writing' (Chase 2005: 651). In families research first-hand accounts of everyday family life and relationships can be useful in building up a composite picture of wider social patterns of experience.

The concepts of narrative and 'life writing' have become increasingly prominent in social sciences research, with interest converging around the metaphor of the story. Ken Plummer suggests that society itself can be seen as 'a textured but seamless web of stories emerging everywhere through interaction: holding people together, pulling people apart, making societies work' (Plummer 1995: 5). Narrative studies aim to understand personal identity, lifecourse and generation, the socio-cultural and the historical world, through narrated experience and its meaning – the ways that individuals package their stories and make sense of their lives. Auto/biographical 'life writing' provides a platform for dis-closures of the self which illuminate the (extra)ordinary lives of ordinary people.

Not surprisingly, there is a strong tradition of feminist work in this area (e.g. Personal-Narratives-Group 1989; Stanley 1995; Swindells 1995). Women's journals have provided insight into many aspects of private life, including their struggle to negotiate the ideals and gendered experiences of motherhood and the family. However, though auto/biographical accounts may tell a personal story, they are neither unique nor individ-ual, in fact to the contrary. As Liz Stanley reminds us, autobiographical and biographical writing needs to be dislodged from its realist preten-sions. These forms may 'lay claim to facticity', but are in truth 'artful enterprises which select, shape, and produce a very unnatural product' (Stanley 1995: 3).

Life stories are typically framed through narrative structures associated with storytelling, including sequence, plot, characters, themes, genres and points of view (Plummer 2001: 185–203). They trace the unfolding of events across different stages of the lifecourse and as a consequence tend to by deterministic, mapping patterns of adult behaviour onto early (childhood) experience. The lifecourse is represented as a passage from infancy to adulthood – the 'seasons' of an individual lifecycle (Sheehey 1995). Stages of the lifecycle are presented as interrupted and/or shaped by interactional moments of transition (Mauthner 2000) or epiphanies (Denzin 1989). While this narrativisation of life may be dominant, it can be resisted and/or contested. Plummer (2001) signals to recent develop-ments in the forms of 'telling' life stories that have disrupted singular ideas of narrative structure. For example, queer theorising reimagines sexual stories beyond the boundaries of heteronormative traditions. New technologies encourage interactivity, and non-verbal visual forms are being incorporated into social sciences research.

These new ways of telling can become the preoccupation of research in and of themselves, but, as Plummer argues, it is more pertinent to study the 'sociology of stories' as this aims to understand 'the role of stories in social life' (Plummer 1995: 31). Rather than focus on the structure and deconstruction of forms of narrative, sociological attention should be directed at what they are saying, because storytelling lies at the heart of individuals' symbolic interactions, evincing the structures at work in everyday experiences of the self. The sexual stories that Plummer presents do not conform to typical forms of auto/biographical life story writing but focus on the narrativisation of erotic, gendered and relational intimacy. He examines the extraordinary proliferation of sexual narratives in contemporary society and how these come into being. This reveals the changing character of sexual experiences, identities and ideologies, focusing attention on the ways that personal (sexual) experience is inculcated through everyday life in a social, cultural and historical context. In this way he demonstrates the artifice that shapes experiences and understandings of rape survival, lesbian and gay 'coming out' and recovery 'self-help' stories.

The underlying tenet of Plummer's argument is that the narrativisation of experience does not simply tell a story, it constructs an account within the language, conventions and social milieu that translates experience. Life stories do not mirror life experiences; they re-present them in particular contexts in culturally intelligible formats. Plummer's analytical framing of auto/biographical narratives demonstrates the utility of this approach in families and childhood research. It shows how the individual experience is co-constructed through the process of life 'stories'. The narrativisation of life events does not contain subjectivity but illustrates the discourses and resources through which individual experience is mediated. As such, narrative inquiry can play an important role in making sense of personal lives and family relationships.

Qualitative research

In the first sections of this chapter I have examined several research approaches used in the fields of families and childhood studies. In the next section I focus on qualitative research more widely and explore how different qualitative methods have contributed to and shaped sociological understandings of families' and children's lives.

Participatory approaches

Increased awareness of methodological and ethical issues, coupled with the pragmatics of researching private and sensitive areas of personal life, has to some extent driven the development of creative methods. The positioning of children at the centre of research has encouraged researchers to be both innovative and responsive, to utilise a variety of different techniques so that children stay motivated and interested. Participatory methods, such as writing and drawing techniques, have been identified as particularly useful as they empower children (Punch 2002), allowing them to take greater control over the research process

(Thomas and O'Kane 1998). It has been suggested that younger children do not know less, they are simply less adept at the unprompted retrieval of information (Wesson and Salmon 2001). Their free narratives tend to be brief when compared to those of adults and older children. A participatory approach can help to focus attention and thereby improve children's recall. The alignment of certain sets of competencies with children and adults respectively is not without controversy (as discussed above), however participatory approaches undoubtedly have some role to play in the study of children's lives and more widely in research of family processes.

There are various techniques which can be bracketed together under the participatory banner. Although they vary widely one from another they do share certain similarities – that is to say, they require *active* involvement by the participant in the production of research data. Researchers have shown themselves to be highly creative in developing participatory methods that ease the awkwardness of the traditional interview format. Alison Clark and Peter Moss asked children to take them on a guided walk through the spaces they inhabit. A 'walking interview' allowed children to account for the spatial and temporal dimension of events as they led the interviewer through their day. The researchers found that walking and talking enabled children to talk freely, uninhibited by 'the sterile environment of a traditional interview room'. The 'physicality and mobility' of this technique brought to the fore children's priorities in their own minds and in the researchers' (Clark and Moss 2001: 28).

Interactive methods can help to break down the hierarchical relationship between the researcher and participants and build a partnership among all concerned in the research process. In family therapy, participatory methods have been extended to include 'sculpting', psychodrama and role-play (Deacon 2000). Sculpting involves one person directing the group to assemble a particular scene or relationship (see Constantine 1978) and/or the placement of figurative representations of the family, such as dolls, into different scenarios (Gehring and Schultheiss 1987). Psychodrama gives participants the opportunity to express their thoughts and emotions in 'spontaneous and dramatic ways' through role-play (Deacon 2000: 6). The method has proved to be particularly useful in the study of events from participants' past (Blatner 1973; Greenberg 1974). Embodied approaches such as these enable researchers to see and assess how the family communicates and manages conflict (Deacon 2000) and provides a route into understanding the workings of the family (Leveton 1992). The use of embodied methods remains rare in sociological research on families, although a few studies of children have begun to explore participatory approaches that include the use of drama (Johnson et al. 1995). In the following sections I focus on techniques that are more commonplace and/or new participatory approaches that are increasing in popularity in family and childhood studies.

Writing methods

Writing exercises can open up the research topic for researchers and participants alike. Incorporating pictures or cartoons alongside written exercises can orient the process towards children and make it fun. Asking children to produce a magazine or newspaper front page which tells their story has also been found to be effective (Deacon 2000). Sentence completion can start with general topics like favourite music then move on to more sensitive, research-oriented topics through progressively directive lines of inquiry. The most long-established writing method used with adults is the diary or log: participants are asked to document their daily activities, feelings, even their dreams (for practical introductions to this method, see Symon 1998; Alaszewski 2005). In psychological studies diaries have been regularly used to analyse social behaviour, interpersonal relationships and routines of emotion exchange (for an overview of selected work in this area, see Larson and Almeida 1999) as a way of revealing family processes in the context of daily life (Laurenceau and Bolger 2005). In contrast Plummer notes that there has been little use of documentary data, including diaries, in mainstream sociological research (Plummer 1983; 2001). 'Sexual stories' (Plummer 1995) and the sexual diary have attracted limited attention particularly on experiences of AIDS (Coxon 1996; Chambers 1998). Diary analysis, however, tends to remain the terrain of life-writing (Cottam 2001).

In sociological studies of family and household, the utility of diaries has tended to be restricted to 'time-use', including various aspects of time management – for example, the division of domestic labour (Gershuny and Sullivan 1998), child care and household time (Hill 1987) and the time parents spend with their children (Bryant and Zick 1996). As mixed methods gain in popularity it can be anticipated that the use of diaries will increase. Advocates show that 'solicited diaries' (Bell 1998) can give access to data on families' everyday routines and encourage participants to reflect on how tasks are divided among family members (Dunne 1999). It is also claimed that diaries have a significant role to play in the study of sensitive topics (Lee 1993) because diary methods not only access inner reflection of self and social interaction, they also elicit data on otherwise private areas of the home, such as the bedroom and bathroom.

Producing a diary can be empowering and encourage greater engagement in the research process by enabling participants to become 'collaborators in the construction of the account' (Elliott 1997: 4.18). It offers participants the opportunity to shape the research by identifying their primary concerns and privileging their own priorities (Meth 2003). As such diary data afford insight into ordinary, everyday sequences of activity and also flag up questions about their meaning and significance. In an early example, Don Zimmerman and Lawrence Wieder combined diaries with in-depth interviews to explore Californian counter-culture. The researchers used participants' diary entries as the structure for subsequent interviews, asking participants about the detail of events and sequences that were documented. They suggest that participants' diaries performed a similar function to field notes, with the diarists becoming 'adjunct ethnographers of their own circumstances' (Zimmerman and Wieder 1977: 484). Post-diary interviews enabled both the researcher and participant to fill in the gaps, with participants adding bits of information or additional experiences they had not mentioned in the diary.

Critics claim that diary data remain decontextualised and individualised, being separated from the social through their private production and domestic context. However, Paula Meth refutes this, and suggests that diary writing in the 'natural' setting of participants' own home offers 'the possibility of a contextualized engagement that takes place within ongoing social realities' which locates 'events and emotions in their social context' (Meth 2003: 200). If the family is largely experienced at home, what better place to document it? It is this blurring of the public–private interface which causes concern for some 'diarists'. Writing a diary can raise anxiety and embarrassment for some about putting 'private' aspects of their family life into words. Others express understandable concerns about how researchers may read and/or judge what they have written. Paradoxically, the intimacy of the method (the participant and *their* personal diary) can also facilitate the telling of stories that have hitherto been experienced as too painful to share among a group or recall in a face-to-face interview. There are obvious limiting factors in using diaries, not least the reliance on literacy. Furthermore, diaries tend to be structured (albeit inadvertently) through public measurements of time and this can artificially demarcate and/or subsume relational experience and emotions (Bell 1998).

As a research tool in studies of family life, diaries are most effective because they draw attention to the co-construction of public–private accounts. They are becoming more commonly used as part of mixed-methods research as a means to enrich and/or substantiate other data

(Alexander et al. 2001; Waddington 2005), contributing to the dynamic picture of family relationships. Diaries may not provide an easy way to access lived experience. As discussed above, the framing of individual experience and the creation of narrative structures around the telling of stories are revealing data in themselves. Therefore, their research value lies in the capacity of the method to capture participants' public presentation of self, their conceptualisation of experience through the structures that shape their lives, including the parameters set by the researcher.

Visual techniques

Diaries discursively frame experience through the participants' affective registers and lexicon. In contrast, visual methods typically aim to generate talk on and around life experiences. Visual research techniques, in particular those that involve task-centred activities, have proved to be an effective way to interview children (James et al. 1998; Morrow 1998b; Gabb 2001). They avoid the need for eye contact and so reduce imbalances of power (Harden et al. 2000). In families research, visual methods are useful in that generational competencies which normally divide parents and children, reflected in adults' greater access to verbal and written language, are overridden. Visual approaches are also useful for working with children who are pre-verbal and with both adults and children whose first language is not English or whose language skills are limited (Clark and Moss 2001).

Graphic methods such as timelines or event calendars can be useful in chronologically charting participants' emotions and experiences, producing data on the lifecourse and relationships across generations (Duhl 1981). Visual methods can also provide data on group interaction. This approach is routinely used in child development studies, when the researcher wishes to observe how parent and child relate and interact with one another through the process of drawing together. A visual approach can encourage children to communicate symbolically and not be reliant on verbal communication. By giving them the opportunity to produce their own data (Deacon 2000) children are positioned as experts on their own lives (Langstead 1994). The flexibility of visual methods means that children's diversity can be readily accommodated (Hill et al. 1996) as methods can be tailored to take into account differences in age and developmental stages.

Researchers in childhood studies typically use visual and task-centred activities to shift the intensity of focus from the one-to-one interview to an activity such as drawing. This can help children to feel more relaxed

(Wesson and Salmon 2001) and facilitate conversation, producing longer and more descriptive narratives (Gross and Hayne 1998). The draw and talk technique can help to structure the child's narration, something that is especially important in research on emotionally charged events or where the focus is on the complexity of a phenomenon, such as family relationships, which may be otherwise hard to verbalise (Gabb 2005a). It can help children put into words difficult and/or abstract ideas. Notwithstanding the benefits of visual methods, they are not a panacea. Not all children want to take part in task-focused activities and it is not uncommon for older children to reject such 'school-like' activities. Children of any age, who dislike drawing or see themselves as 'poor' at this activity, may prefer to talk. After all, many younger children are extremely adept in the art of conversation – talking is often what they do best!

In families research, one graphic method that has received only limited attention is the household portrait. The method was pioneered by Andrea Doucet (2001) in her study of gendered roles and responsibilities among heterosexual couples and extended by Gillian Dunne (1998a; 1998b) in her study of parenthood and domestic life in lesbian households. Household portraits afford insight into families' routines and encourage participants to reflect on everyday processes by visualising normally invisible patterns of behaviour. Doucet asked her participants to sort through different sets of coloured papers which corresponded with colour-coded household tasks and responsibilities. Couples then placed these coloured slips into one or more of the five columns designated by the researcher. She suggests that the method did not elicit data *per se*; instead the technique and resultant materials 'acted as a doorway into [participants'] household and into the issues of parenting and household life' (Doucet 1996: 161).

In *Behind Closed Doors*, I developed a participatory method from the household portrait technique that visually mapped the affective geography of families' interactions. The emotion map method provided a starting point from which to talk about recent feelings and emotional experience and more generally about family dynamics and affective household space. A floor plan of the family home was produced and given to each participant, along with a set of coloured emoticon stickers, representing happiness, sadness, anger and love/affection. Each family member (broadly defined) was designated a coloured sticker to represent them and participants placed these stickers on their floor plan when emotion exchanges occurred. Data were collected from the graphic material produced and through interviews with participants about their emotion maps. A key merit of this approach is that it can be completed by adults and children alike as it is not reliant on literacy skills. In fact, it uses a medium (sticker charts) that children know and which is known to engage their interest. (See figures 1, 3 and 4 for examples of emotion maps and accompanying analysis for the kinds of data this technique can produce.) The method not only generated rich data, but also demonstrated the benefits of research creativity.

Thinking outside traditional methods and playing to the strengths and interests of participants remain key factors in childhood research and are beginning to extend more broadly to studies of family relationships and everyday life. Another example of such methodological creativity can be found in the expanding use of photography in research. Photographs are directly linked to the material world and so can raise issues about the changing concept of family life (Deacon 2000). Cameras offer a form of communication which appeals to children (Clark and Moss 2001). Like other visual methods, photographs readily gain their full attention, helping them to relax as they have something to look at other than the researcher (Hazel 1995). While it is true that there has often been no visual dimension to many research projects (Bolton et al. 2001) there has been a notable increase in the use of photographs as a research tool over the last decade.

Various approaches can be adopted when using photographs in field-work. Picture prompts have been used successfully with very young children who may not have the vocabulary to communicate their feel-ings effectively (Hill 1997). Auto-photography encourages participants to generate original images which can be used to address personal and sensitive issues such as identity and self-esteem (Noland 2006), cross-cultural identity formation (Ziller 1990) and children's ideas of kinship (Mason and Tipper 2006). The construction of photo stories or 'photo novella' can facilitate dialogue around the meanings and significance of a participant's *own* story and this can promote 'deeper levels of reflective thinking' than can be achieved in interview methods alone (Hurworth 2003: 3). Showing images to children can enhance their memory retrieval and, by using 'family snapshots', wider discussion of family relationships can be opened up (Rose 2003). Photo interviews or photo elicitation has been successfully used to promote discussion in anthropological, sociological and historical projects (see Schwartz 1989), generating data on a social level.

There are inevitably some limitations to photographic methods, including ethical issues around sampling, privacy and the validity of the data (see Becker 1978; Blyton 1987; Wang and Burris 1997).

These concerns are often exacerbated in audio-visual (video) recordings. However, advocates argue that the advantages easily outweigh the limitations as the technique can 'challenge participants, provide nuances, trigger memories, lead to new perspectives and explanations, and help to avoid researcher misinterpretation' (Hurworth 2003: 4).

Participant observation

The research potential of visual methods is becoming widely accepted (Rose 2000). However, in sociology the use of video material, recording family life and/or the everyday worlds of children, is only just beginning to be identified as another participatory resource (Neale et al. 2007). This may be due in part to the reliance on verbal interview techniques in sociological qualitative studies of family life. It is also probably partly because its analytical utility has yet to be proved as ethical concerns around informed consent, privacy and confidentiality remain hard to reconcile. Nevertheless, in the field of visual ethnography there is a long-standing tradition of film/video observation (Prosser 1998) and in *Behind Closed Doors* this form of data provided another dimension to the family intimacy picture.

In anthropology, audio-visual observational data have been used for many years to analyse kinship within and across different cultures. Ethnographic material is collected over long periods of time living in the field as part of the community of study, observing what has been enigmatically called the imponderabilia of everyday life (Malinowski 1992). Ethnography pays attention to the minutiae and then interprets the meanings and experiences which the observed 'social actors' assign to these situations and experiences (Burgess 1984: 78). This work informs much sociological family research, including debate concerning the ethics and efficacy of ethnographic observation. However, the richness of material means that I cannot hope to account for it in just one paragraph: see Jennfer Mason (2008) for a sociological engagement with 'our fascination with kinship' and Janet Carsten (2004) as an exemplum of anthropological kinship research.

Observation techniques have been used in both quantitative and qualitative sociological research. In quantitative work, systematically gathered observation data can provide accurate (statistical) information in a standardised format (Friedman 1990). In this form the data are particularly useful in the preliminary and pilot stages of research (Brewer 2000). But it is arguably in the area of qualitative research that observation data can begin to shine. Ethnographic research lends itself particularly well to the study of everyday 'private life' because a close relationship can be formed between the ethnographer and the 'researched' through their personal interactions (Adler and Adler 1993). In some instances researchers have capitalised on their 'insider status' to enhance these personal interactions – see, for example, Kath Weston's (1997) study of lesbian and gay 'families we choose' and Esther Newton's (1995) historiography of a lesbian and gay community. This insider status is taken a step further in auto-ethnographic accounts of childhood compiled from the memories and documentary evidence of the researcher (Okely 1996). However, this autobiographical *reconstruction* of childhood remains distinct from contemporary research on children's experiences today.

In ethnographic methods the terms 'observation' and 'participant observation' are commonplace. The distinction between the two approaches is not simply academic. Observation refers to objectivity and distance as the professional researcher sits apart from the participants and records (on video or in written notes) the activities of the research subject. To be a participant observer, the researcher will have had developed close contact with the group and may have established 'an ongoing relationship' (Crichton and Childs 2005: 3). Of course, there are many commonalities in these approaches as well, not the least the pragmatics of recording data.

In observations of any kind, the immediacy of the situation places researchers in the role of supreme editor. They decide what is significant and/or irrelevant. It is up to them to choose what is recorded and what omitted. Ideally, the only information that is censored is that which is too personal or which may place the researcher or the researched in a compromising situation (Adler and Adler 1993). The main problem that arises from such researcher censorship is that the editorial decision may be biased by a sense of loyalty to the research participants. This sense of being compromised is mitigated when the researcher's difference from and/or similarities to the participants are clearly defined throughout the study, and it is a shared activity which brings the two sides together. For example, in a healthy eating project participant observation was effectively used to study children at mealtimes in school. In this scenario the adult researcher was evidently not a child but sat and ate with the children. The food itself provided a natural topic for discussion which allowed for observations to be made of what and how the children ate (Mauthner et al. 1993).

Authenticity in observation data remains contested and it is known that participants who are being 'watched' are likely to 'act up' for the benefit of the researcher or the camera. It is unimportant in the end whether this 'act' is something they normally aspire to or is a performance especially for this occasion. What remains of academic interest are the ways that they represent themselves.

Interviews

Despite the growing popularity of creative and/or participatory approaches in families and childhood research, interviews remain the default method in most social science qualitative studies. There are many techniques or research methods which use them. Questionnaires are in fact highly structured interviews that ask the same detailed questions of a large group, the results of which typically are then analysed as statistics. Structured interviews that aim for standardised data ensure that each participant is asked the same set of questions. Less directive approaches, including semi-structured and unstructured, 'open' interviews, tend to elicit more individualised accounts. Interviews can directly focus on personal experience, or subjects can be approached indirectly. For example, researchers have asked participants to use metaphors to describe experiences and feelings or to talk about specific events. These mediated 'verbal pictures' encourage people to describe one thing by analogy to another, less sensitive, familiar metaphor (Kopp 1995). This can elicit data on participants' perceptions and emotions that may be otherwise hard to access (Cade 1982).

Interviews normally involve a face-to-face encounter, but as technology has advanced so too has the use of computers as a research tool. Email and networked interviews can be used when face-to-face interviews are impractical (for example, due to geographical distance) (Murray and Sixsmith 1998). Other distance methods, such as telephone interviewing, may help to access hard-to-reach groups and/or the physically disabled (Sturges and Hanrahan 2004). In this context, distance methods are a pragmatic solution to a research problem, but there are also wider reaching benefits to an online approach.

From the 1990s, research has engaged with the various forms of computer-mediated communication (CMC), including email, MUDS (Multi-User Dimensions) or MOOs (Multi-User Object Oriented), the Web, IM (instant messaging), SMS (short messaging service via mobile phones) and blogs (for an overview, see Markham 2005). The plethora of community fora, chat rooms and blogs devoted to discussion of the trials and tribulations of parenthood all testify to the significance of the internet in motherhood, fatherhood and family life research. Discourse analyses of these online mediations are likely to form an integral part of the research agenda on twenty-first-century families and relationality.

The advantages of using the internet as a medium for gathering data on social phenomena have been explored by a number of researchers (e.g. Fox et al. 2003). Researchers have used online environments to stand on the sidelines (also known as lurking) to observe the ways that people discuss topics such as mental illness (Davison et al. 2000) and personal identity issues (McKenna and Bargh 1998). Other researchers have adopted the stance of participant observer, taking part in online discussion forums, posing ('passing') as one of the group. This role may be no more purposeful than the one traditionally occupied by the interviewer, however the difference is that the researcher's academic identity remains unknown to the rest of the group. As such the participant online observer is open to accusations of deception. Most of these concerns can be offset through the use of online message boards which are designed and moderated by a researcher.

Participant message boards do still encounter certain online-specific issues and even these data can be contaminated (Fox et al. 2003). In web-based research it is impossible to be certain whether the questions have been answered by the target population. Indeed 'passing' as someone other than yourself – man/woman, old/young – is common on the internet. Body language and intonation are absent (Hewson 2003). There is no way of knowing the context of participation. The participant may be playing about with a group of friends or could be otherwise distracted (Stone and Pennebaker 2002). These factors mean that it is impossible to maintain a consistent level of control over the research environment.

Conversely, the anonymity afforded through online research has been identified as a facilitating factor. Because participants' identities can remain unknown it is claimed that they may be more inclined to disclose sensitive information that is otherwise perceived as too embarrassing or difficult to speak about face-to-face (Murray and Sixsmith 1998). The utility of online research in the area of childhood studies may be considerable (Buchanan 2000). Research on children's internet use has demonstrated their familiarity and ease within a virtual environment (Valentine and Holloway 2002). In particular, it is claimed that online research methods appeal to teenage participants because it provides them with a familiar medium and guarantees a degree of anonymity which can help them to overcome any shyness and reticence.

Notwithstanding these benefits, while children are commonly portrayed as confident and able users of computers and the internet

(Thomson and Laing 2003) it should be remembered that this is not true of *all* children. Many disadvantaged groups have little or no access to PCs and/or broadband at home. Web-based research privileges those who have access to a computer (Fox et al. 2003). The result may be that only people with high levels of computer literacy will be included in the sample (Turney and Pocknee 2005). Even when there is a computer in the household, who gets to use it and when is often restricted, especially in families with two or more children. In this context privacy is highly unlikely and therefore assurances of confidentiality cannot be guaranteed.

The internet and online research may be moving up the research agenda and undoubtedly have great appeal for some researchers. But to a large extent the interview format chosen will depend on the epistemological stance of the researcher and/or the purpose of the research – for example, whether the aim is to discover the *extent* of a problem or to gain an *understanding* of it. Moreover, notwithstanding the popularity of new approaches, the unstructured face-to-face interview remains emblematic of qualitative research. Qualitative social researchers use interviews extensively because they allow flexibility for both the participant and the researcher as either can change the direction of the exchange. The researcher can be responsive to the participants' embodied/verbal replies while participants' free-form 'rambling' or tangential answers give insight into what is relevant and important to them (Bryman 2001: 313). This flexibility helps to decrease the power imbalance between the researcher and the participant and is one of the primary reasons why in-depth interviews have become synonymous with feminist research of women's lives.

Feminists have sought to transform the traditional interview method into an interactive (Oakley 1981) or reciprocal (Edwards 1993) process, leading some to refer to the method as 'a female style of knowing' (Graham 1983: 136). Interviews with children have attracted a similar feminist ethic insofar as they typically aim to minimise imbalances of power and be sensitive to the child's agenda and competencies. To achieve this it is suggested that interview questions should be phrased in an appropriate way that acknowledges the child's maturity, cultural background and level of understanding. Children need to be encouraged to talk about their lives from their own perspectives (Mauthner 1997). Open questions allow children to answer in their own way, giving them some control over how much information they are willing to reveal. The researcher has to listen to these answers and not pre-empt or guess what children may be feeling.

A useful way of interviewing children is to ask them to describe an ordinary event or experience, for example what happened during the day. This can lead on to more directive questions about specific events and/or to talking about more abstract ideas such as their feelings. This graduated approach avoids the question-and-answer routine, which many children dislike and which can lead to misunderstandings between the researcher and the child. The language used in interviews should be age-appropriate, especially around sensitive issues such as the body and sexual development (Mauthner 1997). By encouraging children to use their own vocabulary, their own ways of communicating, and then asking them for clarification, their meanings are ascertained above any (preconceived) ideas of the researcher.

Children are most likely to give a full and open account when the researcher has established a rapport showing that they are trustworthy (Hill 1997). This may require several interviews, starting with informal 'getting to know each other' sessions before broaching the research topic. The context of the interview will also affect what children reveal (Thomas and O'Kane 1998). It is advocated that the location should be private and child-friendly with familiar toys on hand, with somewhere nearby for their responsible adult to wait (Mauthner 1997). Letting children know what is going on, telling them about the research and providing some personal information about the researcher can encourage a child's natural curiosity and help to drive the conversation. Incorporating interviews into a mixed-methods approach has proved to be extremely effective in research with children.

In recent years there have been moves to open out in-depth interviews beyond the semi structured 'conversation with a purpose' typical in much feminist sociological research. The 'free association narrative interview' (FANI) (Hollway and Jefferson 2000) and 'biographical-narrative-interpretive method' (BNIM) (Wengraf 2001) have been developed in psycho-social research with the aim of accessing participants' accounts of real events and emotions. Because of the growing use of this approach in parenthood, families and relationships studies, and my own use of biographical interview methods in *Behind Closed Doors,* I want to unpack some of the main themes and principles that underpin it. The FANI and BNIM approaches examine how the psyche affects the social, and vice versa, and explores how these two elements shape thoughts and behaviour. This book is not the place to account for differences between the two approaches, but it is fair to say that these tend to derive from their disciplinary origin and their relative positioning along the psycho-social narrative. In this sense the FANI approach leans more towards psychology and the BNIM approach more towards sociology. However, both share underlying ideas, suggesting that the psycho-social subject is, in essence, formed through a marriage of the 'discursive self' and the 'defended self' (for a detailed description, see Hollway and Jefferson 2000).

Psycho-social methods aim for an interactive encounter that recognises the situated, experiential and emotional context of participants' stories and the ways that past experiences affect understandings and representations of self. They do not set out to discover explanations but to elicit stories; not to generalise feelings but to remember specific relevant events (Hollway 2001). Importantly, in the narrative interview approach it is the responsibility of the narrator (the participant) to make the significance and the meaning clear to the listener (the researcher) and in doing so to create a shared meaning. Traditional approaches to interviewing tend to use a question-and-answer framework – the interviewer sets the agenda and directs the interview. Despite attempts by many feminist researchers to widen interview styles into less structured formats, interviewers remain in control of the interview.

The BNIM and FANI approaches aim to empower participants in the telling of *their* story by being wholly non-directive. The researcher typically asks the participant a single, 'open' question at the start of the interview in order to facilitate recall about the research area, structured through their own experience and understandings, framed in their own terms of reference. After asking this initial question the researcher's role is to be an active listener; that is to say, to listen and not interrupt; facilitating not directing (for a practical guide, see Wengraf 2001). The researcher moves the session on but does not lead the participant or influence the narrative course of the interview. The researcher can ask questions which arise out of the participant's story, but these interjections are more akin to intra-narrative prompts than an attempt to steer or orient the interview.

There have been many issues raised about social researchers using psycho-social methods. Some psychologists worry that most researchers have not had the relevant training and may therefore be ill-equipped to handle the method. Sociologists have fewer concerns about the process of data collection and more about the analytical framework. Advocates of psycho-social methods claim that collecting stories from participants' lifecourses provides the researcher with more information than even the interviewee suspects. The selection of a particular story, the details that are emphasised and the manner in which the story is told all signify and represent choices made by the participant. These choices unwittingly reveal a lot of important information and provide invaluable data for the researcher.

It is this *interpretive* aspect of the psycho-social approach which represents the biggest epistemological challenge for sociological researchers. Rather than seeing participants' stories as their own – framed in their own terms – a psycho-social approach looks for readings behind participants' stories of self, meanings that may be unknown or unacknowledged by the individual (the defended subject). For many sociologists, this can ring alarm bells around issues of research ethics and power. Is it ethical for the researcher to identify someone else's subjectivity for them? Should we – can we – do this? Sociologists tend to frame people's perspectives in their own terms – *their* lives, *their* perspectives – and many are resistant to reading things into participants' stories of self that can be only presumed to be there, hidden from the individual.

To look for the story behind the story implies that the researcher knows more about the participant than they do about their own lives and subjectivity. It artificially separates social reality from the lives of participants and erases the interrelationship between the macro-societal (discursive) and the micro-societal (lived, supposedly 'natural' way of thinking/being). Moreover, the opening up of the participant to themselves, focusing their attention on potentially novel emotional connections, also raises ethical issues about the possible *negative consequences* of the interview on the interviewee. Concerns have been expressed that the approach may cause an individual to relive painful experiences and/or raise an issue that had been previously 'buried' or not thought through. Participants may disclose information in the safety of the intimate, intense interview context without thinking through the repercussions of these disclosures. In families research, this kind of 'emotional unburdening' can create problems among family members and this may adversely affect relationships long after the research has finished.

I do not want to discount the substance of these concerns, some of which I share, however I also do not want to overplay them. It is relatively easy to overcome some of them through careful handling of the interview encounter and sensitivity on the part of the researcher. Furthermore, as illustrated by *Behind Closed Doors*, if the move towards a psycho-social approach is oriented around the means of data collection rather than interpretation of unconscious processes, then the areas of contestation are significantly lessened. In the end, what this approach requires is great care and attention to the research process, something that should exist in all sensitive topic research. I hope that my discussion of the kinds and quality of data that can be elicited through the use of biographical narrative interviews (see chapters 5–7) demonstrates why some sociologists in the field of family studies are now considering this research approach.

Vignettes and photographic scenarios

So far I have examined the presentation and framing of individual, first-person accounts. The next and final two approaches aim to generate data on the social level. Vignettes present small scenarios that illustrate research themes in the third party, away from the sensitivities of personal experience. Participants are typically asked to respond to 'descriptive sketches' (Schoenberg and Ravdal 2000); to create an ending to the 'story' which demonstrates how they, or a character portrayed, would act in the situation. A vignette needs to contain enough contextual information to give participants an understanding of the situation, but be vague enough to invite individual responses (Barter and Renold 1999). Vignettes can be generated from a range of sources including previous research findings, real life histories and experience, or take the form of moral dilemmas. There is growing support for the idea that vignettes are most productive when they resemble 'real life', that is to say, the scenarios that are presented are conceivable, even mundane (Finch 1987).

Photo elicitation or photo interviews work in similar ways to vignettes and can produce similar kinds of data (Bendelow 1993). In addition, discussion of photographs can raise issues of representation and highlight the mediation of experience and family relationships. This can lead into broader discussions on the role and purpose of cultural discourses, and, where appropriate, introduce the ethics of representation. For example, how and in what contexts should images of children be shown? The use of vignettes and/or photo interviews enables the researcher to avoid many of the ethical and emotional difficulties encountered through participants' recall of their personal lives. These methods provide an acceptable means of talking about the private in public (Finch 1987) by generating responses on a social level (Schoenberg and Ravdal 2000). As such they are ideally suited for research on sensitive issues as they can help to desensitise and depersonalise the situation (Hughes and Huby 2001).

Photo and vignette discussion can work effectively as an ice-breaker, putting participants at ease while introducing the research topic, or as a means of winding down interviews, switching the focus from the personal to more abstract issues (Barter and Renold 1999; 2000). This strategy is strongly recommended in research that involves sensitive topics (Kelly 1992). Childhood researchers have used vignettes to explore the ethical frameworks and moral codes that inform children's thinking about the family (Mauthner 1997). They have also been used to explore attitudes surrounding sensitive social phenomena such as mental health (Aubry et al. 1995), racial integration (Farley et al. 1980) and abuse of the elderly (Rahman 1996). Vignettes are increasingly utilised in health care research and have proved to be extremely useful in cross-cultural studies because they help to overcome communication problems (Schoenberg and Ravdal 2000) and enhance understandings that transcend cultural barriers (Greenhalg et al. 1998).

Many of the earlier studies that employed the vignette technique were from a quantitative perspective, with responses to vignettes being used to supplement data from large-scale survey questionnaire (Barter and Renold 2000). In this format, participants were typically introduced to a number of scenarios, asked a number of questions and then selected their response from a range of predetermined (often multiple-choice) answers. Vignettes in quantitative research provide large quantities of data on complex and sensitive issues, such as the experience and assessment of child abuse (Miller et al. 1990), recorded in a standardised form. As with all quantitative methods, the limitation of vignettes in this context is that nuanced answers and/or finer details remain hidden as participants' responses are limited to the answers available to them (Finch 1987; Barter and Renold 2000).

In both quantitative and qualitative research, vignette data should not be interpreted as a representation of people's actual lives. What people *believe* they would do in a vignette scenario is not always the same as what they *would* do if they were in the situation in real life (Hughes 1998). Janet Finch (1987) argues that while the difference in perception and experience is not straightforward, neither is it problematic. She suggests that we should not become preoccupied with inconsistency between belief and action. It is not necessarily the *action* that is of primary interest (this will always be situation-specific). Instead it is the processes of meaning-making and the interpretations used in reaching the outcome that are of greater importance (Barter and Renold 2000). Vignettes can help to unpackage individuals' perceptions, beliefs and attitudes by eliciting data on the socio-cultural repertoire they draw on.

Focus groups

The other approach which typically makes use of third-party scenarios to elicit data on opinions and beliefs is the focus group. Focus groups have been variously defined as in-depth group interviews; a structured group discussion on a given subject; or simply an informal, topic-specific discussion among a group of selected individuals. The main benefits of focus groups are their ability to access detailed articulations of individual and collective points of view and the insight they afford into the processes and practices of arriving at/failing to establish a consensus. The levels of disagreement/agreement provide an indication of the strength/weakness of certain normative views. Discussions in focus groups are typically dynamic, exposing the nature of the sense-making praxis among individuals as a result of group challenges and debate (Wilkinson 1998). It is the nature of this interaction and the quality of the data produced which make focus groups so amenable to research on and with families (Smithson 2000). By far the most common use of focus groups is in conjunction with in-depth interviews or surveys, due to the breadth of the former and the depth of the latter (Morgan 1997). Used in this context they enable researchers to follow up, explore and/or test findings from other methods.

In social sciences research, focus groups are most commonly used at either end of the research process. In the early stage they are used to explore initial hypotheses or as an aid to generate ideas prior to the development of more structured instruments such as questionnaires or interview schedules. In the latter stages of research they are used in large-scale studies as a follow-up device to pursue particular topics or issues that have arisen or to add to the richness of a small-scale project. Another factor that increases the popularity of focus groups among social science researchers is that the method can capitalise on the existence of homogeneous groups, such as work colleagues, classmates or family members, facilitating discussion which in other contexts occurs 'naturally' among them, although it should be noted that while focus groups reproduce the sort of 'natural talk' generated through ordinary conversation, the guidance, intervention and agenda-setting of the moderator/researcher makes it anything of the sort. Hence the analogy of a meeting rather than a conversation is more appropriate (Morgan 1997).

There are some disadvantages of using focus groups in terms of the validity or reliability of their data – something that arises because of the particularity of the interactive event and unavoidable influence of the moderator. Attitudes among participants tend to become more polarised as a result of group discussions and as such the data may be skewed (Race et al. 1994). Moreover, the method can be ineffective in accessing accounts of individuals' private attitudes, practices or experiences when these differ from normative or public discourses. Participants may feel compelled to conceal personal differences and/or tell a public, socially sanctioned story. As such it is not uncommon for focus groups to generate different data from those produced in individual accounts such as one-to-one interviews or outside of the research context in everyday life. Thus it is important to treat focus group data as not necessarily right or wrong, accurate or inaccurate, or representative of the participant's 'real' views on the topic of discussion, but as products of a particular performance of an interactive social event (Smithson 2000). While participants' inclination towards normative discourses is not exclusive to focus groups, it does remain a particular and defining characteristic of the technique.

The dearth of research on the effects of participation in focus groups places a question mark over their appropriateness as a research method in sensitive topic research. Nevertheless, focus groups have been widely and successfully used in highly sensitive areas, including analysis of people's attitudes to sex and sexual practices (Morgan 1997). In the end, as with most methods, it is more likely that it is the practical limitations which debar the use of focus group methods in sensitive topic research more than any methodological limitation. In research projects where recruitment is difficult, composing homogeneous groups may simply be unachievable. In this context more creative forms of composition and/or a stretching of the methodological imagination may be required. For example, later I illustrate the kinds of data that can be generated through intra-familial, family friends and sibling group discussion. While the composition and structuring of these group discussions can be only loosely defined within a focus groups framework, to separate them entirely is both arbitrary and counterintuitive. It is the process of decision-making which remains crucial among group interviews and as such they have more in common with focus groups than with first-person individual interviews.

Framing research and analysing data

So far I have examined methodological approaches that have shaped the studies of families and childhood. In this final section I consider the framing of research and the different analytical approaches that have been used to unpack and examine these data. I introduce case study and cross-sectional analysis and the move towards a more integrative paradigm in mixed-methods research. Many of the approaches and methods previously described lend themselves more or less readily to different analytical strategies. For example, it would be hard to imagine why case studies would be routinely used in quantitative survey research on household composition. Conversely, qualitative mixed-methods data on everyday experience lean more towards case study or cross-sectional analysis than to statistical analysis of socio-historical trends. I examine some of the challenges faced by researchers using these different approaches and point to emergent methodological trends in the analysis of empirical and mixed-methods research data.

Case studies

Case studies can be seen as symbolising the intellectual repackaging of biographical and/or lifecourse narratives. Case studies are not concerned with the narrativisation of experience *per se* so much as the ways that different components of an account combine to present a particular story or version of events, experience and/or emotions. In this way the approach is as concerned with deconstruction as it is with narrative construction. A 'case' may be singular (one person or instance) or complex (involving interrelated individuals, groups and/or events that pertain to general phenomena). In family studies, the case being studied tends to be a single family, kinship network (however loosely defined) or group of families with a trait in common (Greenstein 2006). Generally speaking, single case studies are widely used in medical research and are a useful methodology in other practice-based areas that examine the individual and their social context, such as social work research (Kazi and Wilson 1996; Greenwood and Lowenthal 2005). The aim of the case study approach in practice-based research is twofold: to address an identified problem; and to evidence any strategies and/or hypotheses that are advanced. The use of case studies in sociological analysis of family life tends to be closely aligned with practice-based research that uses this method to explore interrelationships between the personal and the social (Chamberlayne and King 1997) away from a positivist paradigm that aims to resolve particular 'problems' and/or critical events.

Structuring research analysis around particular case studies, however, poses ethical problems. In case study research on groups (friendship, sibling, families) the researcher can become drawn into the relational matrix of participants as individuals present their story and sound out difficulties and/or anxieties that have been hitherto unvoiced (Hey 1997). Melanie Mauthner (2000) in her study of sister relationships found that she had to adopt the role of 'silent mediator' in order to manage the participant–researcher dynamic. Through the research process, some researchers have forged friendships with participants that extend beyond the research encounter (Skeggs 1997). In contrast Mauthner aimed to leave the field and sister relationships as she found them – intact – in order to minimise the effect of participation. Rather than perform the empathetic role traditionally advocated in feminist research (Oakley 1981), she practised selective reciprocity. She limited disclosure so that she did not become emotionally exhausted and could preserve a private life that was not drawn into the field. This approach acknowledges the 'intellectual autobiography' of the researcher (for an overview of these debates, see Maynard and Purvis 1994; Stanley 1990) but stops short of reflexivity wherein the subjectivity of the researcher is integrated into the research process (Fontana and Frey 2005).

Another challenge posed by the case study approach is safeguarding participants' anonymity and confidentiality. There are various strategies that, when combined, can help to preserve confidentiality among individual members of a case study. But, as previously stated, caution must be exercised before making promises of anonymity that cannot be guaranteed. Nevertheless, certain procedures are good practice. Summarised accounts can be separated from pseudonyms in order to break the identifiable narrative thread. Demographic details can be changed (provided that the extent of the alterations does not manipulate the data). Themes can be illustrated through anonymised examples which are not attributed to individuals. Case studies can be shaped around one perspective without corroborative or dissenting commentary from other sources; presenting a first-person account rather than interpretive tales about others.

A case study approach is useful in the analysis of family life because it can focus attention on an individual participant's understanding of their experiences; their versions of relationships with other family members and wider kin and friendship networks. While triangulating data was originally used to check the validity of material, especially across qualitative and quantitative sources, in contemporary research this usage has been changed. Today it is more likely that the triangulation of data is used to identify different realities, to clarify meanings of particular events and/or social phenomenon (Stake 2005: 454). It is no longer simply used to make comparisons between datasets and/or among cases, but instead examines the 'thick description' (Geertz 1973) within the relational and contextual dynamics of a particular case. As such the triangulation of case study data does not aim to produce one interpretation of an event, scenario or relationship. Instead it can identify multiple perspectives and understandings of the same case (Silverman 1993). This means that caution is needed before generalisations are made beyond the particular case study. However, using the approach in this way is not its primary purpose – the usefulness of the case study method lies in its particularisation of experience and not in its representation of the social. Studies that aim to trace the patterning of experience and/or make comparisons between data are more likely to utilise a cross-sectional analytical paradigm.

Cross-sectional analysis

The examination of data across cases and/or methods allows for trends to be identified through the systematic cross-referencing of material. If case studies are seen as vertical strands of data, however complex and 'thick' these may be, cross-sectional analysis looks at data along a horizontal plane, slicing across the dataset. The aim of cross-sectional analysis is to examine the relationship between categories (or variables). Categories are set up through a consistent indexing system, ('categorical indexing'; see Miles and Huberman 1994) and provide the framework with which cross-sectional analysis is undertaken (for a practical guide to sorting, organising and indexing data, see Mason 1996).

Cross-sectional analysis is widely used in comparative analysis and research that uses survey methods. It has proved to be particularly useful in historical, cross-cultural and/or cross-national studies. For example, socio-historical studies have traced gendered patterns of behaviour among families (Pfau-Effinger 2004) and transitions to adulthood (Mitchell 2006). Cross-cultural studies have challenged normative understandings of family (Edholm 1982) and motherhood (Glenn et al. 1994). A focus on racial identity, cultural origin and difference has shifted the agenda away from Western lifestyles and ideas of 'choice' (Collins 1994). This highlights the ways that transnational families extend beyond the parameters of contemporary theorising on changing kin patterns and individuation. Instead, they require a more complex, non-linear approach (Smart and Shipman 2004).

In the UK, cross-national studies are becoming more popular. This is in part because the European Commission has funded several programmes and invested in cross-European networks whose remit it is to examine social and economic developments in EU member states. Wider interest in and the utility of a comparative model is evidenced through a journal devoted to this approach – *Journal of Comparative Family Studies*. Cross-national analyses are useful in that they challenge cultural perceptions of both social phenomena and theoretical/conceptual frameworks. They can sharpen the focus of analysis and bring to the surface new perspectives (Hantrais 1995). For example, cross-national studies of households living in poverty have demonstrated how context and family settings shape families' experience of deprivation (Kerr and Bcaujot 2003; Hansen et al. 2006) and the dynamics of child poverty (Jenkins et al. 2003).

There are, however, problems which cross-national studies typically encounter. The first is logistical. Coordinating a study and research team across different cultural and institutional contexts presents managerial challenges. The next is the issue of comparability. Data are collected in different member states, shaped and structured by national conventions, and as such standardisation is difficult. Finally, there may be a lack of shared understanding about the central concepts and/or social contexts within which the research phenomena are located (Hantrais 1995). All of these factors can be resolved, but doing so may require the researcher to make significant compromises in both method and methodological approach.

The most common challenge faced by researchers using a cross-sectional approach is how to handle the complexity, or to extend Geertz' (1973) phrase, 'the thickness of description', that is produced through the ever-expanding variety of methods employed in this field of study. In the case of longitudinal qualitative research this is made even more complex because the continuous process of change among lifecourse data needs to be accommodated (Smith 2003). Working across data with multiple perspectives on relationships and/or family scenarios raises issues of authenticity and power relations. Accounts do not necessarily present a unified narrative, in which case, 'How does the researcher tell a story from multiple accounts?' (Mauthner 2000: 295). In any research project there is always the potential problem of dissonant data – when data do not make sense or when one account or group contradicts another. In families research dissonant data are typical, hardly surprising given that who constitutes 'family' remains contested. The interconnections of kin ties shift along the lifecourse and in response to life events.

In cross-sectional research *among* families the problem is all the more thorny because the issue of dissonance and/or complementarity refers to both intra- and inter-familial accounts. Amaryll Perlesz and Jo Lindsay consider how researchers can interpret family data when each member of the family presents their personal experiences from their own perspective. They suggest that rather than gloss over or discount areas of disagreement, conflicting accounts can provide 'fertile ground for analysis' (Perlesz and Lindsay 2003: 26). Although the triangulation of dissonant data can be hard to handle, such tensions are useful in developing understanding of relationships and family life. The process of triangulation focuses attention on subjectivity and meaning and can increase 'sensitivity to the variable relationship between an account and the reality to which it refers' (Seale 1999: 59). It is this multidimensional layering of data which characterises mixed-methods research.

Integrating data in mixed-methods research

Any number of methods can be combined in mixed-methods research and these can be analysed as case studies and/or through a cross-sectional approach. Some have advocated tackling a research problem with '*an arsenal of methods*' (Brewer and Hunter 1989), and, in various combinations, all of the qualitative methods detailed above have been used, producing rich data on family relationships and intimate life. Traditionally, the mixing of different methods has mirrored the format of cross-sectional analysis using the combination of methods to highlight dissonance among data. In this framework the analysis of these data was seen as a means to cross-check the validity of qualitative material and triangulate qualitative and quantitative datasets (Denzin 1988). However, recent debate in the UK, generated in part through ESRC Research Methods Programme, has reframed mixed methods away from these early concerns and developed a more nuanced understanding of triangulation (Moran-Ellis et al. 2006) which involves the 'integration' or 'meshing' of methods that transcend the qualitative/quantitative divide (Mason 2006). In the fields of families and childhood research the combining of methods is now commonplace.

Mixed-methods research is becoming ever more eclectic with a richness and diversity of approaches (Bryman 2006). Alison Clark and Peter Moss advocate the use of 'a portfolio of tools' which can be adapted to the requirements of a project and/or research subject. They suggest that the combined 'ingredients' of a 'mosaic approach' enables young people to express their feelings and ideas with confidence (Clark and Moss 2001: 54). It is important not to exaggerate the results of mixed-methods research. Studies have demonstrated that while the choice of method is important, there is no *a priori* link between method and construct or between method and epistemological position (Temple 1994). Thus, while methodology is consequential and may influence the parameters of a study, it does not follow that the complexity of approach necessarily alters the resultant substantive data.

In fact, it may be more productive to think about mixed-methods research as a means to clarify both the research topic and how different aspects of the topic may be theorised and studied (Brannen 1992). This suggests that the analytical focus must shift towards a more integrative paradigm that examines *synergy among data* rather than focusing on dissonance between different methods. This enables researchers to capitalise on the multidimensional data produced through a mixed-methods approach; to broaden understandings about dynamic living systems through studying the inconsistencies and ambiguities of past and present family relationships. Set within this wider framework a whole picture of the individual and how family members interrelate begins to emerge.

For example, in the *Behind Closed Doors* project I found that the combination of methods produced a dynamic account of everyday intimacy and affective practices in families. Solicited diaries mapped structure and routine, while household emotion maps graphically located these events in spaces and places around the home. A psycho-social narrative approach to interviews enabled participants to determine the structure and content of the life stories they told. Semi-structured, more directive interviews picked up the threads and addressed thematic questions about particular events and experiences. The intersections between public and private spheres and how external factors (such as social policy and normative values) shaped parents' understandings of intimacy and sexuality were examined through discussion of vignettes and images. Observations gave both a glimpse of how family members interact with one another and what 'performance' of family they chose to make public. Focus group discussion within families added to the picture of how internal, 'private' family life was managed and demonstrated family processes as opinions and consensus were negotiated among the group.

The integration of these methods produced a *multidimensional picture* of the complexities of family relationships. It pulled together the interiority of affective experience, the intergenerational and gendered dynamics of family intimacy and the affect of external socio-cultural factors on 'private' life. A case studies approach tends to pull together the vertical threads of a story, while a cross-sectional analysis examines the horizontal connections between different threads. The combining of mixed-methods data connects these different threads and weaves together the vertical and horizontal axes. Connections are forged between spatial and temporal dimensions as biographical, lifecourse, everyday, personal and social data are integrated, producing a holistic account of family and relational life.

4
Conceptualisations of Intimacy

So far I have explored methodological approaches and conceptual frameworks in families and childhood research. Intimacy has been addressed through this analysis but has not been unpacked in a critically rigorous way. In this chapter I review conceptualisations of intimacy in family relationships and examine how the 'interiority of family life' (Smart 2004b: 1048) has been evinced in sociological research. As Lynn Jamieson says, 'Intimacy is at the centre' of contemporary family interpersonal relationships (Jamieson 1998: 1) – or more pertinently stated, at the literal and metaphorical *heart* of the matter. I map out the emergence of intimacy as an area of academic interest and, in particular, how this work has shaped the field of family studies. I do not trace the historical emergence of patterns of intimacy because Jamieson (1998) has already done this and I can add nothing further.

While there has been some, albeit limited, attention to the cultural–national contextual particularities of intimacy and family relationships (Throop 1999; Yan 2003), I have only included sociologically informed work focused on Western culture, especially UK and US societies. Within this I engage with debates grounded in the British sociological tradition more than those of the US. That is to say, I conceptualise families as affective spaces of intimacy within which meanings and experiences are constituted by family members in an historical socio-cultural context rather than in accordance with naturalistic understandings of reproductive and/or socialisation function (Smart 2004b). In this framework I characterise key interventions and themes within sociological debate. I refer to both the meta-theorisation of intimacy and (predominantly small-scale) qualitative research of interpersonal relationships.

I propose that sociological studies of intimacy and sexuality in families typically fall into four critical junctures: intimacy is bound up with

sexuality and (hetero)sexual relationships which characterise the functioning of families; the democratisation of interpersonal relationships
has led to transformations of intimacy; intimacy and family relationships are embodied practices experienced in particular spaces, largely
in the home; practices of intimacy demonstrate the interrelationship of
the public and the personal, constituted through acts of intimate citizenship. While the ordering of these four junctures is, generally speaking,
chronological, this does not mean that each debate is contained; the
themes inform each other in a dialogue, albeit at times a fractious one.
This chapter is presented in four sections around the ideas that characterise these junctures. I explore both the substance of these ideas and
their various intersections.

In the first section I introduce the early analytical versioning of
intimacy. This work focused attention on the emotional coupling of
heterosexual relationships and concomitant materialisation through
familial interactions. Critical attention to the character and framing of
intimacy extended the boundaries of intimacy research, beginning to
separate sexual identities and the patterning of intimate behaviour from
the reproductive narrative. I examine notable research that unpicked the
naturalising discourses of the heteronormative paradigm, in particular
the work of Stevi Jackson (1982). In her analysis of childhood and sexuality Jackson resisted the dominant child development model and claimed
that children's sexuality was socially constituted. This work situated the
formation of sexuality across the lifecourse and in so doing paved the way
for subsequent analysis of same-sex relationships and lesbian and gay
parenthood which effectively disassociate intimacy, sexuality and the
reproductive imperative.

In the second section I examine what has been termed 'the transforma
tion of intimacy' (Giddens 1992) and corresponding arguments around
the extent of and/or changes in the patterning of intimate life. Central
to the materialist feminist critique is a heightened awareness of the ways
that everyday 'family practices' constitute a sense of relatedness. This
focus on practices of intimacy has led other researchers to claim that
viewing intimacy through the lens of family and kin is no longer viable.
Diversity among contemporary patterns of care and intimacy requires
a more inclusive relational paradigm oriented around ideas of friendship. This fundamentally undermines the heterosexual/homosexual
dichotomy and the (socially constituted) distinctions between different
kinds of feeling and relationships. In this way anyone, or to push the
point still further, anything, can constitute an intimate because it is
the quality of a relationship which is significant and not its functional

purpose. I examine ideas of asymmetrical reciprocity as a means to make sense of these extended and extending emotional connections.

In the third section I examine work that coalesces around ideas on practices of intimacy. I focus attention on research of embodied relationality – the ways that parents and children demonstrate love and affection and the mediation of intimate experience. Cultural understandings of risk and the setting of boundaries around intimate conduct form a crucial part of this analysis, with emotions and academic concerns heightened around adult–child intimacy. This foregrounds the significance of different relational contexts. I explore how parent–child and carer–client relationships are differentially framed. I examine the parameters and consequences of location and, in particular, the role of the family home in shaping interactions and practices of intimacy.

In the final section I focus attention on the interrelationship of the public and the personal – the ways that practices of intimacy are constituted through acts of intimate citizenship which in turn shape the social world. I interrogate public–private dualisms and demonstrate how research on the 'economy of intimacy' (Zelizer 2005) and women's everyday 'emotion work' (Hochschild 2003) contests the separation of the two spheres. I consider how practices of intimate care evince the artificiality of affective distinctions. In the next and final strand of work I examine research which pulls together emotional–social worlds around ideas of intimate citizenship. Through analysis of the work of the sexualities scholar Ken Plummer (2003), I examine how ideas of the 'intimate citizen' enmesh the socio-cultural and individual subjectivity through everyday processes, constituting interpersonal relationships as reflexive sites of agency.

Intimacy and affective function

Defining and studying intimacy as a discrete category of human experience remains a source of some considerable debate in the social sciences, first emerging as a 'problem' in the late 1970s and early 1980s. At this time intimacy was variously defined as comprising elements of affection (Berger and Calabrese 1975), altruism and solidarity (Levinger and Snoek 1972), interpersonal openness (Altmann and Taylor 1973) and commitment (Huston and Burgess 1979); a constitutive dimension (Walker and Thompson 1983) and/or a valorising component of the relationship (Huston and Burgess 1979). Writing at this time on the topic of intimacy was often situated in the context of sex research, the most notable studies in this frame being those by Alfred Kinsey and colleagues (1948;

1953) and William Master and Virginia Johnson (1966; 1970). The coupling of intimacy with sexuality and sexual/sensual relationships was not unpicked. Authors such as Ronald Mazur talked about 'creative intimacy' as a means to celebrate 'polymorphous sensuality', the pursuit of sex for enjoyment and interpersonal enrichment, set apart from social roles and caring practices (Mazur 1973). Analysis of intimacy and family lifestyles examined emergent 'alternative moralities' and 'family pluralism' through the lens of changing patterns of sex, sex roles and family life: 'The need for intimacy and enduring commitment has outlasted the social institutions that provided for them in the past, and their replacements have not yet been invented' (Skolnick and Skolnick 1974: 18).

Debate between the feminist scholar Mary Jo Deegan and symbolic interactionist Joseph Kotarba (Deegan and Kotarba 1980) characterised research parameters of the time and demonstrated where critical ideas were beginning to dismantle the academic boundaries. Deegan's intervention centred on the (theoretical and relational) interdependency of intimacy and sexuality, as well as on the ethics and means of researching such a sensitive topic. Kotarba (1979) observed visitor–prisoner interactions during prison visits. He claimed that the 'accomplishment of intimacy' in such a highly visible, confined context demonstrated the processes of 'public personalisation' and the mediation of intimate realities.

This research was criticised by Deegan because, she claimed, Kotarba presupposed that intimacy was distinctive, characterised by a set of behaviours that could be observed and determined by the researcher in episodes of interaction. She also challenged the way he linked intimacy with heterosexual couple relations and in so doing set these apart from other familial (presumably non-sexual) relationships It is worth noting that these comments were made against an historical backdrop wherein the causal factors which shape female sexual socialisation were topical (Estep et al. 1977) and homosexuality was characterised, especially in psychoanalytically informed literature, as a pathological and/or troubled form of self and identity (Weeks 1986). However, it is important not overstate the significance of this historical context as more recently another study of inmates and their partners (Comfort et al. 2005) adopted a markedly similar focus, conjoining sexuality and intimacy.

The framing of intimacy in and through sex research was characteristic of this period. This sexuality-oriented approach to the study of intimacy was structured around the 'coupling' of intimacy and sexual relationships. This model laid the foundation for a sustained focus on the emotional functioning of heterosexual relationships which more often than not was located within the context of marriage. This work concentrated on various internal and external factors that affected the marital relationship. These included the consequences of perceived competition between heterosexual partners (Sanders and Suls 1982); the ways that courtship rituals enhanced couple intimacy (King and Christensen 1983); and responses to extramarital sexual permissiveness by wider society (Saunders and Edwards 1984). The sharing of feelings, in particular hurt feelings, between marital partners in the context of clinical therapy was recognised as a dimension of intimate experience (L'Abate and Sloan 1984). But the significance of mutual disclosure as a formative site for constructions of intimacy was not explicated until the 1990s, most notably in the social theorising of Anthony Giddens (1992) and through the materialist feminist work of Lynn Jamieson (1998), work which I detail in the next section.

Notwithstanding the tantalising threads presented in this area, the characteristic emphases in studies of intimacy in the 1980s remained the construction of sexual identities, proclivities and transmission of intimate behaviours through interpersonal familial contact. Contributions from psychologists and sex therapists did address the social contexts of intimacy, for example the commodification and fetishisation of human sexuality in modern consumer culture (Baker 1983). In more sociologically framed work, the constitutive role of socio-cultural discourses in creating unequal power dichotomies in male–female relationships was highlighted (Saunders and Edwards 1984; Larson and Allgood 1987), analysis which has been added to in more recent studies of heterosexual love and sexual relationships (Jackson 1993; Duncombe and Marsden 1996; Langford 1999; McCabe 1999).

Among the early intimacy research literature there were few exceptions to the focus on (hetero)sexual relationships, but one text does stand apart. Stevi Jackson's analysis of childhood and sexuality (1982) shifted the gaze away from adults and the reproductive function of parental relationships towards children's experiences of sexuality. Even though Jackson's study did not address the concept of intimacy *per se*, the scope and importance of her analysis does warrant further attention. The pairing of childhood and sexuality as something other than an occasion of abuse, crisis and/or risk was previously unimaginable. Jackson was fully aware of the sensitivity of her topic and the repercussions that might proceed from her theorising: 'To write about children and sex is to bring together two sets of issues that are highly emotive, that readily provoke moral outrage and righteous indignation' (Jackson 1982: 1).

Few subjects are as universal to shared everyday life experience as the intimate, erotic, interpersonal experiences which occur in childhood. Paradoxically, to this day, there is little sociologically informed research which tackles this. As such Jackson's early intervention is all the more remarkable. The crux of her argument is that both childhood and sexuality are socially constituted. Children are separated from adults through cultural meanings ascribed to age and emotional–physiological development; a socialisation process through which gender and sexual conformity are instrumentally attached to (normally genital) presentation. In other words, childhood and sexuality are understood via their functional link to the human reproductive system, a scientific account which forecloses any alternative because of its invocation of the 'natural' ordering of the (two) sexes. Jackson's foundational analysis reoriented the research paradigm by decentring the adult–sexual couple as the nexus of sexuality research. Her work has informed much subsequent sociological sexuality inquiry; work which further contests the naturalisation thesis by evincing variability in cultural and historical norms (Weeks 1986; Jamieson 1998).

Alongside Jackson's work wider attention was being afforded to children, but this interest tended to be focused on the chronological transmission of intimate practices through family relationships (Thompson et al. 1985). This conceptualisation of intimacy was founded on 1970s child socialisation and psychological development work which examined this intergenerational phenomena, especially the relationships between parent and child (for a critical engagement with this work, see Hollway 2006). The child development model of intimate attachments that evolved retained a functionalist perspective, linking the special (often read as 'natural') parent–child relationship with an effective model of parenting. These attachments were then analysed through a Freudian model of parental authority and subject formation. However, the simultaneous attention to the formation of sexuality across the lifecourse alongside the development of identity and subjectivity opened the way for interrogation of the derivation of adult intimate–sexual identities and behaviours. In particular, critical shifts in the conceptual paradigm emerged through analysis of homosexuality, focusing attention on constitutive parental influences and childhood experience – for instance, how children's strong identification with a father figure may affect their adult sexual orientation (Heilbrun Jr. 1984); the affect of parents' homosexuality on children's sexual development (Harris and Turner 1985; Golombok 2000); and, later, the primacy of homosexual adult relationships as the anchor to family life (Schreurs and Buunk 1996).

Early sociologically informed accounts of same-sex parenting were less concerned with tracing the origins of sexuality but explored how lesbian parents balanced their sexual and maternal lives (Hanscombe and Forster 1981). Somewhat ironically, subsequent additions to the field have tended to shift the focus away from intimacy and affective relationships and onto gender and sexual identity (Lewin 1993; Dunne 1999). Only recently has attention been drawn back to love, sex and intimacy in lesbian couples (Blyth and Straker 1996) and same-sex family analysis (Weeks et al. 2001; Gabb 2004a), something I return to in the next section in an analysis of 'families of choice'. The study of gay and lesbian intimacy in the 1980s may have been narrow in scope but it did serve to dislodge the narrow focus on marital relationships and heterosexuality. It led to a greater critical awareness of the influence of factors such as equity, autonomy and emotional interdependence. These characterise the democratisation thesis and constitute a foundational principle in contemporary sociology (Giddens 1999; Plummer 2003). I examine arguments within this framing and theoretical versioning of intimacy in the next section, ideas which I have grouped together in the second critical juncture around the detraditionalisation of intimacy.

The detraditionalisation of intimacy

The detraditionalisation and/or democratisation theses which emerged in the 1990s provide the backdrop to much contemporary debate on intimacy and affective relationships. Whether applauded or refuted, the ideas in these conceptual frameworks comprise the lens through which intimacy is now commonly analysed and understood. In this section I unpack key debates and address areas of contestation. These critical debates at times have served to polarise opinion; however, it is important to acknowledge areas of agreement. While opinions diverge on the extent and contemporaneousness of transformations of intimacy, there is general consensus that since the 1960s there have been changes in patterns of intimate relationships – notably romantic-sexual partnerships – across much of the Western world (Jamieson 1998; Budgeon and Roseneil 2004; Williams 2004; Gross 2005). Lone-parent families (Silva 1996), step-parent families (McCarthy et al. 2003), friends as family (Nardi 1992), families of choice (Weston 1997; Weeks et al. 2001), blended families (Portrie and Hill 2005) and brave new families (Stacey 1996) all testify to the reconfiguration of traditional forms of intimacy and interpersonal relationships, while paradoxically reinforcing the underlying status of families as a social unit in which affect and emotions reside (Morgan 1996).

The professed changes in patterns of intimacy have been understood by social theorists in a variety of ways: through the role of social movements, notably second-wave feminism (Castells 1997), globalisation and the liberalisation of attitudes (Giddens 1992), individualisation (Beck and Beck-Gersheim 1995) structured through late capitalism (Illouz 1997; Hochschild 2003); or a consequence and constituent of postmodernity (Bauman 2000). While I examine various different opinions across this field, I primarily focus on Giddens' idea of 'transformations of intimacy', not because I give greater credence to his conceptual framework above and beyond others, but because his ideas have stirred up an intense debate that teases out many points which cut across wider discussions on the detraditionalisation of intimacy.

Giddens suggests that transformations of intimacy have occurred throughout contemporary Western society and that these transformations reflect a 'wholesale democratisation of the interpersonal domain' (Giddens 1992: 3). He bases his argument on contemporary therapeutic ideologies which, he claims, have fostered a culture of self-fulfilment by which individuals judge the merits of intimate relationships. Giddens' argument is that the separation of sex from reproduction has brought about the possibility of a 'pure relationship' in which men and women are equals. He sees the pure relationship as part of a generic 'restructuring of intimacy' (Giddens 1991: 58), which has replaced familial ties of obligation. The relationship now exists 'solely for whatever rewards that relationship can deliver' (ibid.: 6); when a partnership ceases to 'deliver', couples simply separate by mutual consent.

For Giddens, the 'liberation' of sex from the affective and caring stranglehold of reproduction represents 'a revolution in female sexual autonomy' (Giddens 1992: 28). Freed from the needs of reproduction, sexuality is decentred, which leads to flexibility and choice, or in Giddens' terms, 'plastic sexuality'. Advancing his argument, he points to the prevalence of 'episodic sexuality' among gay men, suggesting that their poly-amorous practices and/or intimate encounters sever 'the connections which link sexuality, self-identity and intimacy' (ibid.: 146). The individual is a 'reflexive subject'; someone who is able to move within and create a 'narrative of self' (ibid.: 75).

Since then, much has been made in the theoretical literature of the sociological triad of breakdown, democratisation and continuity as foundational to the study of family intimacy (Gillies 2003). For example, extending his postmodern metaphor of liquidity, Zygmunt Bauman

(2003) frames interpersonal relationships as affinities that are structured through latent, insecure, frail and impermanent bonds of love. This affective fragility characterises modern societies and consequently requires the individual to proactively manage the parameters of their ever-shifting intimate landscape.

Theoretical literature in this emotionally precarious area situates risk, anxiety and uncertainty at the centre of contemporary experiences of intimate relationships. This is attributed to the fragmentation of traditional family structures which proceed from the escalation of individualism in modern culture. Ulrich Beck and Elisabeth Beck-Gernsheim suggest that in this cultural context of serial adult-sexual relationships, it is children who have become the reliable source of love (Beck and Beck-Gersheim 1995), something which can adversely affect the adult–adult relationship (Beck-Gernsheim 1999). As a consequence of parental anxiety over child welfare, new patterns of family communication and changes to the constitution of contemporary extended kin networks, it is claimed that family intimacy has become increasingly democratic and participatory (Passmore 1998). This has led to an ethos of negotiation and disclosing intimacy between parents and children.

Critics of the detraditionalisation thesis do not reject the idea of changes in the affective patterning of relationships *per se*, but claim that proponents have overstated the case. For example, Neil Gross (2005) contests whether individuals and groups who live outside the (heteronormative) centre do in fact become 'arch-inventors' of contemporary patterns of intimacy as characterised by Weeks and colleagues (Weeks et al. 1999). He points to the proliferation of wedding-like ceremonies and the 'wedding industry' (Lewin 2002) which, in the UK, is targeting the 'pink pound' following the enactment of civil partnership legislation. Citing examples across a breadth of research projects and survey data, Gross demonstrates how powerful the ideal romantic-sexual couple remains in the cultural imaginary. Marriage persists as a 'guiding cultural ideal' for much of the Western population, drawing attention to the resilience of patriarchal beliefs and practices (Gross 2005: 297–301).

Gross argues that while there is some evidence that regulative traditions such as 'lifelong, internally stratified marriage' are in decline, this has not meant that 'reflexivity, understood as unbounded agency and creativity, has rushed in to fill the void.' Radical social change is delimited through the prevalence and embeddedness of 'meaning-constitutive traditions'. These 'establish limits on what may be expressed to oneself and others in a situation, influencing the thinkability of particular acts and projects' (ibid.: 295–6). Gross suggests that the detraditionalisation of intimacy is underspecified and empirically problematic, points which echo and have been extended by others, many of whom come from a feminist standpoint.

In a critical engagement with ideas of the 'pure relationship' and 'plastic sexuality', Lynn Jamieson argues that Giddens marginalises childhood and parent–child relationships and effaces the classed, gendered and ethnic dimensions of parenting and socialisation, dimensions that constitute the material and embodied context of everyday family life (Jamieson 1998). The reflexive process (self as project) advanced by Giddens is said to lead to self-obsessed individualism – a 'luxury' from which many are excluded. Jamieson argues that Giddens' patterning of (s)elective love in contemporary relationships remains an ostensibly theoretical account of interpersonal democratisation; obscuring the relational basis which underlies most people's affective lives. While public stories of intimacy are in circulation which emphasise mutuality and reciprocity as structural principles of relationships, Jamieson argues that 'there is no clear evidence that disclosing intimacy is increasingly the key organizing principle of people's lives' (ibid.: 2). There is a complex relationship between stories and lived experience. People incorporate and recycle public stories into their own narratives of self, but the authentic self and the story of self are often separable (ibid.: 12).

Jamieson maps the historical emergence of contemporary family relationships and highlights the shift in emphasis in the study of personal or primary relationships from the structural analysis of relational bonds to the more qualitative perspective of personal intimacy based on affective and communicative disclosure. In the early twentieth century parent–child relationships were not typically presented as emotionally intense (Jamieson and Tonybee 1990). 'Good mothering' was characterised in functionalist terms – a job which needed to be done and for which women were 'naturally' suited. Proponents of functionalism, such as Emile Durkheim (1858–1917), believed that women's move from the workplace into the home was an evolutionary outcome, necessitated by the increasingly complex basis of society. In the 1940s–1960s Talcott Parsons (1959) extended such thinking, arguing that effective childrearing depended on specialised skills, which only women possess. In order for children to 'fit' in society and the rapid social changes it was undergoing, mothers were charged with using their innate maternal bond with 'their' children to socialise them into becoming good citizens. Thus it was only in the 1950s that motherhood and the mother–child relationship became characterised as such an emotionally charged relational experience, with the focus on caring for the physical and psychological well-being of the child.

In contemporary Western society the parent–child relationship has become one of ongoing negotiation and intimate knowing: 'intimacy now encompasses constantly working with the child, to know and understand him or her' (Jamieson 1998: 47). Jamieson suggests that this relational process compels parents (as a couple) and parents and children (as a family) to develop mutual understanding through 'talking and listening, sharing thoughts, showing feelings' (ibid.: 158). This process is not solely dependent on verbal communication – the articulation of intimacy. Rather, it is 'deep knowing and understanding' which characterise disclosing intimacy (ibid.: 9) and these 'patterns of disclosing intimacy are part of an emerging future' (ibid.: 159).

At first glance, Jamieson's argument on disclosing intimacy in parent–child relationships appears to have some parallels to the one advanced by Giddens. Taking a heavy steer from child development literature, Giddens suggests that it is the quality of the parent–child relationship which is paramount, 'with a stress upon intimacy replacing that of parental authoritativeness. Sensitivity and understanding are asked on both sides' (Giddens 1992: 98). The parent–child relationship is structured around dialogue. He advocates that it should approximate the pure relationship and draw on free and open communication. This does not dissolve parental power but shifts it from authoritarianism to authority, which, he says, can be 'defended in a principled fashion' (ibid.: 109). The relationship between parent and child should be democratic, irrespective of the child's age: 'It is a right of the child, in other words, to be treated as a putative adult'. When the child is too young to enter into negotiations, 'counterfactual justification should be evident' (ibid.: 191–2). Where Jamieson and Giddens substantively diverge is on the extent and realisation of this democratic ethic, particularly in terms of gendered and generational power relations within family interactions.

Jamieson points out that 'Parenting is rarely a gender-neutral activity and often exacerbates inequalities'. On a day-to-day basis 'mothers typically remain much more emotionally and practically involved with their children than fathers' (Jamieson 1999: 488). Moreover, reiterating earlier feminist arguments (e.g. Delphy 1992), she contests the disassociation from wider generational structures wherein parents (both mothers and fathers) as adults exert significant power over their children. Jamieson (1998) notes that the new and much-heralded ethos of mutuality among partners and families has been observed to be a smokescreen that masks the traditional imposition of parental control through socially sanctioned authority.

Some mothers may enter into complex negotiations with older children, in an attempt to practise empathy, understanding and communication (Brannen et al. 1994). Others may even aim towards a goal of pseudo-democracy with younger children through careful reasoning (Walkerdine and Lucey 1989). However, the crux of Jamieson's argument is that *despite* these efforts, 'Mutually intimate mother–child relationships are not necessarily the consequence' (Jamieson 1999: 488). While (predominantly white, middle-class) mothers and their teenage children may equally subscribe to the discourse of openness and honesty as the route to intimacy and democracy, there are tensions around the areas of communication, disclosures, secrecy and surveillance (Gillies et al. 2001). *Knowing* children easily slips into wanting *knowledge about* their activities, as a means to protect and/or control them. The 'twin ideals of democracy and intimacy necessarily clash in parent–teenager relationships ... because both parties have opposing goals in the trading of information' (Solomon et al. 2002: 965). Wider social–generational power relations remain intractable. Furthermore, there is little to suggest that strategies such as these are universal; in fact, the opposite is true.

Furthermore, ideas of mutuality routinely come unstuck when the topic of conversation is 'sensitive', that is to say touches on the personal–private issues of intimacy and sexuality. Research has shown that fathers often find any discussion of sexuality with their children especially inhibiting (Kirkman et al. 2001). There is substantial evidence to show that the axial cultural constructions of intimacy and gender socialisation in the context of 'family sexuality' is still a potent mix (Gabb 2001), especially when it comes to parent–child understandings and/or communication. Research indicates that there is significant variation across class and ethnicity about what it means to be a good parent and what constitutes a good relationship.

It is the omission of material conditions in theoretical accounts of democratisation and mutuality which receives most critical attention. It is claimed that this serves to expunge the messiness of everyday lives as macro-societal and micro-personal worlds coalesce. Nowhere are these intersections and material loose ends more keenly experienced than in the process of 'divorce'. Giddens may treat children as 'the putative equal of the adult' (Giddens 1992: 191), but these ideas quickly begin to unravel once parents separate. While couples in a pure relationship may part with impunity, children cannot be as readily cast aside; child care responsibilities, financial obligations and parent–child emotional attachments continue.

Research has demonstrated that after divorce, women often face financial hardship. In many instances men are content to retain traditionally defined masculine roles such as breadwinner and hands-off parent (Brannen and O'Brien 1995). There is some evidence to suggest that non-resident parent–child relationships can be sustained across households and that children are able to accommodate the idea of two homes quite readily (Smart et al. 2001). Other studies highlight how many non-custodial fathers lose touch with their children, especially over the course of time (Cherlin 1992). The reasons for losing touch may be due to waning interest or because contact is either too hard to negotiate and/or too painful to continue, but the result is the same. The mother becomes the constant source of emotional attachment and in many cases the only regular source of financial support.

Notwithstanding academic differences, shifts in the research agenda away from a structural analysis of categorical relationships to more qualitative perspectives of interpersonal intimacy reflect wider social changes in the affective patterning of relationships, wherein marriage, divorce and remarriage are commonplace. The move away from structuralism and/or functionalism to personal interaction focuses attention on the ways that everyday practices of intimacy constitute a sense of relatedness and family. However, some argue that this stops short of where we are now and seek to extend the argument still further. This strand of research suggests that it is no longer viable to understand intimacy through the lens of family and kin. Contemporary relational patterns of care and intimacy undermine this heteronormative framework and require a queering of sociological thought (Budgeon and Roseneil 2004).

Proponents of the queer trajectory claim that transformations of intimacy and care are eroding the heterosexual/homosexual dichotomy (Roseneil 2000), out of which comes 'a certain logic of congruence' (Weeks et al. 1999: 85). The relationship – the desire for intimacy – is important in its own right, structuring everyday lives and lifestyles. 'Families of choice' (Weeks et al. 2001) and 'families we choose' (Weston 1997) demonstrate variety among the patterning of relationships. These include voluntary affective attachments within which friendship networks can become 'de facto families' (Altman 1982). These elective families are 'something new sociologically', an 'index of changing social possibilities and demands' (Weeks et al. 1999: 90). Friends are the source of consistency and support, something that was previously taken for granted as a function of families or kin networks.

Central to this friendship ethos is a contestation of individual's finite capacity for intimacy. Supplementary and, in some instances, substitute affective structures, such as 'friend-like relationships' (Pahl and Spencer 1997), networks of friends and/or non-resident partnerships, have been cited as increasingly common – the contemporary source and repository of care and intimacy (Roseneil and Budgeon 2004b). Same-sex friendships have been shown to be as important for men as they are for women, although differences between the genders have been identified (Yaughn and Nowicki Jr. 1999; Roy and Benenson 2000). The universalism of the 'friends as family' model among lesbian and gay communities (Nardi 1992) has been queried (Lewin 1993; Gabb 2004b); however, there is general consensus that a functional framework, wherein one model fits all, no longer reflects the pluralism of interpersonal networks and relationships – if indeed it ever did.

The gender–sexuality scholars Sasha Roseneil and Shelley Budgeon draw together many of the ideas around the detraditionalisation of family and the queering of intimate relationships in an edited collection of articles in *Current Sociology*. They acknowledge that the category of family still has salience, but contend that even in its changed and diversified form, it is 'increasingly failing to contain the multiplicity of practices of intimacy and care which have traditionally been its prerogative and its *raison d'être*' (Budgeon and Roseneil 2004: 127). They suggest that 'there are fundamental shifts underway in the social organization of intimacy and sociability ... which are both constitutive and productive of these conditions of social change' (ibid.: 128). Rather than position these within the largely pessimistic framework of individualisation and breakdown (Bauman 2001; 2003) they propose that a range of personal relationships are now being shaped which successfully provide intimacy, care and companionship across the lifecourse.

Focusing attention on 'non-standard intimacies' (Berlant and Warner 2000) highlights the blurring of boundaries and the fluidity between different categories of relationship. In doing so, it decentres the conjugal relationship as the nexus for research on intimacy. 'This queering of the social calls into question the normativity and naturalness of both heterosexuality and heterorelationality' (Roseneil and Budgeon 2004b: 138–41). The essays in this collection examine different aspects of contemporary intimacies. For example, the editors explore how sexual partnerships are deprioritised as friends provide care, support and intimacy in times of emotional, physical and practical need (Roseneil and Budgeon 2004b). Similarly, couples who retain separate households ('living apart together' – LATs) are shown to destabilise the dyadic relationship model and traditional ideas of family as defined through the household (Levin 2004), as do those who create 'personal communities' of friends and families structured on the concepts of choice and commitment (Pahl and Spencer 2004).

Another contributor, Sue Heath, suggests that young people are looking to the communality of shared housing for intimacy and support in ways that challenge the conventional heterosexual couple and in the process create 'neo-tribes' (Heath 2004). The American family sociologist and gender–sexuality scholar Judith Stacey (2004) proposes that gay men's recreational sex creates 'families of choice' which provide the possibility of greater reciprocity of care over the course of the lifecycle. Same-sex relationships challenge traditional (legally institutionalised and culturally reified) forms of citizenship and require new language beyond family values orthodoxy (Adam 2004).

In this vein, the emphasis on relationships as diverse composites of various social and personal practices, taking place in a variety of social and historical contexts, has led researchers to explore how different styles of attachment may be indicative of wider social competency. There has been what might be classified as an 'intimate turn' in the study of families and interpersonal relationships. This represents a paradigm shift not only in the study of families and kinship, but in the very qualitative meaning of family life. Affinities are being examined through a new lens which is helping us to understand intimacy as a discrete subject for analysis, evaluation and judgement. 'Family' has lost its empirical status as a permanent and fixed feature of social reality (Williams 2004). Instead it is regarded as a changing socio-cultural phenomenon with localised epistemological underpinnings. Family is something you do as opposed to something you are (Gillies 2003).

The new emphasis on the discursive and participative nature of families draws attention to hitherto private narratives of intimacy and sexuality. In so doing it poses a fundamental challenge to standardised and/or normative understandings of intimacy (Plummer 2003). Among other things, the democratisation of intimacy thesis has helped generate great diversity in the taxonomies of emotional intimacy. Some work still tries to quantify and measure distinctive types of intimacy (Hook et al. 2003), suggesting that intimacy is one part of an individual's wider affective register alongside interrelated feelings such as passion and love (Baumeister 1986). But there is other literature and research which endeavour to de-emphasise the distinctions between different kinds of feeling and relationships (for example, erotic and non-erotic relations).

This work allows friends, lovers and children to be brought together under a single rubric (Weeks et al. 2001: 107) and queries cultural understandings of love and desire (Gabb 2004a). Similar conceptual moves have been made in various related areas of intimacy research, including studies of early years and pre-adolescent children (Brilleslijper-Kater and Baartman 2000), experiences during adolescence (Feldman et al. 1998) and relationships between siblings (Mauthner et al. 2005; Edwards et al. 2006). The significance of ethnic and cultural context (Cicirelli 1994; Chamberlain 1999) and interrelationships among members of religious faith communities (MacKnee 2002) have also been examined.

There is now a body of research that has shifted the focus away from families and/or couples as the loci of intimate relationships. This work typically conjoins intimacy with reciprocity, expressed through diverse relational transactions. This framing of relationality is shaped around a mutuality of purpose and a levelling of difference among those who reciprocate. However, as Jean Duncombe and Dennis Marsden point out, 'Asymmetry in intimacy and emotion work may be the last frontier of gender inequality' (Duncombe and Marsden 1995: 150). Mutuality does not account for intimate relationships that are imbalanced, as are many relationships between men and women, parent and child, siblings, rich and poor, sick and healthy. To date this conundrum has yet to be resolved in analyses of intimacy.

One avenue that might provide fertile ground in the analysis of socially differentiated intimates can be found in the philosophy-oriented work of the political scientist Iris Marion Young. Young contests the need to affect symmetry between self and other in order to understand another's standpoint. She argues that 'moral respect and egalitarian reciprocity' is not dependent on a desire for and/or an achievement of symmetry in positions of self and other. Instead it relies on the acknowledgement of *differences between self and other*, notably differences in history and social position (Young 1997: 351). The crux of her argument is that the presupposition of symmetry and sameness obscures constitutive differences. Multidimensional relations with one another should not be worked over to appear as similarities and reversibility; we should aim to acknowledge the specificity of differences.

Young develops the idea of asymmetrical reciprocity as a framework through which 'mutual acknowledgement' of others' interests can be appreciated: 'each position and perspective transcends the others, [and] goes beyond the possibility to share or imagine' (ibid.: 351). Building on the work of Emmanuel Levinas (1981) and Luce Irigaray (1974), Young explores how subject differentiation can establish respectful (spatial and temporal) distance of self from other; a distance which requires creativity in order that both parties can effectively communicate. As such she positions communication as 'a creative process' – a dynamic exchange in which 'I am open and suspend my assumptions in order to listen'. This process of listening and being open to others' standpoints achieves 'moral humility'. It acknowledges that there is a great deal that we do not know or understand about others' perspectives; it is a 'humble recognition' of our own situated position (Young 1997: 354–5). Beyond this, moral respect and openness to the other requires 'some sense of mutual identification and sharing' but, more importantly, it also requires 'a moment of *wonder*, of an openness to the newness and mystery of the other person' (ibid.: 357).

Wonder 'does not try and seize, possess, or reduce this object, but leaves it subjective, still free' (Irigaray 1974: 13). Respectful wonder represents not only openness to others, it also 'means being able to see one's own position, assumptions, perspectives as strange' (Young 1997: 358). It decentres taken-for-granted social positions as the focus for knowledge and interpretation. Young does not develop her thesis in the context of intimate relationships, but it could have great purchase in making sense of structural differences among intimates and in wider conceptualisations of intimacy and affective exchange. A model of asymmetrical reciprocity as the cornerstone of all intimate relationships not only acknowledges difference between intimates, but also makes such differences a creative and dynamic factor within these relationships.

Taking the argument a step further, the feminist science and technology scholar Donna Haraway (2003) considers the material and conceptual possibilities of relationships between 'companion species' in which asymmetry is foundational. Research in family and childhood studies has examined the significance of human–pet relationships, notably around children's creation of family and kinship (O'Brien et al. 1996; O'Connor et al. 2004; Mason and Tipper 2006). Reading these studies through Haraway's 'companion species' paradigm, it is possible to see how pet–human relationships fundamentally challenge the boundaries that have tended to define and delimit the academic imagination around studies of intimacy. For Haraway, dogs, like cyborgs, are part of a 'queer family of companion species' (Haraway 2003: 11). The building of a home and a relationship between dog and human is 'a kinship-making apparatus that reaches into and draws from the history of 'the family' in every imaginable way, literally' (ibid.: 95).

Haraway does not seek to advance a post-humanism agenda, which merges the boundaries between self and other to include dogs as one of us. Dogs are not surrogate children. 'My multi-species family is not about surrogacy and substitutes; we are trying to live other tropes, other metaplasms. We need other nouns and pronouns for the kin genres of companion species, just as we did (and still do) for the spectrum of genders' (ibid.: 95). She contests the tendency to anthropomorphise the pet/dog-owner/human relationship arguing that this misreads and disparages the real relationship. This is not about 'unconditional love', which is in itself an historically specific fictive creation, it is about 'seeking to inhabit an inter-subjective world that is about meeting the other in all the fleshy detail of a mortal relationship' (ibid.: 34).

The framing of inter-subjectivity in Haraway's thinking is not based on an illusory claim to equality, but on 'significant otherness' structured through respect and trust. This extends Young's ideas on asymmetrical reciprocity. It moves beyond simple understandings of affect and the relational to include multidimensional emotions that transcend 'naturalcultural' boundaries: 'all ethical relating, within or between species, is knit from the silk-strong thread of ongoing alertness to otherness-in-relation. We are not one, and being depends on getting on together' (ibid.: 50). If we accept that differences have an enduring constitutive role in the designation, understanding and experience of relationships, then accounting for the asymmetry of emotion exchanges cannot be side-stepped. The paradigmatic shift offered by Young and Haraway has not (so far) been taken up in the conceptual field of intimacy studies, but it undoubtedly could play an important role in future inquiry. In chapter 5 I tease out a few ideas from *Behind Closed Doors* data that raise questions about the boundaries and boundary management of intimacy through analysis of family–pet relationality. This demonstrates the value of Young's ideas of asymmetrical reciprocity in making sense of multidimensional relationships.

Embodied intimacy

Notwithstanding the diversity of forms, practices and conceptual understandings of intimacy, what is common to all is the corporeality of experience, ranging from the sensation of touch to our physical reaction to others' articulation of feelings. Words alone may be spoken, but they elicit a physical sensation in the recipient. Mutual disclosure may be an intimacy of the self, but 'the completeness of intimacy of the self may be enhanced by bodily intimacy' (Jamieson 1998: 1). In this section I examine embodied practices of intimacy and family relationships. There have been relatively few studies of how families *do* non-verbal 'bodily intimacy', that is to say, the embodiment of intimate practice. Moreover, the primary focus of research in this area remains sexuality more than wider experiences of intimacy. However, the work that has been done adds a crucial dimension to understandings of intimate conduct and family relationships.

Fundamental to analysis in this area is a querying of 'the body', a terrain that remains hotly contested (Turner 1984), with the differences and particularities of the pre-discursive, the phenomenological and the lived body being unpicked (Crossley 2006). As part of this argument it is suggested that 'the body is a masculinist illusion' which does not exist in any single or simple form. Instead it is more accurate to talk of bodies in the plural (Longhurst 1995). I leave to one side this complex area and take for granted for the purposes of this book that material bodies do exist through social experiences and understandings of self and other. As such I am talking about the embodiment of intimacy and bodily intimate practices rather than the body as something in and of itself.

There is a wealth of interest in studies of embodiment, body practices and bodily boundaries, exploring the body and society (Turner 1984; Scott and Morgan 1993), body shape (Bordo 1993), bodies and sickness (Brown 1995), embodiments of gender and sexualities (Ingram et al. 1997) and class (Dowling 1999), to name but a few. Studies of the body and emotions have also come to the fore in the study of intimacy, as seen for instance in the importance of body image on heterosexual interpersonal functioning (Wiederman 2000). Much of this work is situated in the (inter)disciplinary context of geographical studies, which have encouraged explorations of the complex interrelationship between embodiment and spatiality (Rose 1995). Feminist theorising has been hugely influential here (Simonsen 2000), drawing attention to the 'sexed body' as a 'critical component in the matrix of subjectivity' which foregrounds and evinces the 'understandings of power, knowledge and social relationships between people and environments' (Longhurst 1997: 495). Notwithstanding the importance of this literature, David Morgan suggests that 'the systematic linking of family sociology and the sociology of the body remains to be achieved' (Morgan 1996: 113) – an observation which still rings true.

In childhood studies and child welfare literature significant attention has been paid to policing the (affective and physical) boundaries of the child. In one of the very few studies of 'normal family sexuality', the psychologists Marjorie Smith and Margaret Grocke (1995) examined children's sexual knowledge in 'ordinary families', illustrating how boundaries between abusive and non-abusive parenting are hard to define. Behaviours thought to be indicators of abuse, such as 'excessive masturbation, over-sexualised behaviour, an extensive sexual curiosity or sexual knowledge and genital touching', were found to be common in their sample. They therefore question whether these signs alone are sufficient to suggest abuse (Smith and Grocke 1995: 83). Other research has explored the range of parental behaviours towards children across the general population, paying particular attention to practices of physical punishment. This work has demonstrated that, in the UK, the use of corporal punishment is almost universal (Smith et al. 1995; Nobes and Smith 1997). Findings of this kind highlight the arbitrariness of boundaries around ideas of appropriate conduct and intimate behaviour. They point to differences between public valorising of the rights of children and private practices of sexuality and adult–child interactions.

Sociological research has tended to pursue a different line, focusing attention on the constitution and incumbent meanings of the parent–child relationship. This work suggests that the amount and nature of physical contact between adults and children signifies children's social position (Jackson 1982), showing how they are denied any concept of 'bodily autonomy' (Kitzinger 1988: 85). In families the body is socialised with reference to broader structures of power and control. Bodies deal out or receive punishment, signify the gendered hierarchies that exist between 'husband' and 'wife' and represent the generational hierarchy of adult–child relations. Certain body parts take on particular roles, many of which are dual-purpose. Eyes can 'speak volumes'; they can say 'I love you' or they can show annoyance, distress and hatred. Hands may caress, express love and tenderness, they can care for and connect with others. Paradoxically they may be clenched in a fist and inflict pain or be withheld to separate self from other (Morgan 1996). Teenagers' assertion 'talk to the hand' is a potent symbol of how demonstrative hands can be and is an example of how (powerless) children may use their bodies to distance self from other.

Genital and other erotic areas of the body, such as women's breasts, are accorded a particular status in Western culture. This normative (moral) modelling continues into the home and is inculcated through ideas of 'good parenting'. Social norms of modesty dictate what must be concealed from children's eyes, especially once they reach puberty and become aware of their own sexuality and sexual identity. Children likewise learn to manage the sexual potentialities of their bodies. From an early age they learn that their 'privates' must be kept hidden and that areas 'down there' are too secret even to name (Gabb 2004a). To know these codes and perform the necessary shifts in public and private personas marks the acceptable social citizen from anti-social others (Goffman 1969).

Studies of motherhood have demonstrated how moral anxieties about body space and the proximity of others' bodies alter during maternity (Young 1990) as sensuality and physical contact are understood to reinforce the mother–child bond (Gabb 2004a). Women's embodied experiences of menstruation, childbirth and lactation challenge bodily boundaries of self and other (McDowell 1993). Research on fatherhood has shown that some fathers try to create this sense of embodied connectedness by engaging in bodily activities such as cuddling, sleeping with their child or bathing together (Lupton and Barclay 1997). However, David Morgan argues that the 'pleasures and erotics of family living cannot . . . be detached from issues of risk and danger' (Morgan 1996: 124). These sentiments are typical of sociologically informed work. Psychological literature has looked at parent–child sexuality and intimacy in the context of children's sexuality development, focusing on mother–child attachment (Bowlby 1969), the differences among mother/father–child relationships (Fox et al. 1991) and children's sexual behaviour and psychological development (Sandfort and Rademakers 2000).

In sociological debate, studies of children, intimacy and sexuality tend to be framed around ideas of 'risk' (Ennew 1986; Scott et al. 1998), sexual abuse (Kelly et al. 1998) and paedophilia (Wyre and Tate 1995). This research draws on arguments which situate child sexual abuse as 'a man thing' (Itzen 2000), with some work even claiming that non-abusing fathers experience sexual arousal or 'inappropriate' interest in their daughters (Williams and Finkelhor 1995). Beyond this predatory male paradigm, it is primarily in the area of children and sexuality research, set aside from intergenerational relationships, where the sexuality = risk equation appears to be challenged. For example, studies which focus on sex education (Measor 2004) and how young people experience and understand sexual relationships (Allen 2004; Sharpe and Thomson 2005) in the context of heterosexuality (Holland et al. 1998) and emergent lesbian and gay sexualities (Epstein 1994) shift the agenda away from risk and danger. These analyses are extremely important in developing sexual health and sex education policy and are building a picture of *intra*-generational intimacy and sex/uality learning. But the jigsaw remains incomplete because this research typically focuses on adolescents away from their families, in youth centres and at school. As such, negotiations around *inter*-generational sexuality and intimacy remain uncharted.

There is controversial sexuality studies literature on 'man-boy love' (Sandfort 1987) and intergenerational intimacy (Jones 1990) which argues that relationships between adult men and children can be consensual and fulfilling: an integral part of non-Western culture (Herdt 1981). Attempting to bridge the gap between ideas on 'child love' and the more policy- and/or feminist-oriented work on child welfare and abuse, Ken Plummer (1990) has suggested that we should adopt a social constructionist approach to understandings and analyses of these practices. This would afford greater insight into the 'historical diversity and situational ambiguity of "sex" and make inroads into the divisive debate on children and sexuality' (Plummer 1990: 232). Some research has attempted to follow this path, looking at how and why children and sex/uality have become culturally synonymous in the Western world (Kinkaid 1998); how the media construct (innocence–sexual) dualisms which are especially unhelpful to debates on children and sexuality (Walkerdine 2001; Jackson and Scott 2004). Other research in sexuality studies (discussed earlier) attempts to challenge distinctions between erotic and non-erotic relations, by bringing friends, lovers and children together under a single affective rubric. Ideas on 'sexual citizenship' add another dimension to the debate, problematising socio-cultural understandings of sexuality and children by denaturalising the sexual (Weeks 1998). These ideas are examined in more detail in the next section.

Research on how parents and children negotiate sexual–familial identities in their everyday lives highlights the cultural specificity of codes of conduct and decency (Robinson et al. 2004; Gabb 2005a). This approach brings out the construction of affective boundaries within families and the differential experience of intimacy–sexuality management. Most families are not directly scrutinised. It is primarily only those in receipt of benefit and/or in regular contact with the health service due to children's ill-health/disability who are open to routine inspection and surveillance. The same is true of those who live outside the conventional boundaries of heteronormative families (Gabb 2005b). In such cases, to assess whether some degree of sanction or intervention is 'justified', families are measured and in turn measure themselves against 'the norm'. This template and way of doing family is popularly produced in advice on how to manage the trials and tribulations of parenthood and become 'good enough' parents (Winnicott 1965).

Parenting advice is mediated knowledge – firsthand experience passed down from mother to daughter, health visitor to client. Professional 'knowledge' is imparted through handbooks and magazines. Expert advice is delivered in the form of reality television such as *Super Nanny* (Channel 4), *Little Angels* (BBC3), *Driving Mum and Dad Mad* (ITV1) and instant access (frequently sponsored) websites such as http://www.

thinkbaby.co.uk; http://www.parenting.com. Opinions and personal experience is shared via blogs and online parenting communities. These multifarious 'simulations of intimacy' (Plummer 2003: 21) and normative strands of advice are supported and given credence by official documentation in the area of social policy (Bramwell 1998). Such advice and guidance are clear about embodied boundaries and typically advocate the need to protect children from 'risk', especially sexual predation. However, while sex education literature aimed at teenagers describes intimacy and intimate relationships as part of everyday relational life, being linked with but not dependent on sexuality and sexual relationships (Farrington 2000), parenting guidelines seldom address the tricky terrain of 'normal family sexuality' and intimate familial relationships. Instead these resources tend to focus on healthy living and unruly behaviour.

Parents have to rely on 'instinct', while all the time taking on board media hyperbole around tragic instances of child abuse and adult–child predation which inform social policy and the cultural climate around what is appropriate behaviour. Thus David Morgan argues that in this uncertain climate all physical contact between adults and children should be seen as risky practices, even interactions that are mutually consensual and enjoyable to all parties, including comforting, rough-and-tumble, routine caresses and embraces, because physical intimacy is always *at risk* of being misunderstood. In this precarious cultural context it is not surprising that uncertainty prevails: parents, especially fathers, are confused about what is expected of them (Morgan 1996).

In the areas of child welfare and non-familial (institutional) care there are clear guidelines on adult–child, carer–client bodily boundaries which delineate the parameters of in/appropriate behaviour and intimate conduct. For example, in a guidance booklet on 'safer caring' (Bray 2003) written for the British Agencies for Adoption and Fostering, it is recommended that foster carers should not touch a foster child in ways that could be misconstrued; this includes cuddles and kissing goodnight. Carers should enter the child's bedroom only when asked and male carers should always be accompanied by a female adult in such 'private spaces'. These guidelines are aimed at short-term carers of children who (may) have been previously abused. The strategies mentioned are intended to protect carers and the local authority rather than provide therapeutic responses. However, their directive and discursive framing illustrate the anxiety around embodied forms of intimacy and communication.

In a similar vein research of non-familial, institutional care demonstrates the ways that boundaries of body work are managed to evacuate sensuality from formal acts of intimacy. In a study of the experiences of older and disabled people who are reliant on professionals and service providers for their care, Julia Twigg (2000) explored 'the intimacy of body work' that is involved. She suggests that ordinarily 'bodily closeness contains the capacity to create intimacy'; in the carer–client relationship it can signify social relations. For example, the 'power dynamics of bathing' demonstrate inequality as the powerful carer stands, fully clothed, over the powerless, naked client, occupying the formerly private space of the bathroom (ibid.: 180). Only through the enforcement of bodily boundaries can both the care-provider and the client feel separate from one another, thereby dissipating the intimacy of the encounter. In contrast, research on sexuality and families has demonstrated how bodily boundaries between self and other are typically blurred (Gabb 2004a; 2005b). Family bodies are familiar to one another; they grow up together, boundaries shift as children mature, but physical and affective space remains shared. Physical expressions of intimacy are encouraged as part of families' healthy interpersonal communication. The 'civilising process' of sexuality education takes place in the home. As such the parent–child embodied relationship is like no other in that 'family members have bodily licence' (Morgan 1996: 134).

Most research in this area, possibly because of its predominant academic location in geographical studies, typically foregrounds the mutually constitutive relationship between people and the places they inhabit: 'bodies reinscribe and project themselves onto their sociocultural environment so that this environment both produces and reflects the form and interest of the body' (Gross 1992). It is claimed that embodied family intimacy cannot be removed from the sites in which these interactions occur as the context shapes what form practices take and the meanings attributed to them. Given that the primary location of most forms of family intimacy is the home, it is no surprise that most of the spatial analysis in this area examines the domestic environment.

Work has shown how the home is structured along a public–private axis (Allan and Crow 1989) which shapes and is shaped by the encounters which take place in this context. There is a dynamic interplay between the public and the private in family homes, something that is so fundamental that it shapes the architecture of this built environment. As David Bell argues, houses constructed in the nineteenth and twentieth centuries were 'designed, built, financed and intended for nuclear families – reinforcing a cultural norm of family life with heterosexuality and patriarchy high on the agenda' (Bell 1991: 325). The layout and descriptors of rooms physically and metaphorically represent normative models of the reproductive, monogamous family unit, with 'master' bedrooms and smaller spaces for the children.

Home functions as a sign and is loaded with connotation. It alludes to privacy, 'a place where inhabitants can escape the disciplinary practices that regulate our bodies in everyday life' (Johnston and Valentine 1995: 99), but home is not without surveillance: 'the public world does not begin and end at the front door' (Allan and Crow 1989: 5). The boundaries of this public–private environment are permeable. Homes are not neatly carved up into public and private spaces, but represent a series of overlapping front and back stages with doorways, windows and gardens bridging the spatial (public–private) divide (Morgan 1996). Spaces are often semi-private, for example the bathroom is private for the occupant when the door is locked and a place of intimacy for activities such as couple bathing (Gabb 2005b). However, the bathroom can rarely be seen as an exclusively private space because people outside the family are routinely invited to make use of the facilities when they are visiting.

To explain the spatial messiness of everyday domestic living, Gillian Rose has developed the idea of paradoxical space: 'spaces that would mutually exclusive if charted on a two-dimensional map – center and margin, inside and outside' – but which are, on a routine basis, 'occupied simultaneously' (Rose 1993: 140–59). An embodied approach to the study of family relationships and the context within which physical interactions and intimacy occur bring to the fore the tensions, ambiguities and contradictions evident in our everyday experiences of family. These factors arise out of the contested barriers between what constitutes public concern and what remains legitimate private practice. In the next section I focus on the fourth and final juncture outlined at the beginning of this chapter. I examine how ideas of 'the public' and 'the private' feed into conceptualisations of intimacy and understandings of intimate relationships.

Intimate citizenship

In the journal *Sociology*, an article by Joe Bailey (2000) and subsequent riposte by the feminist family sociologists Jane Ribbens McCarthy and Rosalind Edwards (2001) interrogated the concepts of public and private in part around ideas of families and intimate (parent–child) relationships. This debate underpins subsequent formulations of intimate citizenship (Plummer 2003) and thus warrants further note above and beyond general sociological interest. Bailey suggested that we are seeing 'an advocacy for the private' in sociological studies and that fascination with the private is a sociological response to an 'exhausted or evacuated public realm' (Bailey 2000: 382–3). He situates the public and the private as being in a dichotomous relationship; an analytical distinction which is 'multi-dimensional and extensive' (Bailey 2000: 384). The private is associated with the interiority of self – human nature. For Bailey, feminist scholars and the sociology of the family have colonised conceptualisations and studies of the private, focusing attention on 'the emotional valency of one-to-one relationships in a sociological understanding of the institutions and society which contain them' (Bailey 2000: 392).

In their response, McCarthy and Edwards outlined how they, and other feminist scholars, have used the concepts, arguing that the public and the private are not distinct. They point to the way they have addressed these concerns in their own research by referring to 'social practices and orientations' which social actors 'do'; 'practices that create, invoke and depend upon certain values and expectations' (McCarthy and Edwards 2001: 770). As such they demonstrate the interrelationship of the public and the private and advocate using the term 'the personal' as opposed to the private to get away from ideas of interiority. This rescues the private from 'a total identification with intimacy and the self . . . "The personal" is also social' (McCarthy and Edwards 2001: 773).

Interrogations of the public–private dualism are important to the analysis of interpersonal relationships because this binary thinking has created artificial boundaries around different experiences and understandings of intimacy. The gender–sexuality scholars Lauren Berlant and Michael Warner argue that 'ideologies and institutions of intimacy which promise individualised self-fulfilment conjure the private as the only sphere where this may be achieved' (Berlant and Warner 2000: 317). The investment of intimacy in the private disavows civic engagement and situates the public as separate to intimacy. As a consequence, only in the imagined 'fantasy zone' of the private can good (intimate) citizenship be realised because the boundaries between (private) intimacy and (public) politics situates these two spheres as mutually exclusive. However, in practice, as Lynn Jamieson points out, in everyday experiences of intimacy, the public and the private intersect at many junctures. There are innumerable ways of 'doing intimacy' which may or may not require different levels of boundary work but which do not render these different practices as distinctive entities.

Jamieson's argument is that it is not the public–private *categorisation* of the intimate encounter which is of significance, but the temporal parameters within which individuals, couples and families affectively operate. It is the *finite limitations of time* which shape people's intimate boundaries and not principled ideas of public–private category management. That is to say, it is the scarcity of time as an affective resource that necessities the creation of defined *kinds* of relationship and forms of intimacy rather than any sense of public–private boundaries around emotional capacity. Time is an emotion resource that needs to be factored into analysis of the ways that people create and manage their intimate networks.

Many studies of intimacy and intimate relationships similarly seek to undo the public–private dichotomy, falsely reasserted by Bailey (2000). Research on intimacy, intimate relationships and affective communication in the workplace often tackles head on the boundaries between public–private, self–other (Hochschild 1983; Marks 1994; Kakabadase and Kakabadse 2004). Another area where these intersections have been brought to the fore is in analysis of economies of care and affect. Viviana Zelizer (2005), a cultural analyst of economic processes, dismantles the doctrine of 'hostile worlds' which positions relational intimacy as distinct from economic transaction. She suggests that as world markets expand, monetised social relations are invading all spheres of intimate life (Rifkin 2000). 'In a normative version, the hostile worlds view place rigid moral boundaries between market and intimate domains. It condemns any intersection of money and intimacy as dangerously corrupting.' Such separation is based in the 'dichotomous theories of sentimentality and rationality' that can be traced back to early nineteenth-century industrial capitalism. Today, this model of theorising runs aground when confronted with contemporary debates on such topics as payments for egg donation, the sale of blood and human organs, or the purchase of care (for dependent children, the elderly, disabled and/or sick friends and relatives) (Zelizer 2005: 22–6).

What Zelizer finds surprising about the hostile worlds debate is the failure to recognise how intimate social transactions routinely coexist with monetary transactions. She suggests that intimacy and intimate relationships are not fragile but robust sets of practices which thrive among a material culture where economic self-interest and money structure so many aspects of our lives. In contrast to the 'hostile worlds' thesis, Zelizer argues that 'across a wide range of intimate relations, people manage to integrate monetary transfers into larger webs of mutual obligations without destroying the social ties involved' (ibid.: 28). It is through 'connected lives' that individuals manage 'the mingling of economic activity and intimacy. By creating, enforcing, and renegotiating extensive differentiation among social ties, their boundaries, and their appropriate matching with commercial media and transactions of production, consumption, and distribution' (ibid.: 40–1). She illustrates her argument by tracing how economic transactions are found across the spectrum of intimate life, from courtship through to marriage, in caring relationships between friends, relatives, the cared-for and the carer. Thus it is not that monetary exchange is absent so much that affective payments have to be packaged in acceptable and distinguishable forms of social transaction.

For Zelizer, intimacy and economy are interwoven, so the moot point is not whether or not money corrupts, but rather 'what combinations of economic activity and intimate relations produce happier, more just, and more productive lives' (ibid.: 298). This, she contests, breaks down the traditional hostile worlds dichotomies which erroneously separate economic transaction and intimate personal relations and more honestly represents the caring economies that do exist. In this framework payment for care does not render these caring practices 'relationally second rate', but recognises that carers ought to be paid for the affective work they do (Nelson 1998: 1470).

The emphasis on care as central to intimate lives echoes previously discussed ideas on reciprocity (Stacey 2004) and the reframing of intimacy beyond family (Budgeon and Roseneil 2004). Where Zelizer adds another dimension to this debate is in her interrogation of the nature and *valuing* of relational work, which builds on earlier ideas developed by Arlie Hochschild on women's 'emotion work' (Hochschild 1989) and the 'care deficit' (Hochschild 1995). Hochschild pulls together these ideas in *The Commercialisation of Intimate Life* (2003) when she discusses how the gendering of emotion exchanges structure family relationships. This finds concordance with other research which has clearly illustrated how women sustain families and households through their domestic labour (Delphy and Leonard 1992), shoring up relationships between fathers and children (Seery and Crowley 2000) and maintaining wider kin relations by 'keeping in touch' (Leonardo 1987). The activities that women routinely do, such as feeding the family, not only serve a pragmatic purpose, but also perform a symbolic function, with mothers literally constructing a sense of family through their everyday family role (Devault 1991).

Building on this work, Hochschild extends the gendered analysis of women's emotion work and explores how the affective 'economy of gratitude' foregrounds intersections between public and private worlds. She argues that individuals 'gift' emotion work to others in an affective exchange which goes beyond what is normally expected – gifts being supplementary to necessity. But the gifts that are given are not decontextualised, in fact the opposite. Gifts are shaped by their social milieu and are understood by men and women through different 'cultural prisms'. How these *social meanings* are negotiated in this gift exchange represents the 'economy of gratitude' (Hochschild 2003). Whereas Zelizer retains a focus on the financial value of relational care, Hochschild is more concerned with the economic purpose of sustaining interpersonal (family) relationships, the distinctive roles of men and women and the affective economy of families (Hochschild 1989). 'An economy of gratitude is a vital, nearly sacred, nearly bottom-most, largely implicit layer of an intimate bond. It is the summary of all *felt gifts*' (Hochschild 2003: 105).

The economy of gratitude functions like all other economies and for the process of gift giving and receiving to work, individuals must share an understanding of their role in the gift exchange process. For example, a woman may feel grateful for the gift of additional child care contributions from her husband, but if switched around such activities would not be seen as a gift, as they are likely to constitute part of the woman's routine role in the family. As such Hochschild is concerned with the (gendered) ways that care is provided in families. The dimension which Zelizer brings to this analysis is how society affords symbolic recognition to the financial cost of such intimate care. Moving between different forms of intimacy and interpersonal relationships, Zelizer demonstrates how Western society puts a value on care by defining the parameters of an intimate relationship. These definitions are consolidated via social understandings of the role and value of the relationships, for example a daughter caring for her mother, a mother caring for her child, a housekeeper caring for a family that is not her own. Like others working in this area (e.g. Fineman 1995) Zelizer suggests that who gets paid for transactions of intimacy and the emotional value of relationships is repeatedly decided through social policy and the courts.

Zelizer demonstrates that it is through contested cases in law that the boundaries between intimacy and economy are drawn, placing people and relationships on one side or the other. She illustrates her point through analysis of the process of compensation payments to the families of victims of 9/11. These families sought more than financial recompense; many also wanted public recognition of their loss and their special relationship to the victim: 'the medium and modality of compensation represents not simply quid pro quo cash value but the meaning of the relationship is involved' with significant value being assigned to relational work (Zelizer 2005: 305). Thus Zelizer talks about the 'purchase of intimacy', a term which does not simply refer to financial exchanges around intimate care but how these coalesce with conceptual understandings and social meanings ascribed to these practices of care and affect. This analytical framework evinces how the public and the private coexist at many levels. In an era where a compensation culture is prevalent, maintaining intimate relationships has a financial cost attached. This does not devalue the feelings or quality of care that is given (typically, between family members, as a gift) as suggested by proponents of the hostile worlds thesis. Instead it acknowledges, financially, the 'emotion work' of women that has been traditionally provided free of charge. Situating Zelizer and Hochschild side by side facilitates insight into the processes through which values are attached to this gendered emotion work, care and intimate exchange. Intersections between the public–economic and the private–personal–intimate are central to this analytical paradigm.

The heteronormative structuring of emotion exchanges are examined as part of Zelizer's and Hochschild's affective economic analyses, but sexuality and relationships are not the primary foci. It is in the field of sexuality studies that the public–private interplay in understandings and experiences of sex and intimacy is fully addressed. Analyses of same-sex families and homosexual interpersonal relationships call into question the taken-for-grantedness of heteronormative models which evacuate the public from desire and 'affairs of the heart'. In order to critique this artificial separation, some scholars have advanced the idea of 'intimate citizenship' as a means to flag the empirical and conceptual interrelationship of these two spheres. Debate in this area is wrapped around gay activism and equal rights. It is claimed that sexual or intimate citizenship is 'an attempt to give meaning to the recognition of diversity ... It is a useful metaphor for new claims of rights, and for rethinking the balance of entitlement, recognition, acceptance and responsibilities' (Weeks et al. 2001. 196). Jeffrey Weeks unpacks the term, saying that the sexual has been situated at the heart of intimate personal life, while citizenship resides in the public sphere within broader social communities. The 'sexual citizen' is a hybrid being who usefully breaches the public–private divide (Weeks 1998). Analysis of sexuality and citizenship in this aligned form focuses attention on the heterosexual and gendered underpinnings of citizenship status (Richardson 1998).

In the study of 'families of choice' the linking of sexuality and citizenship enables new possibilities of parenthood and family constellations to be innovatively explored: inventing 'new ways of living that can influence the available possibilities for thinking and doing citizenship' (Weeks et al. 2001: 199). Entering cautiously the terrain of sexuality and children, some have even used the idea of sexual citizenship as a means to extend citizenship status to all, including children. This has led Weeks to suggest that by highlighting the denaturalisation of the sexual, ideas of the 'new sexual citizen' help to advance debates around relationships between adults and children and in families (Weeks 1998). In a more contentious form, this argument is extended by David Evans (1993), who inculcates wider calls for social acknowledgement of children's rights as a means to position children as sexual citizens in their own right.

There are merits in using the term 'sexual citizenship', as a way to foreground the interrelationship of public–private discourses around the affective register of families, but there are also limitations. This has led others to prefer the term 'intimate citizenship', suggesting that it is better suited to the breadth of intimate experience. Intimate citizenship is more inclusive and embraces a wider spectrum of issues which include, but are not structured through, sexuality (Plummer 2003: 65). The term is grounded in contemporary understandings of citizenship (Janoski 1998). These incorporate the UN Charter of Human Rights. The Charter sets down 'a plurality of rights and obligations [that] are shaped through participatory, differentiated social worlds (& communities), each with contested status and continuing tensions that need resolving' (Plummer 1999: 1). It is developed through a feminist appreciation of the material and relational world in which we live. As such it draws on ideas of democratisation and individualisation, but does not see these as without responsibility and commitment, instead 'it requires the reflexive working out of those chosen ties in everybody's 'do-it-yourself biography' (Weeks et al. 2001: 197).

It is in the work of Ken Plummer that ideas of 'intimate citizenship get thoroughly unpacked. He argues that citizenship carries legal weight, while identity carries social and cultural weight. The term intimate citizenship reveals the legal referents that structure personal lives and are constituted through private practices. For Plummer it is this relationship between private actions and public debate which is of central concern: 'how our most intimate decisions are shaped by (and in turn shape) our most public institutions' (Plummer 2003: x). He uses the term intimate citizenship as a sensitising concept (Van den Hoonaard 1997) to draw attention to the linkage between the personal and the public. He suggests that it represents 'a potential bridge' (Plummer 2003: 15), which ensures that these areas can no longer be conceptualised and understood as 'separate autonomous spheres' (ibid.: 68).

Plummer then moves on to advance earlier ideas of sexual citizenship by using the term 'intimates' to describe anyone who is engaged in practices of intimacy. He acknowledges that the term 'intimate' has no single meaning but suggests that it facilitates clarity of analytic purpose in that it enables intimacy to be seen as something people embody, as intimates. This references back to Lynn Jamieson's ideas of the 'intimate mother' and the 'intimate father' (Jamieson 1998), differentially gendered parenting positions through which women and men *do* intimacy. But beyond this, what Plummer aims to achieve is to materialise the doing of intimacy at a deeper level than simple practice, seeing it as part of the understanding and doing of self. He argues that intimacies are not only about close relationships with friends, family, children and lovers, they are also about self-knowing; an appreciation and acceptance of our physical and psychic selves (Plummer 2003). His conceptualisation of intimates and intimate citizenship pulls together the public and the private. He illustrates intimacy as both an embodied practice and part of individual subjectivity.

While Plummer's ideas connect with the democratisation thesis with its (theoretically informed) equality of rights agenda, his conceptualisation of intimate citizenship simultaneously draws on Jamieson's relational matrix which is embedded in social structures. He acknowledges that families are the nexus for the reproduction of gender relations and patterning of power structures between adults and children. 'The intimate zone is, through and through, socially produced, maintained and transformed.' Even the most private aspects of family lives are 'ultimately engulfed in legislation regarding marriage, divorce, child care, and pensions, not to mention wider social ideologies of familism' (Plummer 2003: 70). Plummer does not see this gendered and generational framework as something which reduces the transformative potentialities of families, instead he argues the reverse.

Plummer suggests that practices of intimate citizenship are forging new ways of being intimate and doing intimacy in the context of moral, decision-making families. In this way intimate citizenship acknowledges the material conditions of intimates and the public–private tensions which structure these relationships. However, rather than seeing these as disempowering for parents and children, he recasts them as dynamic processes. As such he brings us full circle. He demonstrates how intimacy is bound up with ideas of sexuality and sexual relationships. Whereas theorising in the 1970s and early 1980s struggled to move beyond seeing intimacy as the emotional functioning of heterosexual and family relationships, Plummer situates intimacy and interpersonal relationships as reflexive sites of agency. He argues that private intimate relationships and family practices are shaped by, and in turn shape, public institutions. In doing so he separates intimacy from the sexual by showing how families' acts of intimate citizenship – their *doing* of intimacy – feed back into ways of *being* family in contemporary society; how intimacy is no longer a functional determinant in families but a means of expression and affective fulfilment. Intimate citizenship draws attention to the critical tensions between the public and the private and enables ideas of 'creative intimacy' (Mazur 1973) to be relocated *within* contemporary forms and experiences of family.

5
Mapping Intimacy in Families

In this chapter I aim to open out key theoretical debates on intimacy. I return to some of the ideas and understandings of intimacy that were presented in chapter 4 and ask questions of these conceptual frameworks through empirical data from *Behind Closed Doors*. It is not my intention to find fault with any one model, instead my aim is to critically engage with these various conceptualisations in order to demonstrate where theory–data tensions may arise. Researchers in the area of family studies tend to approach fieldwork with an open mind rather than setting out to prove a particular hypothesis. In fact, it comes as little surprise that in research that has employed deductive reasoning, testing theoretical models against data, researchers have quickly found that data extend beyond the parameters of theory. For example, when Libby Plumridge and Rachel Thomson (2003) examined two longitudinal datasets using Anthony Giddens' ideas of reflexivity and self-identity, they found that while these ideas and conceptual 'tools' were useful as a starting point, they had to be operationalised in order to address empirical research. 'In practice the data outgrew the theory, which we found spoke primarily to a particular theoretical interpretation of social change, rather than the ways in which lives change in practice' (Plumridge and Thomson 2003: 221–2).

Plumridge and Thomson's findings echo earlier work by Lynn Jamieson (1999) who examined Giddens' democratisation thesis against the gendered and generational materiality of everyday family life. Here too the development of a theoretical perspective was seen as conceptually limited and limiting, glossing over the complexities of lived experience. The same is true of Jane Ribbens McCarthy and colleagues, who claim there is a fundamental flaw in the theoretical postmodern idea of 'democratic families'. This, they argue, 'remains a fundamentally "public" concept that is being imported into the "private" sphere in ways that misrepresent people's family lives and misshape our understandings of those lives' (McCarthy et al. 2003: 146). They suggest that it is connectedness and a sense of parental (moral) responsibility that underpin family relationships and not individual self-fulfilment.

It is all too easy to set up theoretical frameworks and then knock them down with evidence from empirical research. While the *Behind Closed Doors* project could be seen as more inclined to this theory verification/falsification model it was never my intention for this to be a one-way process. Instead, I demonstrate how and in what ways data fit with theoretical models or push against, and in some instances breach, the boundaries of existing frameworks. The ideas that emerge serve to inform, illustrate and contest particular ways of thinking about intimacy and also generate dynamic intersections between these frameworks. Thus in this chapter I employ 'inductive reasoning' (for a review of different analytical approaches, see Blaikie 1993; and for a practical guide, see Mason 1996). In chapter 2 I suggested that conceptualisations of intimacy in families typically fall into four critical junctures around particular themes. In this chapter, through theoretical sampling, I generate and test some of the key ideas within these junctures, using theory *interactively* with empirical data. This iterative approach readily lends itself to analysis of families and interpersonal relationships and it is this iterative aspect that I want to extend in order to explicate the processes of family relationships. This does not simply aim to match fragments of empirical data with particular conceptual models, but to develop insight into sense-making practices of intimacy in families in contemporary society.

I have structured my analysis in three sections. The first examines changes in the patterning of intimacy and the usefulness of the democratisation thesis in making sense of these affective transformations. I focus on the dialogic ethos that underpins contemporary discourses of 'good parenting'. In this analysis I foreground generational and gendered power relations to demonstrate the dynamic complexity of family intimacy. I query gendered assumptions about emotional capacity and take a fresh look at the practices of intimate fatherhood. I explore how cultural 'rules' affect the setting and maintenance of self–other, public–private boundaries around intimacy. This engages with debates around risk management and the shaping of intimate conduct.

In the next section I explore the structuring of intimate relationships both within and beyond the family. I interrogate ideas around child-centred families which characterise parenthood as an altruistic activity. I examine the processes of parental investment in children. I consider instrumental forms of intimacy that are not oriented around the child but around parents' individual needs and/or aspirations. Extending this analysis of the parent–child relationship, I examine how parents and children make sense of family relationships and the discursive framing of these affective ties, notably the invocation of friendship as a means to epitomise relational security. This focus on friendship beyond the rhetoric of familial relationality shifts the emphasis away from ties of obligation to individually fashioned networks of intimacy, shaped around poly-amorous affinities. Taking the theoretical point further I problematise what constitutes intimacy and an intimate relationship through examination of relationships among 'significant others'. Extending the ideas of Iris Marion Young (1997) and Donna Haraway (2003), I decentre the framing of intimacy away from interpersonal reciprocity. I look at the significance of animal–human relationships in pet-oriented households, where pets are considered to be 'one of the family'.

In the final section I interrogate families' routine affective practices. Time is recognised as a crucial factor within the process of creating and maintaining families. I examine the management of time as both a commodity and a gift, and the ways that limitations of time serve to shape the boundaries around public–private experiences of intimacy. I explore the processes of intimate practice and how these form part of everyday family life. These data highlight families' affective communication, the various strategies of disclosing intimacy – verbal, non-verbal and embodied. I consider the significance of families' affective shorthand, symbolic phrases which stand in for more complex feelings and/or time-consuming interpersonal exchange and the experiences of physical intimacy that form part of everyday family routine. The embodied dialogic process conveys different levels of meaning that reflect wider gendered and generational relations. This brings to the fore the ways in which public–private discourses intersect around the boundaries of intimacy and sexuality behaviour and what constitutive factors shape the management of affective family practices. I examine the 'differences that matter', that is to say which factors significantly affect formations and experiences of family intimacy. In particular, I focus attention on the in/significance of sexuality and cultural difference.

Affective transformations

Democratic dialogues

It is claimed that the democratisation of interpersonal relationships has led to transformations of intimacy (Giddens 1992). Parent–child relationships are structured around dialogue, free and open communication, through which parents reason with their children rather than simply enforce sets of rules. As I have shown in chapter 4, the degree to which 'transformations of intimacy' are materialised in everyday family lives remains contested. There is, however, general consensus that there has been a paradigm shift in the traditional patterning of intimate networks and that this reflects a desire for openness and fulfilment in interpersonal relationships. In *Behind Closed Doors* many parents presented themselves through this democratic framework and there was a sense that they genuinely aspired to a dialogic ethos.

> *Andrea* (F6): The most important thing is to talk because how does anybody else know [what you're thinking/feeling]? ... I think it's important that children can come to you and tell you anything, whether it's good or bad.

To some extent the value of retaining open channels of communication was most readily apparent in discussions around managing conflict in relationships. In these instances parents and child alike often spoke about the importance of talking things through, making time to listen to one and another and finding middle ground. Compromise was represented as the best solution although, not surprisingly, this was just as much an ideal as other aspects of interpersonal exchange. However, as others have shown (Jamieson 1999; Gillies et al. 2001; Solomon et al. 2002), the theoretical idea of democracy and the everyday reality of family lives is often vastly different. For example, some parents use conversations with children as both a means to make emotional connection and to gain information about children's private lives that may be useful in their management of boundaries and behaviour.

> *Harriet* (F5): ... If Kelly [daughter, aged 17] is that way out and wants to talk, yes, I will listen, I just stop everything because she talks to me about things ... she will open up and she'll talk about what she feels about things. Particularly because of her age we're concerned about any intimacy she might have with boys, and also with drugs and alcohol. So, at least when she's discussing not always what she's doing herself, but what her thoughts are so you can tell what she's thinking, and that's quite reassuring.

Harriet's description of how she uses parent–child exchanges as a means to gather information about her daughter's activities is interesting not only because it demonstrates the instrumentality of parenting practice, but also because it illustrates how she crafts a democratic model around deeply entrenched generational power relations. Elsewhere Harriet talks about how her family can discuss anything and everything. She suggests that the family ethos is structured through a shared desire for democratic and open communication, something about which she is very proud. In an interview with Kelly, Harriet's daughter, the distance between aspiration and actuality becomes clear. Kelly describes family discussions in quite different terms from those her mother used. Whereas Harriet sees their discussions as an opportunity to connect with her daughter and coincidently gather information, Kelly sees them as an interrogation. These differences in perception bring to the fore Harriet's struggle to reconcile her desire to respect her daughter's growing autonomy with her equally pressing desire to uphold the rules of the household which are informed by her Catholicism.

On first reading it is easy to interpret Harriet's actions and defence of action as those of an individual, controlling mother, albeit one with her child's interests at heart. But they are perhaps more interesting in the way they illustrate the complex relationship between stories and lived experience, the skilful processes through which individuals incorporate and recycle public stories around democracy into narratives of self (Jamieson 1998: 12). The ideas of Arlie Hochschild (2003) on affective gift exchange are particularly helpful here in making sense of what is actually going on. Harriet talks about respecting Kelly's privacy and is happy that she shuts the door when friends and/or boyfriend are in her room. But what she actually describes is *the gift of privacy* and not privacy *per se*. In practice, Harriet's desire for democracy is operationalised in ways that consolidate traditional generational power structures. As the giver of a gift she is able to retain control over what form it takes.

In this instance Harriet is comfortable with allowing her daughter to have a private (bedroom) space, but she retains the right to intrude. She says that she would not dream of knocking as this room is an integral part of the house and as such Kelly has to respect parental rules in this shared space. Harriet endeavours to reconcile this pulling of generational rank with the professed household democratic ethos through invocation of the rhetoric of openness. She asserts that as the parents' bedroom door is always open to Kelly so Kelly's should be too. In order to 'prove' the fairness of her argument Harriet cites an incident when Kelly came into their room in the middle of the night because she was frightened; as this 'intrusion' was acceptable, so too is the mother's demand for free access to her daughter's space. In practice, the rhetoric of openness and principle of democracy are part of this family's practices, but only insofar as they can be fashioned to achieve parental preferences.

Echoing Julia Brannen and colleagues (1994), findings across the dataset illustrated that even when parents did try to foster genuine and complex empathic negotiations with older children, this did not mean that they achieved a sustained, mutually intimate parent–child relationship. For example, in areas such as sexuality behaviour and sex education, strategic use of the rhetoric of openness typically enabled parents to impose their moral beliefs as the normative model. Moreover, some parents seemed to deliberately situate themselves and their parental role as central to childhood development because in doing so they could remain influential and keep their constitutive emotional role in their child's (adolescent's/young adult's) life. In such cases parents' desire for democracy neither aimed for a real levelling of intergenerational power relations nor was it oriented around receptiveness to children's wishes.

Children were not necessarily dupes in this process. Older children especially were aware of the strategies being used and in turn made instrumental use of their family's pretensions to democracy. Wanting the best of both worlds they demanded to be treated as a 'putative adult' as characterised by Giddens (1992: 191–2), but also expected to retain the benefits of being a child. Child care benefits included car lifts on demand, a shoulder to cry on when peer relationships caused emotional distress and reassurance that parents would always be there as and when needed. These findings suggest that the intergenerational power relationship between parents and children is a dynamic one. A democratic ethos that is structured through a dialogic process is always subject to the particularities of familial circumstance and the socio-historical context of these relations. In an era where the rights of children have moved up the policy agenda it should come as no surprise that some children are becoming quite adept at 'playing the (democratic) game' to their own advantage.

The significance of gender

In the 1970s and 1980s intimacy was wrapped around a traditionally gendered, functional model that embedded it within the structuring of (typically heterosexual) relationships and the affective transmission of familial roles. More recent work has moved away from this perspective, pointing to the plasticity of sexuality (Giddens 1992). In this transformative framework sex is separated from reproductive function and instead ideas of mutuality and individual fulfilment shape relationships. Women and men are free to make or break intimate connections in order to satisfy their needs. Feminist work has challenged the absence of material analysis in this model, claiming that many aspects of gendered power relations remain largely unchanged (Jamieson 1999). The primary responsibility for child care still rests with women (Richardson 1993; Sullivan 2000) even in the context of non-traditional heterosexual relationships (VanEvery 1995). These feminist claims ring true with data from *Behind Closed Doors*. Many women spoke of the significant time and energy which they dedicate to domestic and child care tasks, in many cases in addition to paid employment.

> *Helen* (F8): I get up at seven and I get my shower and I get myself done by 7.30 and then go wake the boys and start getting them rousted ... Martin [husband] gets up, well he doesn't, he wakes up, he lays in bed, he'll watch his news, he'll get up at 7.40, he'll have a shower, he'll see to himself, he comes down at eight o'clock grabs a slice of toast and he's out by 8.05 ... whereas I've been up like a whirlwind ... But you see if he had to do that he just wouldn't be able to do it, he just couldn't cope because he hasn't got the patience.

Helen's morning schedule is typically hectic and during this time her husband does not appear to assist with the child care in any way. However, in contrast to the underlying tenet of much feminist work, which focuses on the unfairness of unequal gendered roles, many mothers, such as Helen, frame their role as primary carer in a positive light. Most mothers clearly relished the more intimate mother–child relationship that was produced through their significant personal investment. They knew their children better than anyone else and it is not surprising that children typically cited their mother as the person whom they turn to when upset. Mothers were identified by parents and children alike as the main source of compassion and understanding in families. Beyond this, mothers' investment of time in children afforded them affective compensation. For many women, the mother–child relationship is both fulfilling and unrivalled and provides sufficient recompense for their maternal labour. This adds another relationally-oriented dimension to understandings of motherhood and suggests one reason why the gendered patterning of family relationships remains intact. Notwithstanding the ambivalence which some mothers feel and the distress that can be experienced when parent–child relationships break down, for many women the mother–child relationship remains emotionally rewarding, something that is sometimes lost in analyses of gender in families.

The significance of gender in the dynamic of intimate family life cannot be understated and was manifest in research many ways. For example, women were often highly articulate in their descriptions of their emotions and many had previously worked through their feelings in discussions with female family and friends. As a consequence they typically felt more comfortable than men in presenting an emotional account of themselves. Notwithstanding such differences in affective capability, the presupposition that men do not really 'do' emotions and that gender can be mapped onto affective behaviour may do a disservice to both men and women.

Recent studies of fatherhood have begun to look anew at how men connect with their children. It is claimed that intimate fathering cannot be viewed through the same lens as intimate mothering because men and women have access to different cultural resources and often perform a different work–family role (Dermott 2003). From the responses of participants in *Behind Closed Doors* it is evident that many men do struggle to express their emotions, but this does not mean that they are less feeling. Instead, close analysis of project data showed that many fathers express emotions in ways that are not readily understood or recognisable as affection. Some fathers spoke of intimate exchanges between father and son that remain indiscernible to others who do not have knowledge of the intimate practices and affective repertoire of individual families; but these exchanges nonetheless formed part of their emotion currency.

> *Jeff* (F4): ... Me dad has never been kind of lovey-dovey to me. In a way, I mean I've never missed anything, I know me dad love me to bits, he's me dad and I've done nothing to him for him not to love me to bits. In fact, me dad is proud of me because of the way I've changed and because I've got the kids. He doesn't say it, but I know he is. I can tell he is ... It's intuition, it's just ... it's the way he says it as well, it's kind of, I know what he means, but he's not saying direct, he's saying it indirectly or in whatever way me dad wants to say it, and I'm happy with that ...
>
> [*Interviewer*: How do you show your dad that you love him?]
>
> *Jeff*: I mean, at Christmas I got me dad something he wanted and it was more expensive than what me mam got, but I got me mam what she wanted as well ... and me dad got some tools. I think me dad realises how much I spend on him, he knows, he's not daft me dad, he knows how much I spend and if I spend a bit more I think he knows, in a way, that's my way of saying 'Thanks, you've been brilliant' ...

In this extract Jeff struggles to put into words how he and his father affectively communicate because they do not use the words or gestures which comprise the cultural repertoire of love. His description of father–child emotion exchanges demonstrates the need to examine gendered behaviour beyond normative models, to look outside the box. If the project's research agenda had been more directive and focused on traditional expressions of emotion, the intimate relationship between Jeff and his father could have been read as affection-free. For example, they do not say 'I love you' and they do not hug. But because participants were encouraged to tell wide-ranging stories about their lives, the father–son relationship could be told as Jeff reflected on and worked through for himself how they affectively communicate.

Other accounts of father–child relationships were fashioned in similarly hard-to-read forms. In several of these fathers described their attempts to do affect in different ways, for example through rough-and-tumble play. Intimate play is often the main form of physical affection available to men as their adolescent children, especially sons, refuse father–child hugs. These exchanges remain within the boundaries of traditional masculinity, but they also do important relational maintenance and are surrogates for more explicit (feminine) forms of emotion work. However, fathers still tended to measure themselves and their relationship with their children against other, openly expressive, traditionally feminine models and by these measures they typically found themselves lacking. Men position themselves as almost passive in this process, although several were trying to take proactive or remedial steps.

Data from *Behind Closed Doors* support the findings of recent studies on contemporary fatherhood (e.g. Brannen and Nilsen 2006) which suggest that many men are working hard to break the affective patterning of father–son behaviour learnt through their own childhood and do things differently. Some actively reconstructed fatherhood around a model that is traditionally seen as female, being demonstrably affectionate and talking openly with their children about any topic. One father spoke with great pride about how 'his boys' receive affection quite happily, seeing this as a positive way to raise children and hoping that this emotional competency will stand them in good stead in their future relationships. Fathers' desire for increased parent–child affect can be seen as a response to social pressures which assert increasing demands for greater paternal involvement. Alternatively, wider changes in the rigidity of masculine and feminine roles across society may be enabling some fathers to open themselves up to feelings previously seen as the domain of women/mothers.

While an increase in father–child intimacy was generally experienced as positive, the innocence of such activities was seldom taken for granted. Fathers have to navigate a risky terrain which is shaped through 'cultural narratives' (Kinkaid 1998) of male predation and child abuse which pepper the popular imaginary. In Anglo-American culture it is particularly difficult for men to articulate feelings because they are operating within a feminine-defined affective field wherein male sexuality is characterised as predatory (Gabb 2004a). Emotionality is antithetical to traditional understandings of masculinity: 'Cultural frames name and define the emotion, set the limits of its intensity, specify the norms and values attached to it, and provide symbols and cultural scenarios that make it socially communicative' (Illouz 1997: 3–4). Within this scenario fathers are first and foremost men and as such sustaining an intimate relationship with children can be difficult to achieve. However, what participants' responses in *Behind Closed Doors* demonstrate is that they are doing so in interesting and sometimes ingenious ways.

Intimate transactions and the rules of affection

Analysis of father–child interaction demonstrated the coded presence of masculine forms of intimacy. While there is no singular affective template and the boundaries of parent–child 'touch' remain highly contested (Halley 2007), these and other individually experienced ways of doing intimacy and emotions tend to be structured through culturally inscribed sets of 'feeling rules' (Hochschild 1979). The positioning and maintenance of boundaries around self and other, public and private, is crucial to everyday practices and understandings of intimacy. Data from *Behind Closed Doors* illustrate the various ways that parents established socially informed boundaries around intimate conduct creating their own public–private 'moral framework' (McCarthy et al. 2003).

In response to third-party scenarios which depicted adult–child interactions, parents typically suggested that it was the closeness of the relationship between characters that was crucial, more than what form the intimacy took. Once extended beyond immediate family, adult–child interactions became risky and many parents said that male relations in particular should be kept at arm's length 'just in case'. What is interesting about this is the selectivity of parents' risk assessment. While child abuse takes place primarily in the home or a familiar setting, perpetrated by someone known to the child, this was disregarded by parents. Risk was characterised as something outside of the family, a threat posed by strangers that could be guarded against through due parental vigilance.

> *Jocelyn* (F9): Charlotte [daughter, aged six] ... was always told it was fine to be curious, but private bits are private and nobody else touches them except her, daddy, mummy and that's it.

One reason why parents framed their answers in this way was probably because their construction of a protective circle around physical intimacy and their children was not aimed for the sole protection of the child; it was also intended to protect fathers from unfounded allegations, to protect *their* reputation as parents. The extent of this defensive attitude may be a consequence of participation in the research project which made them more inclined to *prove* their trustworthiness and integrity which in other circumstances would be taken-for-granted. Anxiety or unease around this area was certainly one reason cited by some fathers to explain their reluctance to participate in the study when other family members were keen to do so. Notwithstanding these reservations, data show that cultural ideas of age-appropriateness and perceived levels of threat posed by women/men, mothers/fathers affect the forms and descriptions of parent–child physical interactions and the process of family intimacy.

There is a paradox: on the one hand, there is an expectation in contemporary society that fathers should work to create and instigate activities and means of expression that consolidate father–child intimacy (Lupton and Barclay 1997); on the other, media hyperbole around abuse and risk, and cultural narratives around wider threats to childhood innocence, delimit what forms these embodied expressions may take lest they be misunderstood. To reconcile this paradox parents seemed inclined to leave responsibility with the child as if this in some way lessened any unwarranted fallout.

> *Andrea* (F6): I think it naturally, just well it seems to have naturally [happened] in our family anyway. It starts with themselves not with you, they [children] start covering themselves up or not wanting you to, you know, 'Can you knock please?' and then you notice that if you're getting changed they won't come in whereas before they'd just walk in and chat to you. Suddenly Gordon [son, aged 13] will now hover outside and go 'Are you decent?' kind of thing, so he's naturally just [taking the lead] ... It just feels very natural and obviously their bodies are growing up and it just feels very natural.

What is interesting in Andrea's account is her repetition of the word 'natural'. She is almost washing her hands of responsibility in setting boundaries around age-appropriate behaviour and children's acquisition of increased privacy because her intervention is unnecessary; the process just happens, 'naturally'. In the *Behind Closed Doors* project the idea of the naturalness of certain behaviour was repeatedly cited by parents as the means through which they managed the boundaries around children and sexuality. In counter-fact parents' management of affective and sexuality boundaries draws on culturally constituted shared understandings of normal behaviour. At other times in research they referred to, and in some instances deferred to, any number of mediated sources. These included advice from their own parents, health professionals, handbooks, popular television, faith and culture, to name but a few. This advice was used to navigate everyday boundaries in parent–child relationships. However, amid the plethora of guidance and perceived need for rules and certainty, there remained an uncertain climate around embodied interactions between children and adults, especially men.

The structuring of affective ties

Investment in the child

One dominant discourse that can be traced among contemporary parenting literature is the responsibility of parenthood. This is epitomised in ideas of child-centred parenting. While the parent–child relationship has always existed, it is suggested that parents' investment in their children is novel; a response to the emotional uncertainty and burgeoning individualism of twenty-first-century life. Against this social backdrop it is claimed that parents are turning to their children for lifelong commitment and love. '[The child] promises a tie which is more elemental, profound and durable than any other in society ... the ultimate guarantee of permanence, providing an anchor for one's life' (Beck and Beck-Gersheim 1995: 73). Like Ulrich Beck and Elisabeth Beck-Gernsheim, in the *Behind Closed Doors* project I found that parents tended to invest heavily in their relationships with their children and a child-centred approach to family was typical, something that was perhaps to be expected in a self-selected sample recruited to research this subject.

In participatory self-complete methods most parents oriented their accounts around family life and their children and many saw this investment as something to be proud of, something which made them feel positive about themselves. Parents frequently talked about how days and the weekly schedule were organised around children's playgroups, social and sporting commitments. Parents willingly put themselves out for their children, being their taxi service to and from activities, thinking of their needs above and beyond their own. They arranged shift patterns at work to maximise parent–child time and meet child care responsibilities, proactively monitoring children's developmental and educational progress and taking prompt action when areas of concern arose. All of these and many others besides figured in parents' accounts of everyday family life and were seen as a crucial part of 'being there' for their children

(Gillies et al. 2001). Parents did not appear to resent the responsibilities but saw them as part of their job, of how they wanted to be, as parents.

The child-centred account of families that is advocated in much of the parenting literature is structured around choice and agency and the cultural capital and emotional wherewithal to provide this kind of dedicated parenthood. The data from *Behind Closed Doors* presented so far concur with this somewhat idealised and selfless account. However, this is not the whole picture and parents' investment in their children did not always appear to be altruistic or as beneficial for children as it might at first appear. In many instances parents' purposeful affective activities were not simply designed to provide emotional benefits for children, but also to transmit normative values as shown through analysis of Harriet's data earlier in this chapter. The need to 'protect' a child from danger and risk was used to justify parents' imposition of their rules and codes of conduct. Alongside this, in several families it was evident that parents used mutual disclosure and the closeness of the parent–children relationship to meet *their own emotional needs*.

In one family the mother (Nelushi) openly acknowledged that her investment in her children and the fostering of this intimate relationship was designed to generate affective reciprocity. Investing emotions in her children meant that they owed her emotion in return. It is as yet unknown whether this mother's plans will be successful or whether this form of *instrumental intimacy* will place an emotional burden on her children in years to come. Moreover, it should be noted that her designs may be more imaginary than realisable given that the cultural 'catch up' to which she refers is in fact quite far advanced and certainly will be more so by the time her children reach adulthood.

> *Nelushi* (F10): I can't imagine living in a house without my children being around ... I keep telling my mum before this culture catches up with my children and they're going to leave me at university I want to get back to India because there it's not this way as yet. This culture hasn't yet caught up there yet, people don't leave their parents when they're in college or university. You all live together; it's only marriages or work ... I mean things are going to change 20 years later or 25 years later from now, but you know it just gives me scares on whether they're not going to be with me.

Another mother talked about a similarly instrumental form of intimacy but hers was not a self-oriented investment in the child but an investment in the child for the child's own sake or rather for the sake of the parents' aspirations for the child. Jocelyn and her partner have already made plans for their daughter's career – seeing her as a high academic achiever, a woman who will balance motherhood with a professional career. Jocelyn qualified her forward planning by saying that the main thing is that her daughter is happy; she could be an artist, but she should travel before she settles into a career and family life. As such the direction is of less importance than there being a direction *per se* – a direction that should also include a process of self-discovery. To achieve these goals Jocelyn has devised a plan that includes her daughter doing an additional 2–3 hours of schooling every day, extra study time with her mother that extends over the school holidays.

In order to reconcile parental ambition with the arduous workload that it brings for the child, Jocelyn explains that her plan is necessary because their characters are similar. She invokes a connection between mother and daughter, who become one and the same. However, it could be that her personification of 'sameness' is also a purposeful strategy to sustain class positions. This interpretation finds resonance with sociological analysis of class in the structuring of parenthood and families (Allatt 1993; Armstrong 2006). Jocelyn is a successful career woman in her own right who is currently taking 'time out' to parent full-time. Thus it is not so much that she wants to live vicariously through her daughter so much as wanting to craft her daughter in her own (middle-class) image, using the skills she acquired in her education and upbringing to advance her daughter (Reay 2000). What will happen if children raised in these ways subsequently reject the (classed) model proffered by their parents remains unknown.

To be clear, in discussing the purposeful parenting strategies of Harriet (earlier on), and Nelushi and Jocelyn, I am neither claiming these experiences as typical nor questioning the quality of the mothers' care and/or the extent of their individual emotional capacity. They were all 'good mothers' and there was no indication that either the parent–child or wider familial relationships were damaging. The point I am making is that everyday parenthood and the practices of intimacy through which families operate are not always altruistic. These parents' strategic practices of intimacy are part of the complex picture of family relationships. To edit out sections that paint a not so rosy portrait delimits understandings of relational life and obscures the materiality of everyday parent–child intimacy.

The value of family and friends

So far I have focused on the parent–child relationship more than its familial status. I now want to consider how parents and children experience and understand families. While the empirical status of 'the family' has been called into question (Williams 2004), as I have previously argued its significance in the cultural imaginary and on the political agenda is, if anything, gaining increasing prominence. In *Behind Closed Doors* participants' responses suggested that there was a sense that family, in some shape or form, was important and most parents devoted considerable time and thought to this relational unit. Parents were aware of and in many (acknowledged and unacknowledged) ways incorporated mediations of idealised parenthood and/or remedial advice for unsuccessful models of family relationships into their family practices. But their investment in these cultural resources did not mean that parents bought into an idealised version of family so much as understood parenting as a reflexive project.

Parents tended to measure successful families and 'good parenthood' in terms of individual emotional 'capacity to care' (Hollway 2006) rather than adherence to a prescriptive normative model. For example, several parents referred to the MTV show 'The Osbournes' which depicts the everyday extraordinary family life of the rock star Ozzy Osbourne, his wife Sharon, their children and pet dogs. The Osbourne family was variously described as dysfunctional; nonetheless the individuals were identified as people who were there for one another, who care about each other's feelings and who together make 'a really, really close family'. Several parents described their own families of origin as 'not perfect', but nevertheless they saw them as providing constant support. In these terms they represented an ideal to which they aspired, wanting to emulate these qualities in their own parent–child and family relationships. The parent–child relationship was typically positioned as an emotional space that could be retreated to, the family home was a private sanctuary in which to hide from the challenges presented in the outside world.

> *Helen* (F8): . . . You can always go home . . . there's always a loving warm welcome there for you and they [parents] will understand no matter what's happened. They'll understand and they'll talk to you about it and they'll be there for you and I hope that's the way it will be for our boys, you know . . . It's like an emotional umbilical cord that you know is always there between you and no matter what happens, you grow up and you get your own lives, but that connection is always going to be there and that closeness between you.

Helen uses the umbilical cord as a metaphor to signify a timeless and lifelong familial connection between parent and children that precedes all other relationships; a natural, pre-discursive attachment. This sense of parent–child attachment and the commitment to associated responsibilities that come with parenthood finds accord with studies which highlight the connectedness of families (McCarthy et al. 2003; Smart 2007). However, this does not reassert the centrality of 'the family', but situates children as the means to counteract the fragility of adult relationships. Families are created *through the process of parent–child relationships* rather than being the creator of and repository for these attachments. Data from *Behind Closed Doors* corroborates contemporary research that suggests that expansive *networks of intimacy* have overridden the emotional privilege formerly accorded to 'the family' (Jamieson 1998: 77). This research suggests that the liberation of relationships from a reproductive imperative is hugely significant; once separated from a functional model individuals are free to create their own 'relationship rules' (Holland et al. 2003), forging intimate associations that meet their personal needs (Budgeon and Roseneil 2004).

The disaggregating of intimacy from the reproductive imperative and the loosening of connections around familial relations does not disregard the need to care for dependants so much as recognise that "til death do us part' no longer reflects the reality of many adult–sexual couple relationships. Whether parents have direct experience of divorce themselves, separation, remarriage and step-parenting form part of the cultural narrative of contemporary family life. As a consequence it is argued that friendship has become identified as *the* dependable relationship. Friendships and 'friend-like relationships' (Pahl and Spencer 1997) have taken on a symbolic value irrespective of the individual's level of satisfaction with their own couple relationship. Trustworthiness and friendship have become synonymous. In *Behind Closed Doors*, in an interview with one child/young woman, it is clear that who can be relied on is anyone but boyfriends. The divestment of self within the couple is limited because girlfriend–boyfriend relationships do not last.

> *Kelly* (F5, aged 17): I always put friends first before guys ... It's always, like, I've got family and friends and then at the bottom it's, like, guys.

Children saw friendships as important. They often said that while they could and did confide in their parents, forms of disclosing intimacy were also shared with friends. Kelly sums this up by saying that no one person (or category of relationship) served as *the* repository for disclosure, instead she told bits of her story to different people who were close to her. She gained support from different people, in different circumstances, in different ways. Through this strategy she could ensure that there was always someone available to her, in whom she could confide and who could offer her support when she needed it, in the form in which she needed it. This strategic use of friends and family was shared by many children and parents alike. However, in these same families, friendships were also characterised as a source of parental anxiety. Parents worried about the distractions friendships bring and the 'bad influence' that some friends might have on their children.

In contrast, parents often freely described a variety of adult friendships as adding another dimension to their intimate network. These sentiments typify areas of contradiction in families around the inclusion of friends as part of their intimate circle. Friendships were sometimes kept outside the parameters of family, being valued in their own right – 'friends as friends'. For others individual friends were embedded as part of their kin – 'friends as family'. In general terms, friendships were characterised as meeting the particular emotional or practical needs of individuals rather than families, although in some instances this personal support took the form of family childcare. One mother described a mutually disclosing and close relationship that she has with a colleague at work, a relationship that is spatially, temporally and emotionally contained. The meeting of these two friends affords both women the opportunity to air information about their private life, sharing problems and exploring strategies to manage personal problems.

Other parents talked about how partners could not be expected to meet all their emotional needs. In these cases friends, mothers and/or siblings were identified as their closest confidantes. It may be wise to exercise caution about the extent and contemporariness of these extended networks of support. Historical analyses of intimacy have highlighted diversity and plurality in family relationships alongside wider patterns of social change (Jamieson 1998; Crow 2002). Moreover, cultural shifts around intimate networks do not necessarily undermine the ideals of family so much as shape how interpersonal relationships are understood. This may explain why in the *Behind Closed Doors* project so many parents were keen to describe their partners as their best friends. In some ways there is now a return to the ideal of a 'companionate marriage' with its emphasis on reciprocity and partnership, the origins of which can be traced back to the nineteenth century (Holland et al. 2003). This sharing relationship re-emerged after the Second World War. More recently, the contemporary twist presented in the democratisation thesis is that sexuality has been added to the companionate mix. The companionate (heterosexual) relationship has been cast aside in favour of more diverse poly-amorous affinities.

Notwithstanding plurality among relationships, the endorsement of friendship does not necessarily obfuscate the ideal of the couple as the enduring adult relationship. Data indicate that the invocation of the friendship rhetoric to describe the couple relationship suggests two things: first, that for many people 'couplehood' has retained its primary status as an ideal to which adults should aspire; second, cultural narratives, which cite friendship as *the* reliable relationship, may have influenced how individuals *discursively* represent their lives above and beyond any social shift in the affective patterning of behaviour. Friendships have become synonymous with dependability, the epitome of trustworthy relationships, providing an emotional space that couples should emulate. As a consequence, to demonstrate the strength of a couple relationship men and women may be using the rhetoric of friendship as a means to describe and make sense of their feelings towards one another.

> *Brian* (F7): ... As far as I'm concerned my closest friend is Kate [wife], there's no two ways about it.

> *Andrea* (F6): I think if you're good friends then when the initial honeymoon period's gone you've still got something and it's not just based on attraction or based on lust or whatever, but good friends ... [you] talk to each other. You can tell a friend and be confident that if you tell something that's hurtful that they're not just going to say 'I'm not going to be your friend any more'. You feel able to express yourself. I'm not saying that you should be really derogatory, but I feel, like, with your partner you should be able to express yourself and know that they'll love you anyway.

For some, like Brain and Andrea, their partner is identified as the primary source of comfort and support, and this intimate relationship is perceived to be like no other, although in at least one relationship the viewpoint expressed was not shared between partners and there was a sense that this caused tension in the couple relationship. Corroborating the findings of other research (Yaughn and Nowicki Jr. 1999; Roy and Benenson 2000) these data suggest that it is men who often find it more difficult to form close, intimate disclosing relationships with other men. It is men who are more likely to describe their partners as their 'best friend'. Notwithstanding the emotionally rewarding experiences of 'partner as friend' relationships, data in this area suggest that it may be apposite to examine the ways that the *rhetoric of friendship* is being invoked alongside broader claims around a paradigm shift in the structuring of relationships *per se*.

Significant others

It is evident that there are many different networks of support and intimate relationships both within and beyond 'the family' and these are experienced in ways that resist uniform interpretation. Some look inwards to family members and beyond to extended kin. Others turn to different relational connections which take a variety of affective forms, including friendship networks, faith-based communities and (in some cases) pets. All of these were identified by participants, to a lesser or greater extent, as repositories for and sources of intimacy. These multifarious affective strategies not only demonstrate the need for a pluralistic approach, they problematise what constitutes intimacy and an intimate relationship.

In the detraditionalisation and democratisation theses, a model of mutuality and reciprocity is presupposed as fundamental to new formations of individualised intimacy. But as empirical research has shown, the reality is that structural factors cannot be erased from families as individual family members live within the context of broader social relations that work continually to reinstate hierarchical structures. This recognition of difference calls into question the presupposition that parents and children share the same intimate narrative of family life: 'Diversity is charted not just of types of household but of family practices and experiences across and within households' (Jamieson 2005: 195). In chapter 4 I demonstrated how ideas of 'asymmetrical reciprocity' (Young 1997) are useful as a means to account for individual subjectivity and diversity among the mutual exchanges between differently positioned subjects. Here I want to draw on data from *Behind Closed Doors* to evince the dynamism of extended and extending families in ways that require us to develop these ideas of asymmetrical reciprocity further; ways that challenge the conceptual boundaries around *who* or *what* counts as an intimate.

Analyses of non-corporeal relationships (for example, between individuals and their god) and cross-species (human–pet) relationships add a new dimension to family studies (Mason 2008). But so far these kinds of relationships remain on the margins or are typically excluded altogether from intimacy research, especially in social theory. Previous studies have shown that for many children (Morrow 1998b) and adults (Roseneil and Budgeon 2004b) alike it is the *quality* of the relationship that is significant and not simply biological and/or familial relatedness. The importance of pets for children and the significance of human–pet relationships in children's creation of family and kinship has been thoroughly demonstrated

(Morrow 1998a), but while it is accepted that intimate relationships are not always between like subjects, it appears that species difference is one step too far. However, as Donna Haraway (2003) argues, dogs and people often live 'joint lives', sharing a 'significant otherness' with one another. For many children and adults, the pet–human relationship is not a substitute for more meaningful interpersonal exchange but a relationship in its own right.

Responses from participants in *Behind Closed Doors* illustrate the need to rethink how boundaries are drawn around intimacy and intimates, to include *all* the relationships that are important in people's lives. This does not afford companion species relationships excessive significance, but aims to ensure that traditional forms of family connection are not superseded by new but equally bounded structures and processes that focus on the categorisation of contemporary relationships.

> *Henry* (F5): Oh he [Scott, pet dog] is a big part of the family. Everyone loves him and he's just lovely . . .

As Henry's comment illustrates, in pet-oriented families animals often do not exist on the affective periphery, but are included in how intimacy is experienced. In these families children acknowledged any number of animals as part of their family including dogs, cats, a hedgehog, tortoise, guinea pig, squirrel and even a snail. To these children species is indeed irrelevant. For many parents and children alike, pets were described as part of family life. Dogs routinely cuddled up with their owners, resting their heads in laps in the most 'private' (sexual) areas of bodies. Cats slept on beds and provided comfort and reassurance when stroked. While partners and children could not always be relied on to be there at the right time in the right way, pets were seen as a source of unstinting attention and affection. Practical arrangements such as holidays and deciding where and/or when to stay at a partner's house required pets' needs be incorporated into family routines. Pets joined in and shaped physical exchanges of affection such as rough-and-tumble play.

Emotion map data showed how different categories of individuals are afforded different degrees of privileged access within the home in ways that reinforce the traditional affective stratification of households. For example, parents kept friends separate from private spaces associated with either the intimate couple and/or a privacy of purpose (bedrooms and the upstairs bathroom). These private spaces typically served a 'paradoxical purpose' (Rose 1993) for immediate family, being portrayed by participants as without boundaries, open to all those whom they love. For Harriet this includes mother, father, child and pet dog.

117

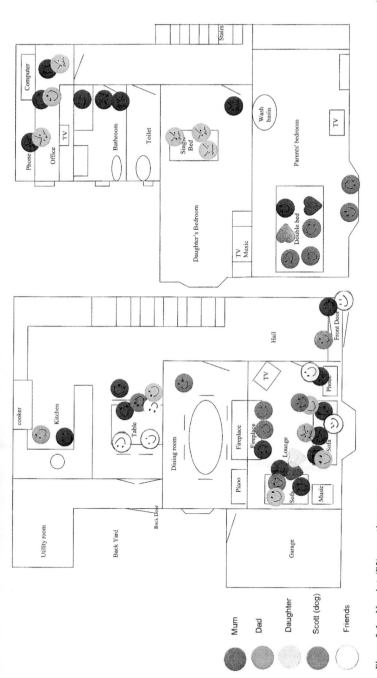

Figure 5.1 Harriet (F5) emotion map

Morning 'family cuddles' in the parents' bed were remembered by Harriet with great fondness. But Kelly is now a young woman, keen to develop her independence and she tends to make use of this intimate space only when she is emotionally 'needy'; when she turns to her parents for solace in the form of a supportive hug and/or simply wants to be with them for reassurance. However, the tradition of 'family intimacy' is upheld by Scott, who is always keen to oblige and leaps (literally) at the opportunity to join Harriet and Henry in their bed. The pet dog is not only part of family life, as Henry says, he is 'one of the family'. As such, in this family the boundaries of intimacy are simultaneously open and closed. Friendships remain experienced in a semi-public social context while the pet/dog–owner/human relationship has no spatial boundaries and spans public–private divides.

In many families, beyond the pet–human relationship, owning a pet was seen as generating affective benefits for interpersonal relationships. For example, taking the dog for a walk provided 'couple time' when parents could enjoy child-free moments together – making time for mutual disclosure. Older children used the opportunity of walking the dog in similar ways, as an opportunity for 'courtship', spending time with their boy/girlfriends away from the regulatory gaze of parents. Alternatively, dog walks enabled children to have time away from their siblings creating an opportunity for individual parent–child intimacy. In households full of children, where time was heavily scheduled, these occasions for one-to-one mutual disclosure were regarded as particularly important. Pets formed affective links that extended beyond the household, something identified as particularly important in the context of relationship upheaval. When previous partnerships had broken down custody of pets had become either a source of conflict or conversely the brokering of 'custody' helped to retain and rework affective ties through shared contact arrangements. Pets also served a significant role in the management of conflict within families. One family acknowledged that the pet dog was used as a diversionary device during tense situations and the father took him for a walk in order to calm down. Rain or shine, dogs were always happy to oblige and go for a walk.

It is important, as with studies of other relationships, not to idealise pet–human connections and in some families pets were identified as a source of tension. While taking the dog for a walk may have affective benefits, the necessity of this daily routine can mean that the 'dog walking rota' becomes a source of arguments. In some instances different opinions on the rules around pet behaviour translated into animals being identified as belonging to one person more than another. This left the 'non-owner' feeling resentful about privileges afforded to an animal which overstepped their comfort boundaries and/or ideas of how pets should behave. In two families the children's incessant demands for a pet were a regular cause of family rows between parents and children and between parents as conflicting viewpoints were negotiated. In one family the dogs were evidently out of control and were a cause of destruction and mess around the house. But on the whole, for most pet-owning families, pets were identified as an important part of the jigsaw of family intimacy, and parents and children talked of loving them. As Haraway (2003) says, this may not be the same kind of love one feels for a partner, parent or child, but it is nevertheless experienced as love and therefore should not be factored out of the affective equation.

Pets were not typically credited with an equal status in families, although for some they were experienced in this way. Nevertheless in pet-oriented families their affective role and the pet–human relationship remained significant. An estimated 52.7 per cent of British households own at least one pet (PFMA 2003), which suggests that pets are certainly not marginal in terms of their presence in everyday lives. Given all of this, their exclusion from conceptualisations of intimacy which claim to interrogate the boundaries around personal relationships is all the more intriguing. Perhaps one reason for the omission is that much of the research in this area derives from social theory with its focus on individualisation and interpersonal relationships between self and other. Alternatively, research that comes from the area of sexuality studies with its focus on sexual identities and communities again precludes cross-species relationships from the analytical gaze. What is clear from participants' accounts in *Behind Closed Doors* is that for many, pets are an integral part of the overall picture of family intimacy. As such they should be included in the mapping of intimate networks within and beyond families; the conceptual frameworks need to be extended a little bit further.

Intimate practices

Quality time

Notwithstanding differences among scholars around the conceptual boundaries of intimacy, there is consensus that it is through everyday practices – activities of care and affect – that families are materialised, rather than through structural determinants that reify traditional kinds of family. Time is recognised as a crucial factor in the process of creating and maintaining a sense of family (Morgan 1996). Indeed, it has been suggested that it is limitations of time which shape boundaries around intimacy and relationships more than the emotional capacities and/or ideological stance of individuals (Jamieson 2005). It is therefore not surprising that the significance of time and need for effective time management strategies were notable features in data from *Behind Closed Doors*. In fact, time was seen as *the most* valuable resource in many families. Irrespective of the activity that was taking place, for many parents and children it was spending time together which created family.

> *Andrea* (F6): ... It's times like that that I've felt really happy, times when we've gone to the park and just played with the family ... [It's] the fact that we're together and close and we're doing something all together. It's like when we're all working in the garden together or something like that, which doesn't happen very often but we've had a project to work on and that makes me happy that we're all just together working.

Whether talking about everyday family practices or special occasions such as family holidays, the emphasis was always about the *quality* of the time spent together, as family. To compensate for the lack of individual, available time, several parents endeavoured to fill the affective gap by involving extended family and, in most families, grandparents were identified as integral to affective networks. Parents tended to describe grandparents as occupying a special and enviable position, because, it was generally assumed, they have more 'quality time' to give to children.

Researchers have examined the consequences of increased grandparental involvement in children's lives (Gray 2005; Musil and Standing 2005) and how grandparents' 'gift of time' enables their daughters to return to work (Wheelock and Jones 2002). There has also been some attention to different kinds of 'grandparenting time' (Ochiltree 2006), questioning the presupposition that grandparents' time is otherwise empty and simply waiting to be filled. In the responses of participants in *Behind Closed Doors*, whether it was because parents felt uncomfortable in asking for help from their parents or because there was a belief that the grandparent–grandchild relationship is special, parents tended to justify and/or understand grandparenting time as an affective resource rather than freely available child care. The 'economy of gratitude' (Hochschild 2003) that shaped this affective exchange was not aligned with economic activity and as such the characterisation of intimacy in this context was never in danger of being identified as 'second-rate' (Nelson 1998).

Grandparents were seen as being able to give unadulterated 'kids' time', something that was viewed with jealousy in several cases. However, there were indications that the framing of grandparents' caring activities as an affective resource may serve a convenient strategic purpose for parents. Framed in this way, the parameters of grandparenthood were under parents' control as their family input and affective time could be contained. When grandparents tried to own their time and/or move the boundaries around their role, this sometimes led to difficult and in some cases emotionally delicate negotiations. For example, when grandparents withheld their time and involvement in the day-to-day running of families this had become a source of resentment in at least one family. Conversely, when grandparents overstepped the mark and were seen to be too involved in everyday family life, this was likewise resented. While this balancing act may place grandparents in an unenviable position, parents' unrealistic and unfair expectations may be a response to their everyday busy work–family lives rather than indicative of deliberate intent.

On occasions when grandparent–parent, parent–child or other extended kin relationships became strained, spending time together was seen as a way to generate a sense of family, even though in some instances individual ambivalence could make these events extremely tense affairs. In these and other more relaxed times, the process of preparing and/or sharing food was repeatedly referred to as a means to repair affective 'bonds'. Whether it was over a lunch break at work, a takeaway meal or a more formal dinner party at home, sharing food provided time and space for intimacy. The sociology of food has been well documented (for an overview, see Beardsworth and Keil 1997), so too the cultural meaning (Lupton 1996) and embodied processes of food and eating (Bell and Valentine 1997). Like other forms of emotion currency, food performs a symbolic purpose in the process of creating and maintaining relationships and has an affective exchange value. In *Behind Closed Doors*, in one single-parent household, the mother sought appreciation from her (young adult) sons for the food she prepared for them and in response to conflicts at home she would demonstrate her annoyance by refusing to cook for them. For this mother, food and mealtimes were a crucial form of family emotion currency and perhaps as a consequence of several difficult periods in her life, food was used a means to 'nourish' and care for herself.

In many families parents demonstrated their love for their children through food and often fondly talked about the provision and sharing of food as part of their own childhood memories. Conversely, family mealtimes tended to be reported as the primary site of routine tension and disagreements, something that came to light in many parents' emotion maps. In families with minority ethnic backgrounds, food was seen as a way to maintain cultural ties and/or create bridges between cultures. One mother talked about food as something which connected her Indian-Asian mother to her British-Asian daughter, grandchild to grandmother. It provided an affective cross-cultural chain between generations. She also saw food as a means to integrate her Asian family life with British culture by taking on board Western customs around food and what she identified as the principles of healthy eating. In this and other families, the provision of wholesome food performed a symbolic and practical demonstration not only of parents' 'good parenting' but also of their investment of time and energy in their children. 'Making something from nothing' and creating home-cooked meals takes time, a resource that can be freely given even when money is scarce.

> *Jeff* (F4): We used to have some lovely meals, and what me mam could make out the freezer, some, some days was amazing. It was, it was great, and like bone soup as I used to call it. Chicken carcases, boned up and made into a soup and stew and dumplings and the frame of the meat, like, then the cheapest me mam could get at the time, but it was still nice ... That's how I try and do Mike [son, aged four] and Molly [daughter, aged three] ... 'cos nine times out of ten, if I cook a meal they'll come after they've eaten it and say thank you and give me a kiss and cuddle for it.

Jeff's investment in the idea of 'good parenting' and his attempts to actively achieve this through the means available to him contest more deterministic accounts (e.g. Bernstein 1971) which tend to map class positions onto the patterning of family practices. Irrespective of class background, in *Behind Closed Doors* participants' responses suggested that the giving of the gift of affective time, in this instance materialised through the preparation and sharing of home-cooked meals, was more meaningful than the 'purchase of intimacy' (Zelizer 2005) and was extremely important in the process of creating family. Families worked hard to allocate time to *doing family*, spending 'quality time' together that was not dependent on economic resources. In some instances this was because finances were in short supply, but in most families it was because parents actively sought to disassociate themselves from the idea that affections could be bought, reinforcing the rhetoric of 'hostile worlds' wherein economic and intimate relationships remain dichotomous. They were keen to demonstrate that emotions and interpersonal relationships could not be accorded a monetary value – the parent–child relationship was 'priceless' (Ann, F1).

Parents talked about doing ordinary scheduled and unscheduled activities such as domestic chores, family meals, watching television or having family chats as intimate time which reinforced their relationships and provided the opportunity for mutual disclosure. Routines and structures were put in place to create and manage different sorts of 'intimate time', including keeping some adult time away from the exigencies of family. Many parents talked about the need to carve out time to be together as a couple. In these and many other ways, families typically worked hard to *optimise time* in all respects and as a consequence, by giving children the gift of their time, parents felt individually rewarded through this process of gift-giving. Parents' disassociation of affect from the economic sphere does not diminish the pertinence of work which examines the conjoining of economic–affective worlds (Hochschild 2003; Zelizer 2005). Paradoxically, it demonstrates the degree to which socially defined understandings of intimacy shape our relational worlds; the extent that individuals 'buy into' the privatisation of emotions and intimacy, something which conceals the public basis of relational experience.

Affective communication

In *Behind Closed Doors* participants spoke about many different relationships that required different amounts of their valuable time, including those with partners, friends, mothers and fathers, siblings, grandparents and extended kin such as cousins. Individuals also cited their ex-partner, health visitor and social worker as part of their disclosing network. Children tended to include parents, boyfriends or girlfriends, friends, siblings and cousins. The intensity of these relationships varied from individual to individual but, as others have suggested, one of their defining characteristics was that they were spaces of trust and reciprocity. Mutually disclosing relationships remain at the core of intimate experience (Jamieson 1998; 1999). Disclosing intimacy took many forms including intense conversations, impromptu chats, shared moments of silent intimacy, emotion exchanges that were facilitated through everyday routines such as mealtimes. Mutual disclosure was not dependent on the instigation of deep and meaningful conversations, although some families did try to orchestrate such scenarios through 'family time', but more often than not disclosure and intimacy occurred spontaneously.

One scenario that was identified by many participants as the primary site for such spontaneity of intimacy was chats. These (often trivial) conversations were not typically used as the space for significant emotional divestment and/or information exchange, but provided an opportunity for simply being together. Chats happened all over the family home – in the garden, in the living room, in parents' and children's bed-rooms. Taking place at any time – mealtimes, watching television, visits from children that interrupted a parent's quiet bathtime. Conversations between friends were often framed by women as 'a chat', but in point of fact facilitated quite meaningful dialogue. They afforded mothers a valuable opportunity to talk through issues that troubled them, serving as a vent for their emotions, a platform from which to air their feelings and provide mutual support for one another. Conversations between extended family provided similar systems of support and also consolidated kin networks and the grandparent–parent relationship without being heavy-handed or explicit about this.

A variety of different means of communication were used to facilitate talk, including face-to-face encounters, telephone and email. Children were typically adept at using computer-mediated conversation (CMC) to speak with friends while they were at home. These CMC conversations, facilitated through MSN Messenger, Facebook and/or MySpace were usually inconsequential, but the idea of being 'in touch' with friends was identified by children as extremely important. Some parents, notably mothers, also spoke of the significance of retaining friendships through email. In other circumstances intimacy was fostered through strategies of talking–not talking, with quiet times being identified as moments when couples and families can *feel* close to one another without relying on words – silent encounters based on what Jamieson calls 'a deep knowing' (Jamieson 1998: 9).

> *Harriet* (F5): Retire to living room to enjoy cup of tea … Just sitting together is good, not much conversation takes place, no need.

> *Ann* (F1): Walked into the café and asked Tom [partner] to get some papers to read. Tom said, 'I thought we've come to talk to each other.' I said. 'No, read the papers'. We both laughed!
> I had a coffee and Tom had a beer. We sat reading magazines enjoyed some time to relax together without Ollie [son, age two].

Families' verbal affective shorthand adds another dimension to the inti-mate 'knowing' characterised by Jamieson. Symbolic phrases such as 'hugs and kisses', 'kisses and cuddles', 'love you', even 'cup of tea and a chat' were used as means to express emotions: euphemisms that stood in for more complex feelings and/or time consuming interpersonal exchange. These familiar expressions of intimacy were not throwaways, emotionally empty comments. In the context of hectic family schedules these condensed phrases can be seen as a time-management strategy that ensured emotion work was completed alongside domestic tasks, ensuring that affect did not fall off the family agenda. For example, for Harriet the phrase 'cup of tea and a chat' means intimacy; an occasion for mutual disclosure.

Developing the ideas of Arlie Hochschild, it is possible to see how a cup of tea can serve as a gift – facilitating an exchange of emotion between wife and husband. As described earlier, an 'economy of gratitude' structures this transaction and, as with all gift exchanges, this process can be tricky to negotiate as each partner draws on 'different cultural prisms' (Hochschild 2003: 105). Harriet's (gendered) role is to be the giver of gifts and her husband the recipient. Thus when her gift is accepted she enjoys the connection, when the exchange is reciprocated she is notably pleased, because being a recipient of such a gift falls outside her cultural expectations. When the cup of tea she offers is ignored and left to go cold, she is upset. In these instances, when her gift is unwanted or forgotten, she appears to experience this as a rejection of her gift of affection.

> *Harriet* (F5): Cup of tea in bed first. Don't think Henry [husband] drank his ...
>
> In our bedroom Henry still also in land of nod, tea cooling rapidly.
>
> We sit down together for a cup of tea in living room; catch up on the morning's events ...
>
> Wake quite refreshed, listen to radio. Up to make tea, have breakfast. Wake Kelly [daughter, aged 17] on way back, lights on, TV on, call her. Drink tea, watch some TV. Henry's tea getting cold ....
>
> We both take Scott [pet dog] for his bedtime walk. Cup of tea before bed.

Data such as these illustrate that gift exchanges do not only involve the transaction of material objects, they can also involve the gift of emotion, affect and time. This adds a further dimension to Jamieson's argument, where she claims that scarcity of time shapes the patterning of intimate relationships (Jamieson 2005). In *Behind Closed Doors* participants' described ritualised time-condensed forms of intimate expression as part of their families' emotion currency; a currency that was known and understood by other family members. These affective codes were experienced as a part of everyday family intimacy.

Intimate bodies

Notwithstanding the significance of mutual disclosure in the forging of intimate relationships, parents and children often employ other means than 'knowing' and 'talking' to make and sustain an emotional connection; means that may include embodied forms of expression. As David Morgan (1996) points out, co-residence typically necessitates caring practices which inevitably involve touch. Intimate bodily encounters are commonly part of everyday family routine, especially when children are young. Parents and children use bodily practices to communicate with one another, exchanging many different feelings such as love, gratitude, compassion and remorse, adding a physical dimension to analysis of family intimacy that is often left out and/or shied away from in sociological research. This omission is surprising given that embodied emotion exchanges not only communicate affect they also often perform a symbolic role. Bodily interactions among parents and children add another dimension to understandings of intimacy because the embodied dialogic process not only expresses emotion, it conveys *different levels of meaning* that are indicative of wider gendered and generational relations.

For children, who may not have access to resources traditionally accrued through age, giving a hug can be a powerful tool, refocusing attention onto them. This gesture may be indicative of a child's emotional need or, in other circumstances, may be a strategic ploy aimed at redressing imbalances of power in a family scenario, using the only means available. Notwithstanding differences in motivation, children use their bodies and bodily contact to assert their presence, to say 'focus on me', 'pay me attention'. In this way, though children may be less powerful in the structuring of families, they are not wholly powerless.

> *Andrea* (F6): If somebody looks uncharacteristically worried ... obviously you'd look at their face and also whether they're talking to the others or to their friends. Sometimes they are more cuddly when they want you to talk to them. They come up and need you to put your arm round them, and even if you say 'Are you all right?' 'Yes I'm fine', but you just know that they maybe need a bit of something. Sometimes they will be aggressive with each other ... that is a sign that something's not right.

Children's embodied language needs to be learnt just like any other. As Andrea says, parents read their own children's body language to pick up the visual clues which indicate when things have gone awry. These embodied cues invite intervention without a reliance on words, something that is particularly important for children who may be unable to verbalise how they are feeling. In *Behind Closed Doors* participants typically suggested that bodily forms of intimacy were extremely important and descriptions of parent–child embodied exchanges were fondly remembered by many mothers and fathers from their own childhood. These moments appear to bring parent and child closer together, in part through the intimacy of the encounter; the breaking down of bodily boundaries between self and other (McDowell 1993; Gabb 2004a). As such it is not the activity in and of itself which is important as much as the sharing of bodily intimacy. One mother wistfully recalled sitting in bed with her parents on a Saturday morning, 'picking the fluff out of my dad's belly button' (Kate, F7), while two other mothers shared similar memories of parent–child grooming.

> *Ann* (F1): I speak to my mother by phone at least twice a day ... I try and visit three to four times a week ... I still enjoy giving my mother a kiss and hug. I enjoy my mum combing my hair. It reminds me of a time as a child when she combed my long hair.

> *Helen* (F8): When we were small we would sit on dad's knee and he would cuddle us and I remember doing my dad's hair for him. He used to love to have his hair done and I remember sitting on his shoulders, I mean I love it now I'm the same. He used to love to have his head massaged. I love to go to the hairdresser's. I just love people playing with my hair, I just find it so lovely. Well my dad obviously did, and I would sit on his shoulders and I'd massage his hair and I'd pretend to be shampooing it and I'd pretend to comb it for him and do all this. There was obviously lots of contact there, but if ever you were upset and crying you went to your mum, mum was the one you went to ...

For Ann speaking with her mother by telephone is not enough, she also wants to retain a physical closeness. Her description of parent–child intimacy includes an emotion exchange, 'a kiss and hug', that might be experienced in many loving and openly expressive families, but she also describes another form of embodied experience that is perhaps less frequently commented on. Ann and her mother in part co-construct the mother–daughter connection through bodily practices which position them in the mother (carer) and daughter (cared for) relationship. While it is Ann who now does a lot of the running around and visiting, her mother retains her maternal status by repeating caring affective practices initiated during Ann's childhood. Combing her daughter's hair is a bodily practice that expresses many emotions and has an emotional reward that is hard to replicate in words because it draws on the continuity of their relationship.

In a similar way Helen fondly remembers the embodied relationship between herself and her father involving parent–child touch. The focal point for these parent–daughter bodily interactions was the head and hair. Set apart from sexual areas of the body, the head and hair afford a safe, risk-free embodied form of parent–child sensuality, something that is crucial in father–child exchanges. Gender is a crucial dimension in how embodied emotions are materialised, especially in intergenerational exchanges. What these data show are the ways that bodily interactions form part of individuals' affective repertoire and need to be included if we are to understand the complexity of everyday family intimacy.

Differences that matter

Gender remains an important factor in the shaping of family interaction and embodied affective experience. However, in *Behind Closed Doors* and in my previous research on lesbian parent families, other factors that might be perceived as similarly consequential turned out to be relatively unimportant. While studies of lesbian and gay parenthood (e.g. Dunne 1999) tend to characterise same-sex families as distinct from their heterosexual counterparts, I did not find any discernible differences in everyday family practices that could be attributed to mothers' sexual orientation. There may have been a period of adjustment during which children came to terms with their parents' 'coming out', but the family dynamic appeared to quickly return to 'normal'. Sexuality was not the primary marker of familial and/or affective difference (Gabb 2001; 2005b). Families were more likely to be shaped through individual choices, socio-economic circumstances and demographics than through sexuality *per se*. Indeed, many parents were quite passionate in their assertion of ordinariness.

> *Michelle*: The words 'lesbian family' imply that it's all lesbian, whereas it's not. You know, the house isn't 'Stonewall' covered and we don't all have t-shirts saying 'Lesbian', you know. We are just,sort of, like a normal family really but me and [partner] just happen to both be women ... Obviously, there are differences ... We are a minority family, but I would still class us, yes, as a family.

As Michelle demonstrates, sexuality and sexual identity are not guarantees of identifiable difference in family practices. This does not deny that some same-sex families are 'doing it differently', by living outside the heteronormative family model, but recognises that there are probably an equal number who are 'doing family' in ways that effectively mirror heterosexual counterparts. Like Neil Gross (2005), I query the validity of characterising same-sex families as being in the vanguard of relational change (for a thorough account of sexuality in/difference in lesbian parent households, see Gabb 2004b; 2005a). Corroborating findings from other families research, in *Behind Closed Doors* participants' responses indicated that there were different factors that were far more *structurally* important. For example, like Jo Armstrong (2006), I found that socio-economic context shaped experiences of motherhood and family in particular ways, something that I have explored, albeit indirectly, elsewhere in this chapter. There was also evidence to suggest that the everyday implications of living with disability significantly affect the patterning of family relationships.

Another factor was families' ethnic–cultural background and/or their sense of belonging to a religious community, with differences being especially marked among families who were observant. In one family a British-Asian mother talked about how her faith shaped the ways she cared for her mother when the mother was terminally ill and grieved for her in death. Another Indian-Asian mother talked about the significance of extended kin network in her culture and how these relationships take precedence over all others. It is not that friendships are unimportant in this context, but that they are something distinct from family. Investment in family ties is paramount; keeping in touch requires a substantial time commitment and emotional energy and this shapes everyday family life.

In some ways there was little evident difference between families with minority ethnic backgrounds, those who identified themselves as belonging to a particular faith community and secular families. In fact, religious belief could appear to be of little discernible consequence beyond church attendance as part of family routine. However, in other ways these differences defined both structures of family intimacy and understandings of normative behaviour. For example, data from one family was wrapped in a particular set of discourses that derive from their participation in an evangelical church. The language and framing of this family and their everyday routines were presented through the moral discourse advocated by their faith. Children are 'a blessing' from God; church attendance, family rituals and investment in the parent–child relationship are a requirement.

> *Andrea* (F6): I suppose with our beliefs we look on every child that they are a child of God so therefore you kind of look at it like being trusted. So it's a really important thing because you've been given this opportunity and an opportunity that will give you a relationship forever with this really important job that you're doing, and you can't let them down; you can't let this baby down.

In this family, the parents were keen to demonstrate the amount of time they put into thinking about parenting skills, and their lives and family were evidently child-centred. The father, Barry, claimed that he was not trying to paint a picture of his family as ideal, acknowledging that, by his own measure, his family is 'far from perfect'. But the family all work hard to operate within the parameters laid down by the church for how relationships and family life should be.

> *Barry* (F6): We usually have a family night once a week ... it's something that the church thought of, having 'a family night' ... It's just time that we spend as a family and we don't plan to do anything else ... It's usually church-oriented so it's usually something round a Bible story or a moral principle or something like that. Not necessarily a religious thing, sometimes it's just about being well-mannered or courteous, or something like that. Some sort of lesson or moral, and then we usually play some games and have some treats and things like that. Just some time together. But like I said, it's just a night that we don't plan anything outside the home.

Andrea and Barry describe their faith as providing both spiritual support and practical guidance in family processes. They comply with a model that advocates particular ways of doing family, a template that is undoubtedly prescriptive, but nonetheless it cannot be characterised as autocratic or traditionally patriarchal as might be expected. Barry openly talked about wanting to provide a positive role model for his sons and tries to sustain a physical, emotional and spiritual relationship with all of them. It is Barry who does the cooking in this family and he contributes equally to the domestic chores and childcare of this household. In fact, what emerged from these family data was how their moral framework led them towards a model of family relations akin to that advanced in Giddens' (1992) democratisation thesis.

More so than any other family, this one structured everyday life through clearly recognisable democratic principles. However, in contradistinction to the detraditionalisation thesis, which prefaces individualisation, it was *community belonging* which shaped this family's egalitarian ethos. Their affinity with community-oriented family life reflects some of the arguments advanced by Lauren Berlant and Michael Warner (2000) on queer theorising. Through analysis of lesbian and gay experience, they evince the artificiality of distinctions between public–private, community–domestic intimate life. I am not arguing that faith-based communities may or may not mirror some of the transformative potentialities that have been associated with sexuality-based communities. I suspect that had I interviewed another family from a different faith community and/or among the same congregation as Andrea and Barry, the picture would have been very different. As such, it is not my aim to overstate the case, but, alongside data on sexuality experience in same-sex families, to use it to draw attention to some of the complexities of families research.

In this and in other examples discussed in this chapter, I have tried to show how key debates in intimacy research facilitate analysis of everyday family relationships and/or point to areas where frameworks fail to account for the diversity among families' practices of intimacy. In this analysis I have not aimed to valorise one approach over another. Instead I have looked at areas which push at the boundaries of contemporary understandings of intimate family life in order to extend the conceptual and theoretical research imagination.

6
The Affect of Methods

In the previouis two chapters I focused on the conceptual framing and lived experience of intimacy and family relationships, here I return to methodological debates on researching families, children and private lives. Through analysis of empirical data from *Behind Closed Doors* I demonstrate some of the tensions that exist in families research and the dynamic process of fieldwork and analysis. This book aims to move beyond the parameters of a methods handbook, to explore how sociological understandings of families are produced *through the process of research*. In chapter 2 I introduced the dominant conceptual frameworks of family and childhood research and in chapter 3 the research approaches that informed and shaped these fields. I examined different methodological approaches and research methods and how these have responded to and extended wider social trends in the patterning of relational life. In chapters 4 and 5 I interrogated conceptual understandings of the changing patterns of intimate life and family relationships.

In this chapter I draw together these two parallel, and often distinctive, strands in order to bridge methodological–conceptual debates in the fields of families and childhood studies. Through close analysis of original empirical data I focus attention on the affect of methods. I illustrate how different methods produce distinctive kinds of data and the ways in which these underpin how we make sense of and understand intimacy and family relationships.

In the first section I explore participatory methods (notably visual methods and diaries) and the kinds of auto/biographical data these produce. I detail the innovatory emotion map method developed in *Behind Closed Doors* and examine how these data materialise spatial and affective dimensions of family intimacy. Data from these participatory methods demonstrate the ways that family relationships are framed through public–private affective repertoires within dominant cultural narratives. Observation data similarly capture both the texture of intimate family life and the mediation of lived experience, producing visual–audio data on the crafting of family and relationships. In the next section I consider biographical narrative interview methods which are becoming more commonplace in family and parenthood studies. This approach tends to produce complex and contradictory accounts that span the lifecourse. I demonstrate how this non-directive technique productively orients the framing of intimacy and relational life around individual experience.

Most methods described so far have aimed to elicit information about personal experience and ordinary family life. In the final section I focus on methods that are designed to address participants' perceptions and beliefs at the social level. I demonstrate the efficacy of photo interviews, vignettes and focus group discussion in producing data on the public–private intersections of intimate life. I analyse how group interviews and third party focus group discussion evince the processes through which people make sense of their own family practices of intimacy. These data highlight the significance of the lived context of intimacy, something which reinforces public–private boundaries around forms of intimacy and intimate behaviour.

Representing family life

Participatory methods allow people to represent themselves and their everyday practices in a form they control. They provide time and space for reflection, aiming to ease participants gently into a research topic study at a speed and pitch which are comfortable for them; conceptually and emotionally foregrounding in-depth interviews which may elicit more sensitive disclosures.

Visual techniques

Visual techniques have been identified as particularly useful in families and childhood research as they are non-threatening and participants are not limited by their writing skills and/or vocabulary. Creative approaches of this kind can produce rich data on and around the research subject. In my study of lesbian parent families I was interested to find out how mothers' lesbianism impacted on their children's lives. It would be hard to address this topic head on, especially with young children, and so to work around this I relied heavily on creative participatory techniques to engage children *indirectly* with the topic using methods that were familiar

Figure 6.1   Andrew (aged seven) 'My Family'

to them. The data produced move beyond simple iterations of 'the family' and enabled children to talk about relational processes in their lives. The imaginative ways they approached the topic were at times astonishing. When Andrew was asked to draw a picture of those whom he thought of as family, he explained that he loves to draw but was uncomfortable about drawing his family because 'I'm not good at people, only vehicles'. We agreed that he should draw his family as vehicles (see Figure 6.1).

I talked with Andrew while he drew his picture. This interview was punctuated by silences as he concentrated on the task in hand and included free-ranging conversation about his love of drawing. These sections elicited no data but helped to diminish the sense of 'interview as interrogation' and instead framed the experience as a gentle chat. Thinking creatively about combining the child's interests with those of my own research agenda meant that both Andrew and I got something out of the interview. Andrew enjoyed creating the picture and chatting about his family. This conversation provided me with information about how he framed and experienced these familial relationships. For example, though his picture depicted only his immediate family, when drawing his mum as an aeroplane his thoughts 'drifted' and he began to tell me about a family holiday when they travelled abroad by air. Thinking about who was included in this 'family holiday' led Andrew to talk about his extended family, including his step-siblings and stepmother. He suggested that the step-siblings are 'like a brother and sister' and that he now has 'two families that are linked' rather than one extended kin network, a separation that is structured through two spatially and emotionally distinct homes. Thus his picture of vehicles encouraged a quite wide-ranging conversation that was not contained by the subject represented, but was extended through it.

Other visual methods that have been effectively deployed in the study of families, extended kin relationships and networks of intimacy include the completion of concentric circles, family trees and spider charts (Gabb 2005a). When using these methods, participants are typically asked to place themselves at the centre of the graphic and then add other people (or intimates) to this picture. Proximity to the centre/self denotes the level of closeness and/or the significance of the relationship. In this way it is possible to visualise which connections are experienced as important alongside their individual relational category – parent, step-parent, neighbour, sibling, teacher, colleague, friend, cousin, pet, etc. Another visual approach that is gaining in popularity is the life grid or time-line. Here participants mark significant events and personal experiences along their lifecourse. This method records micro and macro data, illustrating where, when and in what ways personal experiences and social events correspond. Through accompanying interviews, researchers can explore why certain meanings and emotions are ascribed to these notable occasions (9/11, death of a parent, divorce, birth of a child, etc.).

Each of these graphic methods produces visual data in its own right, but their greatest utility lies in their facilitation of conversation around research themes. As such they tend to be used as a means to elicit in-depth qualitative data on relationality and kin creation. In *Behind Closed Doors* I was interested in the processes of family relationships, analysis that moves beyond who is included as kin into the quite abstract realm of emotions, feelings and connections with others. To facilitate conversation I pioneered a technique that would produce material data on *where* affective encounters took place alongside discursive data around what characterised these exchanges. The data produced illustrated the emotional geography of family homes. The pragmatics of the emotion map method are described in chapter 3, here I focus on the data.

All but one of the participants said that they found the emotion map enjoyable to complete. Parents and children commented on how empowering the method was in that they could document an exchange that had otherwise left them feeling frustrated and/or grumpy. Parents of younger children tended to facilitate children's participation with the method but were asked not to suggest which interactions to include or what emoticon stickers to use. The only negative comment came from one father who said that he thought the four emoticon stickers (happy, sad, cross and affectionate exchanges) caricatured the complexity of feelings and the dynamic of the encounter. This criticism has some merit, although it should be said that the stickers aimed to *signify* an exchange and were not intended to work as stand-alone data. In discursive post-method interviews these graphic data were extended to include *when* encounters took place, details about their exact *form*, and more often than not the circumstances surrounding the exchange – *why* it happened in this form, in this context. The breadth of data produced far exceeded my expectations and provided information on the spatial–temporal patterning of affective behaviour around the home.

Some parents used the emotion map data produced by their children to return to disagreements in order to talk through the underlying issues with them in a little more depth. Others, like Joan (see Figure 6.2) aimed to use information from the data proactively. This 'educational' process suggests that the method could have uses that extend beyond academic research and the method has been already identified as having great potential in the context of family support and parenting skills provision.

> *Joan* (F3): I found it interesting doing the map, the floor plan, 'cos I noticed there was patterns in the rooms, especially the kitchen. It seemed like quite an unhappy, grumpy place where I was telling the children off around the fridge, around the cooker and table, the sink ... It starts off quite happy at the table and then we sit down on an evening and by the end of the evening it's just ... I realised a lot ... I think it was the different areas of the house where the kids must think, 'This is a grumpy area, she's gong to tell us off again now, let's wait for it', they must just think that, you know, and try and push it as far as they can get ...

Identifying the kitchen as a hotspot for family tension is nothing new (Halford et al. 1992), but producing such findings in a graphic form as co-constructed household data is methodologically innovative. This kind of information can be readily used with participants to redress negative patterns of behaviour within families. Data from this method were also useful in that they documented the ways that many parents and children created a sense of family through their use of shared space around the home and/or the cohesive process of doing family activities together. Talking the researcher through his emotion map, one father described how his family have weekly 'curry nights' when the family sit down together and share a meal, using this time to talk through the events of the past week. At other times they share family space without any

137

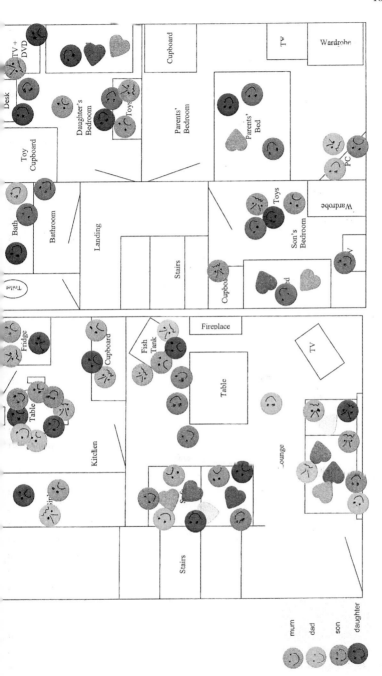

Figure 6.2 Joan (F3) emotion map

interaction. He suggested that both serve a valuable purpose, ensuring that parents and children spend time together just being family. Spatial methods are particularly useful in eliciting data on these *incidental moments*, time shared when nothing consequential happens but which remain part of the emotional geography of family life.

The floor plan provided the parameters of participants' mapping of family emotion exchanges, but these interactions were not confined by discrete areas of the home, such as bedrooms, the lounge or kitchen. The spaces in between these separate areas – notably doorways and hallways – were also afforded emotional significance. Several parents spoke about how exterior doorways accommodated greetings and physical interactions as people entered and left the house, operating as an affective portal that allowed for the transmission of emotions between spaces. Interior doorways performed a functional and symbolic purpose in that they could be left open, creating an affective bridge between parents and children, intimates and non-intimates, or closed to create privacy. This dual purpose appeared to be especially significant for teenagers experiencing the transition from childhood to young adulthood, a period when increasing independence and physical–emotional separation from other family members and the household was being negotiated.

Data indicate that arguments between parents and teenagers often occurred between defined places – being literally and metaphorically framed by their in-between location.

> *Interviewer:* So are there any areas where conflict arises more than others do you think?
> *Kelly* (F5, aged 17): . . . It's usually my bedroom door . . . or in the car on the way to college, which is not in the house I know, but there as well.

The areas that Kelly primarily associates with conflict are located beyond the parameters of particular spaces. It is her bedroom doorway and journeys between home and college which are identified as the 'hotspots' where conflicts arise. These data highlight the need to examine family practices outside confined rooms and the home, to include the movements and areas that extend defined space.

Consideration of what triggered participants' decisions to place a sticker on their emotion map brought to light the process of family intimacy and the cultural repertoires within which families operate. One participant remarked that some rooms were just for necessity, associating these spaces with a privacy of purpose. This characterisation of certain rooms, such as bathrooms and en-suites, was typical and tended to skew the data. The emoticon stickers that were used accurately recorded neither the frequency nor the character of family interactions that took place in these spaces. Moreover, some rooms, especially bathrooms, went left unmarked or had only a limited number of emotion exchanges acknowledged, even though when using other methods they were described as spaces where family interactions frequently occurred. There may be many reasons for families' reticence in assigning stickers to certain spaces, but it is almost certainly true that normalising ideas of propriety alongside the invisibility of mundane, seemingly inconsequential interactions were contributing factors.

Several parents addressed head on understandings of normalcy and what constitutes morally correct behaviour. For example, one mother raised concerns about the potential for assigning the same emoticon to different kinds of interaction. On his emotion map her teenage son (Jack, aged 14) had put a 'love heart' sticker on his bed representing intimacy with his girlfriend. When parents and children in this family elected to share their emotion maps with one another, his mother (Kate) became quite anxious. She was not so much unsettled by the nature of the intimacy which Jack depicted, but concerned that its characterisation might generate potential misunderstandings around the activities represented by *her* emoticon stickers.

> *Kate* (F7): What made me worried was that outside people looking at it might think ... because I do go in and check on them before I go to bed and I wake them up every morning and that for me is a real kind of 'love heart' thing, because they're my babies and I like to check on them, and I wonder if somebody else would misinterpret that looking at an emotion map that maybe there was something dodgy going on. You don't know who's analysing the information and what is normal because some people aren't at all tactile whereas I am, you know, I like to give them a hug and a kiss in the mornings and maybe some people would think that wouldn't be on.

Kate's concerns demonstrated her desire (reiterated in a subsequent discussion of vignettes and photographs) to be seen as a responsible parent; someone who frames her affective conduct within the parameters of 'normal' behaviour. Her data highlight how public discourses on risk and abuse affect individual families. While there is nothing to suggest that Kate has any reason to worry about intimacy in her household, her expressed anxiety demonstrates how everyday intimate practices are moderated and mediated in accordance with normative models; to guard against potential misunderstanding. What emotion map data demonstrated time and again was how public discourses on sexuality and affective conduct get incorporated into families' everyday sense-making practices of intimacy. Like other data from focus groups, vignettes and photo interviews, they illustrate the intersections between public–private lives.

Research diaries

Another participatory method used in *Behind Closed Doors* was the research diary. Diaries afford participants the opportunity to reflect on and consciously craft their account of family. Participants generally commented that this enforced reflection gave them a new perspective on how their family and relationships operate, through daily and weekly rituals; illustrating the *process of intimacy*. For example, Jeff, a single parent, went to great lengths to detail the frequency and character of everyday affective routines in his family. He presented an account of family life that was framed through the discourses of 'good parenting' and demonstrated his commitment to providing a 'good home life' for his children. This was constituted through regular physical expressions of emotion, wholesome, home-cooked meals and quality time spent together as family. In his post-diary interview Jeff talked about how his investment in family makes him feel positive about himself as a parent. Any ambivalence he may experience around the self-sacrifice demanded through single parenthood goes unacknowledged. The 'positive spin' that Jeff presents in his diary may be the truth about his circumstances as he experiences it, or, as with other parents' diaries, it may be that these data are highly crafted, albeit unintentionally in some cases – written with the reader in mind.

> *Jeff* (F4): M&M [Mike, aged four; Molly, aged two] have just said thank you to me for sorting their breakfast out for them. M&M are very happy this morning because we are going to see Grandma and Granddad had lots of kisses & cuddles for them. Had lots of fun and laughs. Had macaroni cheese for tea (that's the kids' favourite meal). Molly went to bed give me kisses & cuddles for me and so did Mike ...

Like Jeff, several participants used the opportunity of producing diaries to detail the quality of their affective routines alongside the frequency and character of these interactions. These data may be a true record of events, and I am not suggesting that the accounts were either inaccurate or intentionally misleading. But it is fair to say that the framing of events typically reflected the dominant cultural narratives within which families operate as much as the events in and of themselves. That is to say, these data say as much about the repertoires of 'happy families' and 'good parenting' as they do about the particularities of lived experience.

Experiences and emotions around conflict and/or sadness were occasionally recorded, but in some cases their inclusion could be read as strategic, serving as a lens through which parents' proactive responses to these scenarios could be highlighted. In contrast, in other families, the picture represented was perhaps more candid and experiences were in many ways less worked over – less reflexive. For example, inequalities in the division of domestic roles and 'emotion work' among mothers and fathers were stated as a matter of fact. I do not wish to suggest that these accounts were more or less authentic than those that were polished. Instead I want to draw attention to the different kinds of data produced through participatory accounts of family life.

> *Joan* (F3): Yeah, the same thing every morning they'll wake up, usually between half past five half past six, I'm up at half past five half past six, down stairs, usually put the telly on breakfast channel, make breakfast, sit and eat breakfast, sometimes it can be really good and other mornings it's not, then it's upstairs get a wash or a bath depending on how dirty they are after their breakfast, dressed . . . and I'm getting ready and washing the pots between eight and half past, I have to leave really at half past to get to school for quarter to, and coaxing Kerry to get dressed isn't too bad, but it's getting her hair brushed!

Data such as Joan's are interesting in that they illustrate the gendered patterning of behaviour that is typical in many families, but beyond this they warrant further analytical attention because they are also of methodological interest. As with Jeff's data, it is telling that in her diary and post-diary interview Joan makes no attempt to unpick *why* these patterns of domestic labour exist. In fact, in both cases, the reasons why their accounts were presented in their respective formats did not emerge until later in the research process. What both sets of diary data did achieve was to alert the researcher to the individual frames of reference and cultural repertoires within which these participants operated, defining factors that could be explicated in subsequent interviews. They provided invaluable background information alongside raising interesting material on individual experience.

Where diaries were immediately useful – producing data that can be otherwise hard to capture – was in their elicitation of families' *affective currencies*. In *Behind Closed Doors* phrases such as 'kisses & cuddles' and 'hugs and kisses' peppered diary data. In one family the phrase 'I love you' was evidently extremely important, being used to hold together kin ties that might be otherwise physically and emotionally distant. As with other participatory methods, though they were completed in the home, diary data were not contained by household, co-residency and/or family. The inclusion of telephone conversations, text messaging, emails and internet chat rooms were detailed among the innumerable intimate connections.

> *Claire* (F2): I told him [son] 'I love you' he smiled and replied 'love you too' which made me happy . . .
>
> Text to Jade [girlfriend] in response to one [received]. As an afterthought, I am thinking of Lance [son, aged 19] staying in London working until Friday so I will text him an 'I love you' too as I know it will make him smile.

As discussed in chapter 5, ritualised exchanges of emotion package feelings in a familiar currency and this affective shorthand often obviated the need for more time-consuming emotion work. Saying 'I love you' meant that the depth and intensity of feeling did not need to be demonstrated: in everyday and cultural terms, these three words said it all. Across the dataset the management of time was an underlying theme for all parents: time as a precious commodity, the need to make the most of time spent together as family, balancing work and family time. Given that diaries are typically shaped through measurements of time (Bell 1998), the prevalence of routines and time management in these data was expected. Beyond this, what these data illustrated was the cultural–discursive framing of temporality and the materialisation of time-limited intimacy.

Diary data on affective time remained ostensibly consistent among parents and children, however in other areas discrepancies between family's data did begin to emerge. When several members of a household completed the same methods it was possible to use comparative analysis to look for patterns across the family dataset. These comparisons produced a rich account of relationships, in some cases illustrating a family story with participants producing a shared narrative that appeared rehearsed. In other instances a 'his' and 'hers' version of everyday family life was produced that was structured through contradiction as each person put forward their individual perspective. However, analysis of individuals' corresponding data also has potential beyond this comparative paradigm. It can say just as much about an individual as it does about (cross-referenced) family dynamics. For example, Brian begins his diary with an explicit reference to sex: 'Woke up sort of wanting a bonk

[sex]'. He later reflected on his comments and said that he was 'acting up' for the research. Looking at Brian's data alongside Kate's (his wife), it is possible to trace patterns of behaviour which illustrate how intimacy and sex are routinely negotiated by this couple.

Kate started her diary the day before Brian. It begins: 'Wake up: Usual few minutes' hug and my head on Brian's shoulder. It's reassuring, relaxing and one of the few quiet, close times of the day'. The following day, the day on which Brian awoke wanting sex, her description is less embellished: 'Usual hug with Brian'. For Kate, sexual desire appears to have quashed intimacy between the couple. She details the events of the day and then rounds off her diary entry with: 'Bath, bed, Brian gets the "intimacy" he's awaited all day!' A comparative analysis of these diary data conforms to the 'his' (sexual) and 'hers' (emotional) marriage that is traditionally depicted. But detailed analysis of Brian's account illustrates that his opening gambit is as much about his initial discomfort with taking part in the research and his inability to articulate emotions *per se*, than with any specific differences in gendered intimate/sexual behaviours. In his post-diary interview he presents a candid picture of his emotional capacities and how he struggled to put his feelings into words.

> *Brian* (F7): It's a bit difficult sometimes to put how you feel into words, I wasn't sure whether I ought to be putting things down like 'I woke up wanting to make love to my wife' and stuff like that, but I thought, well, that's how I felt at the time.

It is interesting to note Brian's changing repertoire. Here he has redefined his sexual desire within the discourses of love and in later diary entries he focuses on mutual intimacy within the couple relationship.

> *Brian* (F7): Had a bath with Kate after sending the kids to bed. We gave each other a foot massage, really nice and relaxing. Boys were both in bed by the time we'd finished so we made love and then fell asleep, both tired.

In chapter 5 I suggested that men often demonstrate their feelings in distinctive forms. Diary data illustrate the complex and shifting relationship between how emotions are experienced and the representation of these feelings. Brian and Kate's data illustrate that comparative analysis of diary data requires great caution in order to resist simplified and inaccurate readings of gendered emotions and the ways that couples negotiate intimacy. As with all methods, they provide only a partial picture. When used in conjunction with other methods, as part of a mixed-methods approach, they can provide a valuable piece of the family intimacy jigsaw.

Observations

The final participatory methods that I want to explore are observations. In families research observation primarily provides two kinds of data. The method can be used to capture the texture of family life, the verbal and non-verbal expressions of intimacy. This can help to familiarise the researcher with everyday processes, showing how family members interact with one another. The second kind of data acknowledges the research process, recognising that observation data do not claim to approximate 'real life' but the mediation of lived experience. This does not reduce the effectiveness of the method but highlights what it is possible to record – the incidences and 'performances' of family that participants present.

There are a couple of factors that are germane to both kinds of observation data. The first pertains to the pragmatics of data collection. Observations are time-consuming. Data collection happens in real time and cannot be compressed through narrativisation. I have already commented on the scarcity of time available to families and as such their reluctance to devote precious 'quality time' to extensive periods of researcher involvement is understandable. Couple this with families' unease at being watched – under surveillance – and the method quickly begins to pose a logistical headache. It is possible to counteract some of the reservations expressed by participants by boosting the appeal of observation recording equipment – getting children to play with the video camera, framing the observation as the production of a home movie rather than CCTV, likening the process to familiar fly-on-the-wall and/or reality television. All of these strategies serve to make the method more appealing without misleading families about the inconvenience and practicalities of participant observation.

The second factor is research ethics, namely what it is legitimate to observe in the area of intimacy and sexuality research. In *Behind Closed Doors* the researchers spent a lot of time reassuring families about the future use and analytical purpose of observation. They discussed what observation data hoped to achieve (the capture of everyday interactions) and suggested the types of activity which might be recorded – mealtimes, a day trip, bedtime routines (for younger children). The final decision about which activity would be observed was left to the families. It was up to them to agree which scenarios were 'recorded' and the means through which these data were collected. Leaving this decision with families aimed to address some of their concerns and anxieties. Moreover, their decision-making process provided interesting data in itself in that it demonstrated the sorts of activities and scenarios through which participants wanted to represent themselves – when they thought they were 'at their best' as family. Some observations were documented through video recordings, produced by the families (auto-observation) or the researcher, others through audio tape recordings and/or field notes.

Without dismissing the significant ethical challenges raised by video observations (discussed in chapter 3), the multidimensional portrait that is created is hard to produce by any other means. These data bring to life how families 'look' and behave, something which can be invaluable if the research process (data collection and analysis) is not completed by the some person. They literally visualise families and sketch the context of otherwise disembodied interviews. These combined audio and visual observation data give a glimpse of lived everyday affective practices and highlight most keenly the process of data selection. In the following analysis I draw on observation data from three families.

A couple of features publicising the *Behind Closed Doors* project were placed in local newspapers in order to recruit participants. The strap-line for one of these features (written by the reporter) was 'Is your family happy?' One response was enthusiastic and immediate. Ann (F1): 'My husband [Tom] and I would consider we have a happy, normal, loving happy family'. In all data collected Ann was keen to reiterate her sense of her family as normal and loving, themes that were particularly dominant in her diary and observation data. Her alignment of these themes with being happy – note her use of the term as both adjective and noun in the initial response – is also interesting. What motivated Ann to volunteer her family in this way remains speculation. She was already a keen diarist and was clear that the material produced through the project was intended to supplement this autobiographical archive which traced the gestation, birth and experiences of her child. Ann's document of her child's life was a reflexive project and she took every opportunity to reflect on family processes and account for events and feelings when things were not going smoothly. Another probable motivating factor could be described as participant altruism. Perceiving her family to be an exemplar Ann wanted to share her experience as a model of good practice. Whatever her reasons, for Ann it seemed important that she represented herself as a good mother and demonstrated this through her attentiveness to Ollie (son, aged two) around whom family time appears to be almost entirely structured.

In video auto-observation data the parents' reference to one another as 'mummy' and 'daddy' illustrates their absorption in the child's world.

When they speak directly to one another it is typically in connection with Ollie and his needs. The portrayal of their family life is not candid and in many ways seems to be highly orchestrated. The examples selected and recorded by Ann and Tom present a particular picture of family, although there is nothing to suggest that these sequences are atypical. Auto-observation video data included Ollie's bedtime routine and there were also researcher's field notes of a trip to the park. The picture painted was one of a happy family which is oriented around the needs of the child, 'needs' that equally serve the parents' 'good parenting' agenda alongside the child's educational development. In a bedtime scenario recorded by Ann, she took time away from the activity to reframe the video camera; to capture the exact picture that she wanted to show of parent–child interaction. Zooming in on the scene she literally and symbolically positioned the child at the centre of family life, with peripheral information that surrounded this picture being cut out. These observation data illustrate the shaping of practices of intimacy. They provide data on parent–child, family and interpersonal relationships – dynamic affective and relational processes in action – alongside the parents' editorial role in the crafting of an account of family. In the end, the composition of their observation data was as interesting as the data themselves.

The authenticity of video observation data is something of a moot point. Most families selected a family mealtime as one of the scenarios that was appropriate for observation. These data not only depicted a conscious crafting of family and relationships, they also revealed a lot about how individuals operated within the context of family. Observations of family scenarios were almost certainly censored and in some instances individuals were on their 'best behaviour' for the benefit of the researcher or the camera. However, this research performance was inevitably hard to control, especially when the 'cast' included children. It was not uncommon for the everyday dynamic of family life to leak out around the edges of the portrait. For example, during observations of a mealtime with one family (F7), recorded on audio tape by the researcher, it was clear that one of the children made strategic use of this scenario to accentuate his demands for increased privacy.

> *Jack* (aged 14): My door doesn't have a handle on it so you can't really shut it properly.
> *Kate* (mother): No, you can't open it easily either.
> *Dan* (aged 12): Yeah, you can.
> *Brian* (father): Yeah, that's one thing we don't have, locks in the house at all do we, on the toilets or anything so.

Dan: I think we should!
Kate: Do you? Why do you say that?
Dan: I've said that for ages!
Kate: Do you?
Dan: Yeah, I think in the bathrooms.
Brian: Why?
Dan: So you don't walk in on me!
Brian: Why?
Dan: 'Cos I don't like it [*said very forcefully*].
Kate: Do you not like it when I walk in either? You don't seem to mind in the morning when I come in.
Dan: Well that's because I can't do anything about it.

Dan's intervention may have been raised in this context because he felt this was a safe environment. That is to say, he was delimiting adverse consequences through the presence of a stranger and/or making use of this somewhat artificial scenario to air views which might in other circumstances have been silenced or ignored. Alternatively, it may have been that the topic would have cropped up 'naturally' irrespective of the family's involvement with the research project. What is clear is that observation data usefully illustrate the ways that sensitive topics of conversation are managed in this family, demonstrating family processes that would be hard to elicit through other methods.

The researcher's field notes add another dimension to these data and provide context and visual description of this family mealtime. She notes that 'Brian sat at the head of the table and did "hold forth" quite a bit, constantly making jokes about their family life'. Describing the mealtime sequence she comments, 'Kate and Brian exchange glances back and forth. They seemed quite taken aback by Dan's statement'. These visual observations suggest that Dan's assertions have genuinely taken his parents by surprise. She surmises that the topic will be returned to 'in private' once both the researcher and the children are not present. The data from observation methods, when combined, suggest that this family does have open channels of communication. The children's voices and opinions are heard, but decision-making tends to take place between the parents, apart from the family. Thus the communication process is filtered through and shaped by generational power structures.

Field notes can provide invaluable information about data, the research encounter and family context. In another family (F3) the researcher used her field notes to set the scene for the interview.

I visited Joan and John in their council house on a large estate on the outskirts of [northern city] … When I arrived I was greeted by Joan and the dogs, one of which had a nappy in its mouth and was busy destroying it and making a mess. The dogs were then banished to the kitchen but remained intent on seeing who the stranger in the front room was, barking throughout the interview.

My first impression was that all aspects of a household with two small children were in evidence, children's toys everywhere, clothes drying, the potty in the middle of the room and the washing machine in full swing in the kitchen. There was a large tropical fish-tank in the corner of the room which evidently was John's pride and joy.

These field notes appear to paint a somewhat chaotic picture of family life in this household. The scene is disorderly and raises questions about family hygiene. But documenting it as she does, the researcher's notes allow for the scene to be revisited and analysed outside the immediacy of the situation. Read again, the notes show that the chaos is due in part to the demands of parenting two young children. The researcher's comment that 'all aspects of a household with two small children were in evidence' is most insightful. Whereas the first set of observation data that were discussed (Ann and Tom, F1) represents a controlled picture of family life, these data appear to be far less mediated. This family has not tidied up in preparation for the interviewer, the everyday clutter and disarray of family life remains where it usually is – so too the parents.

The field notes suggest that Joan and John are not putting on a performance; this is how their family operates. The apparent candour of this picture may not be created by design. It is likely that the unruliness of the scene was indicative of this family's current struggles managing everyday family life and their general lack of access to the social resources and cultural capital readily available to more 'privileged' others. I am not using this example to ascribe categories of families to particular patterns of parenting, something that I have contested at other stages in this book and elsewhere (Gabb 2004b; 2005a). The point I want to make is that it would be easy for the researcher to make judgements about the scene based on socio-economic and educational differences between her and those she encounters and/or between different families in the study. This is not the purpose of field notes. The acknowledged emotional response and her purposefully descriptive commentary are invaluable precisely because they draw attention to the subjectivity of the observation process. Once removed, with the power afforded by hindsight, the noise can be read as a consequence of the washing machine (producing clean clothes for the family) and the dogs whose barking is caused by the arrival of a stranger (the interviewer) and continues because the pets are shut out. These dogs are not members of this family but exist on the periphery, as a disruptive factor, an additional problem that needs management. Their exclusion is a coping strategy. This contrasts with other families who have the time, inclination and wherewithal to integrate the family pet into the research encounter.

Later in the field notes the researcher sketched a picture of the interview context and how the couple interact with each other around the topic of family relationships.

> Joan dealt with their child, and also answered the land line telephone when it rang and answered the door to the postman. John answered *his* mobile phone and then left to help a neighbour. Joan did virtually all the talking about family intimacy although, at their request, this had been set up as a joint interview ... Joan kept [baby] on her knee throughout the interview rather than disturb him by putting him down. This must have been quite uncomfortable for her as she sat like this for over an hour. John made no effort to help or relieve Joan although it was clear that it was not easy for her.

These notes and the snapshot of family life they capture suggest that it is the mother, Joan, who is literally and figuratively left holding the baby. John is conceptually, emotionally and physically removed from the practical and affective demands of family life. John's selective responsibility – making sure that his pet fish are well looked after, answering calls on his mobile phone and going to help a neighbour – means that Joan is left to do the bulk of childcare and domestic tasks. It is hardly surprising that the house remains untidy as she struggles to keep on top of everything. When combined with material from other sources what these observation data illustrate is that, against the odds, Joan is managing to keep this family and household together at all levels. Later in the biographical narrative interviews, the reason for John's behaviour is fleshed out and it becomes apparent why he struggles to engage with everyday family intimacy and emotion processes. Good field notes such as these provide information on the situated context of the research encounter and offer an invaluable glimpse of everyday living. They serve as an aide-mémoire for the researcher and can provide useful information when returning for subsequent interviews.

Biographical narrative interviews

In the *Behind Closed Doors* project, researchers completed open-ended interviews with parents and older children using an approach developed in psycho-social research (see Hollway and Jefferson 2000; Wengraf 2001). This approach aims to enable participants to recall real events rather than impressions of life experience. As discussed in chapter 3 what makes this approach distinct from open-ended interview methods more generally is that the researcher intentionally steps back and takes on the role of 'active listener'. It is the participant who structures the interview; the researcher only asks questions which arise from the participant's story. In families research, giving each participant the opportunity to set their own agenda can be important for many reasons. It means that there is no *a priori* definition of what constitutes interpersonal relationships and no presupposition about which emotional events are significant. Participants can choose what areas and events to disclose and do so at their own pace. This means that they are less likely to feel judged and therefore less likely to give answers they think are expected of them. Given the sensitivity of topics in studies of family relationships these are important factors.

In *Behind Closed Doors* interviews with parents lasted on average two hours and with older children about 30 minutes to one hour. Unstructured interviews were not used with children under 16 years of age. This was not only a pragmatic decision but also an ethical one. As I have discussed at length in earlier sections of this book, researching children tends to be most effective when using a participatory approach. Furthermore, I did not want to facilitate an encounter in which children were introduced to wholly unfamiliar and/or unacknowledged emotions. While it is unlikely that an interview would initiate any response of this kind, to minimise the risk of causing adverse emotional consequences, the unstructured, free association interview method was not used with children.

By and large participants seemed to feel they had gained something from the biographical narrative interview experience and in some cases appeared to find it 'educational' or 'therapeutic'. For example, three fathers independently said that they had learned something about themselves and their families through the interviews. This is in part because the method provides an opportunity for reflection on past and present experiences of family life and relationships. One parent, Claire, took the researcher on a rollercoaster journey that spanned different stages of her lifecourse and incorporated a wide range of emotions. This journey led her to consider what it meant to be a family and to rethink the mismatch between her aspirations for how family should be and the realities of her own circumstances. Her account showed how her experience of family is framed around transition and change – death of a parent, marriage/divorce, childbirth, past and present relationships – charting these events along the narrative of her emotional life. This narrativisation of her life in one sense depicted broken affective lines in the form of damaged and damaging relationships that could not be repaired. On closer inspection, however, it was possible to see how these instances were actually woven together to form a story of continuity.

> *Claire* (F2): I met this other man who was lovely, very nice, very calm, very, had absolutely no problem that I had three children (must have been mad). But um he was just the total opposite, he was so placid, so laid-back, so warm, so kind, so friendly, so enjoyed being with the boys. And I just thought this is lovely and I saw it as a fresh start ... We stayed married for about five years then came to an understanding that it was probably best that we split up and it was [a] very, very ... amicable divorce ... we are still friends. He doesn't come round. He used to, he used to come round quite regularly but it sort of dropped off as his girlfriend made a bit more ownership, and they've got a baby. But I got a text when his baby was born and, you know, nice things like that, so.

The psycho-social approach tends to produce data that foreground periods of transition and/or the different identities and experiences which make up a person's life narrative. This does not suggest that it conforms to an institutional version of the lifecourse wherein experiences are mapped onto phases which are passed through on the journey to adulthood, a proposition that has been effectively challenged in childhood studies. Instead, it produces a biographical narrative of self that is holistic. Using this narrative interview method facilitates a *joined-up approach*. Data illustrate how participants forge connections (sometimes knowingly and at other times seemingly unknowingly) between events; showing how subjectivities are shaped through lifecourse experience.

In *Behind Closed Doors* biographical narrative interview methods were invaluable because they encouraged participants to talk about real experiences producing data on the emotion work invested in the creation and maintenance of relationships. One participant talked about the dynamics of the mother–child relationship, recounting experiences back and forth in time to piece together her story. Starting with the death of her mother, she then moved on to detail experiences from childhood, becoming a mother, and then returned to how she cared for her terminally ill mother. These experiences were not recounted in chronological order but were linked through subjective *thematic* sequencing. One experience linked to a similar one, which linked to a different experience where similar feelings were experienced, and so on. In the course of her interview, she worked and reworked relationships through her recall of past experiences.

The psycho-social approach is particularly useful in facilitating memory work, allowing for connections such as these to be made across the lifecourse, spanning generations. The free association of thoughts, from one relationship to another, from one line of thought to another, allows the interviewee to make connections and produces a *relational account*. In a more structured interview the participant may well have been inclined to produce a more ordered account of experiences that follow a directed and/or chronological narrative structure. Lifecourse data that are produced using a free association approach tend to be cyclic, even iterative, in form, with the interview trajectory shaped through the participants' meandering thought processes.

In *Behind Closed Doors* parent–child relationships were the focus of many accounts, hardly surprising given the scope of the project. Even though free association and biographical narrative interview methods aim to be non-directive, participants are in the end taking part in a project that has a particular focus. While they can decide on which experiences and events it is that they describe, the choice is not free-floating. As such references to experiences of childbirth were predictable. What is more interesting is that in many cases this life-changing event was not afforded great significance, and, beyond this, for others this period was shaped through heightened and conflicting emotions. While some mothers talked about childbirth in almost ecstatic terms (Nelushi (F10) said it was the best experience of her life), several others, and some fathers, found that childbirth was not a joyous event, but one that involved a wider repertoire of emotions including great distress.

In one instance the experience of becoming a mother could not be extrapolated from other events that happened at the same time. Her partner found it difficult to connect with their child due to the onset of a period of deep depression. The baby became seriously unwell. There was terminal illness and death among her extended family and she developed postnatal depression. Though these circumstances may appear extreme, the catalogue of traumatic events that were described was not uncommon and several other parents recounted similar narratives. Contradictory feelings around this period were common and typically included stresses and strains among kin and wider networks of intimacy.

Focusing attention on experiences of heightened emotions, especially those that include emotional contradiction, can reveal *the* story that lies behind the one being told. Case study analysis of the connections and threads across an account can reveal underlying themes that run throughout an individuals' affective story. This does not produce a psycho-social reading of the defended subject, but highlights the need to look across the breadth and depth of data for the participant's autobiography. For example, Jeff, a single parent, talked about the importance of a 'good' family life for children. However, most of the events that he described were taken from his own childhood. On many occasions he spoke as a son more than as a father, recalling tales of happy family occasions that involved his extended kin network.

> *Jeff* (F4): We've had a good upbringing. It might not have been like good holidays, but if we've had a car at the time and it's been a nice day we've always gone to [local seaside resorts]. I know there's not a great deal at most of them, but we had fun and that's what counts. That's what you remember. It's not where you was, it's the fun you had when you was there ... I mean it's, we could go to [seaside] and there'd be a company of us going. There'd be like our family, erm well our mam, me dad's sister, a couple of me dad's brothers, all in separate cars, and we'd just go down in a convoy and just go to [seaside] for the day ...

Using a psycho-social approach is productive in family research because it can trace the patterning of family practice and emotions across generations and explores the building of subjectivity through past and present experiences. Later in the interview Jeff revealed how he recently gained legal custody of his children, a process that involved many assessments and work with social services when he had to prove his parenting abilities. In the light of this information, looking at the whole of Jeff's story, it is not surprising that he goes to such lengths to emphasise his investment in the idea of family. He is currently creating a new family of his own with his two children and defers to the good example that he remembers from his own childhood. In Jeff's data, his transposition of identity from father to child reflects his thought processes as he weaves together past and present experience. In this and other cases, free association and biographical narrative interview data provided a longitudinal perspective that interlaced experiences to produce particularly rich data. When combined, these experiential accounts generated understanding of *why* intimacy and sexuality took the various forms they did in everyday family life.

Public scenarios and private lives

Photo interviews and vignettes can present third-party (visual or verbal) scenarios which allow participants to distance themselves from the situation. Focus group discussion aims to access individual and collective viewpoints and provide data on the dynamic process of group work. Discussions of third-party scenarios can incline participants to say what they think the interviewer wants to hear and/or present what they believe to be the socially acceptable ('correct') answer. Their responses can be quite different from the messiness of their everyday experience. However, through analysis of the data, I demonstrate the usefulness of this approach in family studies. How differences in perception and experience effectively illustrate the process of participants' meaning construction and the cultural repertoires that frame participants' perceptions, beliefs and attitudes.

Group interviews and focus group discussion

In *Behind Closed Doors* group interview data came from discussion *within* families and/or involving friends rather than *between* different families. Groups were variously composed as families (parents and children), family and friends, and siblings. As discussed in chapter 3, it may be stretching the research imagination to include all forms of group interview under the umbrella of focus group methodology. In this chapter, where it is relevant I have differentiated between different group research methods. Elsewhere, I talk more generally about group discussion, which may be more or less 'focused' in character depending on the structure of the exchange. I have analysed data from all forms of group discussion within the framework of focus group research because this approach best serves the multidimensional dynamic data that come from group interaction.

In unstructured group discussion between family members the most noticeable theme to emerge was how parents and children negotiated conflict, employing management strategies that in several cases revolved around the strategic use of humour and/or sarcasm. In one case the family managed disagreements through both verbal and physical strategies of avoidance. Talking about how they negotiate one another in the morning as they all try to get up, dressed and ready for work and school, they detail how they perform an elaborate 'dance' around the house.

They intentionally structure their routines to avoid any interaction that may spark tensions and disagreements.

> *Kate* (F7): we avoid each other I suppose . . . we have sort of evolved a very boring way of avoiding conflict in the morning.
>
> *Jack* (aged 14): The only time we have conflict is
>
> *Kate*:   on a Monday morning.
>
> *Brian*: Yeah, everyone's cranky in this family except for me in the morning [*laughter*]
>
> *Jack*: You make up for it at other times though!
>
> Kate: That's what I'm saying, you don't have extreme emotions because we have evolved this routine in the morning to avoid any conflict. . .
>
> *Brian*: Yeah, but [it's not] just the mornings though, 'cos in the evenings when these two [*signals to Jack and Dan, aged 12*] walk past each other and it's just bloody battling all the time.
>
> *Jack*: That's not quite true 'cos –
>
> *Brian*: Yes it is, it's very true . . . What starts it off, Jack? Tell us Jack. I'll show you, shall I? [*father pushes Jack in the chest*]
>
> *Jack*: Ahhh! [*child feigns hurt*]
>
> *Brian* : Oh, sorry, is that one of your growing up boobs?
>
> *Jack*: Oww! . . .

In these data it is possible to see how a shared 'family story' is presented through quick-fire repartee among all concerned. But on closer analysis what becomes apparent is the way that Brian structures the exchange. He not only leads the banter, but also appears to instigate 'rough and tumble' as an emotion currency between father–child/ren and the siblings. While all family members take part at various points in the verbal exchange, there are indications that not everyone shares the same degree of enjoyment in the 'family strategy'. Dan, the younger son, remains silent for most of the conversation; later, Kate talks about how she finds the relentless banter, sarcasm and routine practical jokes tiresome and annoying. This family's embodied avoidance strategies mirror the way that they manage verbal exchanges.

Focus group analysis of these data shows how the group discursively work their way around a topic, individual perspectives and the sensitive issues that are involved. Rather than tackle issues and individual sensibilities head-on, talking through any areas of disagreement, they literally and metaphorically 'dance' around them. Though Brian claims to have listened and been responsive to Kate's expressed disassociation and discomfort with this strategy, there is little indication that he has modified his behaviour accordingly. Sarcasm and banter remain the way this family communicates; a family ethos that is referred to in other methods at other times. What focus group analysis of these data adds to the picture of family life is that it provides a glimpse of how these individuals operate on an everyday level: the *dynamic process of family interaction*. This focuses attention on the power relations that structure communication and emotion exchange. Elsewhere, Brian acknowledges that he uses humour and sarcasm because he finds it hard to show his emotions, 'I'm not very good at sharing my feelings ... I bottle things up'. What it is evident in these data is that the patterning of affective behaviour has been passed on from father to son. Though Brian may be aware of his inability to communicate affectively this has not stopped *his* patterns of behaviour becoming the norm in the family.

In another family (F6), a group of four siblings asked to take part in a group discussion rather than have individual interviews because together they felt more confident and relaxed. In this group context, discussion was directed by the researcher around experiences and expressions of emotion in the family. The interaction between the children in this group was as revealing as the data produced. Talking about their bedtime routine, Chris, the youngest child, said that he often tries to 'sneak' into his mum's bed because he gets frightened. The researcher asked whether any of the other children also do this, a question that leads the children to tease Frank.

> *Interviewer*: Does anybody else go into mum's bed ...?
> *Chris* (aged five): Frank does.
> *Frank* (aged 12): No I don't! [*children laugh*]
> *Chris*: Yes he does, he do, I know when you trapped my toe you went in mum's bed.
> *Frank*: No I didn't. [*laughter*]
> *Chris*: You went in mum's bedroom. Oh yeah you did, oh yeah you did. [*laughter*]
> *Frank*: No, I went in to mum to say sorry. I didn't stay in her bed all night.
> *Chris*: Yeah you did. Yeah you did. [*laughter*] You did, you did, you did.
> [*Researcher interjects and reorients discussion*]

There is typically a pecking order in sibling groups structured chronologically through a hierarchy of age. Here the youngest child seizes the opportunity to reverse this, teasing his older brother and getting on side with his other siblings to gang up on Frank. These data are interesting in two ways. First, they show how seeking reassurance and affection from the mother is identified as something that only younger children should do. Second, they illustrate the sibling group dynamic. By being openly affectionate and emotionally vulnerable, Frank's hierarchical status as the oldest sibling is undermined. Chris takes great delight in this levelling. The in/appropriateness of demonstrative emotion derives from social understandings of how children should behave at different stages across childhood. 'Growing up' means growing away from embodied expressions of parent–child affection and emotional need. This prescriptive patterning of behaviour relies on children's shared understandings of the social meaning of vulnerability. As such it is not surprising that many older children in this and other families went to considerable lengths to stress their desire for physical and emotional separation from parents as they moved into and through adolescence.

Focus group analysis of these data is interesting because it is possible to see what Sue Wilkinson (1998) calls the sense-making praxis. The sibling banter was light-hearted and all the children laughed. But it is clear that if Frank wants to secure his hierarchical position and prevent this happening again, he will need to modify his emotional behaviour or silence his younger sibling in other ways. It should be noted that at the end of this section of data the researcher steered the conversation away from what was evidently becoming a bullying scenario in which the eldest child could not defend himself against the taunting of his siblings. Earlier mentions of sibling 'rough and tumble' among the family dataset suggest that the reinforcement of boundaries and the hierarchical ordering of the group is ordinarily managed through demonstrations of physical strength. This strategy was not available to Frank in this context. By closing down the discussion the researcher not only tried to protect Frank but also his younger brother from the possibility of subsequent reprisal.

In another context a focus group was set up between Jeff (F4) (a single parent) and his friend Lydia to discuss a series of vignettes and photographs. This group scenario provided an opportunity for the researcher to observe the sense-making processes of these two adults. While the children in the previous illustration invoked underlying (physical) power relations to work through sibling viewpoints, analysis of this next focus group data demonstrates some of the discursive strategies that adults draw on as they move towards common ground and/or guard against individual vulnerability. The desire to keep in step with socially prescribed positions leads two friends to navigate their way through some quite 'sensitive' issues. Their discussion demonstrates how they move towards a shared position that corroborates their individual moral stances and situates their own experiences and understandings of sexuality and intimacy within the parameters of normative behaviour. The discussion is centred on one vignette that describes a scene set in a public park. A young boy is sitting in a children's sandpit and begins to play with his genitalia. The friends, both single parents, were asked how the child's parent should respond to this. Jeff and Lydia immediately framed their discussion within the parameters of their own experience as parents.

> *Jeff* (F4): Mike [son] is nearly five now and when he gets out of the bath he often has a rake [feel] and a pull at it [penis] and it's just like 'get off your brains' like that type of thing, and he leaves it alone. He doesn't do it anyway.
> *Lydia*: Jake [son] does it ...
> *Jeff*: When you change his nappy, doesn't he?
> *Lydia*: Yes, but not so much because I've never really made a fuss of it, you see, so he generally tends not to do it. At his age – he's not quite two yet, so it's different, but I don't really know because obviously you want to get a guideline on the situation, don't you?
> *Jeff*: Everybody's different, so some people would probably tell him off for doing it and other people like Lydia and myself would probably ask him what's the matter. He might just have had an itch or summat.
> *Lydia*: Yes, but also it could be something worse than that, it could be a sign of abuse or anything ... Some people might think that, you know, being too aware, I don't know. I don't think so in this case though.

It is interesting to see how Jeff begins his initial comment by talking about the event as a normal occurrence; the same kind of thing is often done by his own son. Realising he has expressed an opinion before he is certain of others' position on the subject, he instantly retracts. It is only when Lydia says that her son behaves in a similar way that he regains his confidence and joins in, corroborating Lydia's story. This causes her to back down and then move to justify the (intuitive) actions of her son in terms of his age. Once the discussion is centred on Lydia's family, Jeff works hard to support and reassure his friend, finishing off her sentences to show their sense of unity on the subject and to consolidate her status as a responsible parent.

Having established that both of them have witnessed such activities, Jeff positions them on mutual ground. Lydia and he would respond in the same way, which may be different from some people's reactions, but their response is unified, even matter of fact. In case their now shared response could be seen as irresponsible, Lydia seeks to qualify the answer one last time by saying that if she thought there was any 'sign of abuse' she would behave differently. They have reached a consensual point, their shared experience and opinions have been situated within the parameters of normal behaviour, so too their conduct as responsible parents. Focus group data such as these usefully illuminate what are normally private, individualised decision-making processes and how a group works to reach a safe (culturally sanctioned) agreed standpoint.

Vignettes and photo interviews

In *Behind Closed Doors* discussion of vignettes and photographs provided information on the factors that shaped participants' understandings, beliefs, judgements and actions around aspects of intimacy in families and the highly sensitive area of children and sexuality. These methods typically produced data on the socio-cultural repertoire that participants drew on and were useful when combined with data from other methods in that they added another *contextual* dimension to previously described individual experience. Notwithstanding the utility of group discussion, such as the one between Jeff and Lydia excerpted above, in *Behind Closed Doors* the majority of data elicited through vignettes and photo methods derived from one-to-one interviews. This was due to the composition of the research sample and the logistical parameters of a pilot project (as discussed in the Introduction). My analysis of the data from these methods is not structured chronologically around individual vignettes and photographs but through the themes that emerged across the data. This thematic analysis effectively highlights the efficacy of the approach rather than focus attention on the relative merits of the scenarios presented.

Five vignettes and six images were shown to participants. The first three images typically generated a 'so what?' response, usually framed as 'a very nice picture ... no problem at all'. These images depicted a woman cuddling her naked baby, a man cuddling a toddler in a public park and a woman comforting a distressed child. It was my intention that this set of images would work as an icebreaker, easing participants into the method through pictures that would be familiar to them. This was an effective strategy and the ordinariness of these images served as a foil for the next set of three images which were perceived by many parents as more challenging. These showed a man sharing a bath with a young child, a group in which a man and woman (who appear to be naked) are playing with a child on a double bed, and an image, 'Virginia at four', by the photographer Sally Mann which depicts her two daughters (one of

whom is naked) posing for the camera. These scenarios typically generated the most data and focused attention on sexuality management, the
perceived need for boundaries around intimate practices between adults
and children, and the ethics of representing children's sexuality.

While it did appear on first reading that the first set of images produced little or no data, on returning to the data some time later I noticed
that the normalcy of participants' responses meant that their critical
value had slipped under my analytical radar. In fact, the lack of response
was significant in itself. When parents did comment they immediately
sought to create familial connections between figures in the pictures. The
woman was typically characterised as a mother, the man as a father, the
children as their own offspring and the group as a family. When pressed
on why they made these connections and what would it mean if they
were not true, participants repositioned themselves, sometimes reading
the adult as a surrogate carer. At other times they outlined why the scenario could be risky if such embodied intimacy did stretch beyond the
family.

The overriding point being made was that it is best to 'keep the intimacy within the family' (Claire, F2). This viewpoint was expressed as
much by those parents working in the field of child welfare as those
with no professional experience in this area. No parents commented on
the fact that most cases of child abuse take place within the family even
though this is relatively well publicised in the media. Abuse was characterised as something that involves strangers, something that parents
can guard against through sealing the boundaries of intimacy around
their family. In this way parents were highly selective in the cultural discourses they invoked, using repertoires that told the story they wanted
to hear – in this instance drawing on a myth that families pose no risk
to children.

Discussion of the second set of images teased out where parents set
boundaries around intimacy and sexuality and what other cultural discourses were invoked to manage these. The sensuality of naked bodily
contact and the pleasures of these embodied forms of intimacy did
generate a degree of anxiety in some parents. However, once familial
connections had been established, the perceived riskiness of a scenario
was not dependent on the activity *per se* but rather on whether there was
any perceptible unease in the faces or poses of the characters depicted.
Many parents commented that the scenarios presented were typical
in their own household and sought to justify their normalcy through
personal experience. Managing the boundaries around children and sexuality was framed as responsive; it was the child's sexuality development

that shaped changes in family intimacy and demonstrations of affection between parent and child.

Perhaps as a consequence of the mixed-methods approach used in *Behind Closed Doors*, or because of the research subject itself, vignettes and photo interviews produced data that moved between participants' justifications of their opinions and their own family practices and recollections of childhood experience. This lifecourse perspective demonstrated the complex processes of sexuality management around intimacy and emotional interactions between adults and children. It is also interesting to note how many parents summarised their responses to particular vignettes and images with closing phrases such as 'No problem with that'. This closed down any possible uncertainties and expressed a degree of surety that belied the complexity of their deliberating answers. Having asserted their opinion, they wanted to secure their answer, to underscore the point being made, making clear that they were in no doubt as to the right course of action and the correct codes of conduct that structure the 'rules of affection' (Hochschild 2003).

> *Henry* (F5): We used to have our kids in the bath and they just love it; they're not bothered about seeing mum and dad naked or anything. I think again, there's nothing wrong with that ...

The images that were characterised as a family playing on the parents' bed and a father and his child sharing a bath brought back fond memories for many parents of times from their own childhood, experiences that were looked on as special moments. In email correspondence with a researcher, Ann (F1) said that before their son was born she and her husband lived in a house that had a big bath in which they would often bathe together to relax. She also described 'a romantic weekend away' when the couple stayed in a bed and breakfast that had a huge Victorian bath – 'we enjoyed a bath together'. She suggested that these relaxing times and the sensual enjoyment of 'skin to skin contact' are similarly experienced in shared baths with her son – moments of relaxation and closeness that she relishes. These sensual pleasures do not need to be justified as Ann is secure in her position as a 'good mother'. Her enjoyment of intimate contact with her son does not suggest any risk, because risk is gendered. Within the cultural imagination, as a woman and mother she poses no threat. The spectre of male sexual predation in the popular imaginary lay beneath the surface of many responses to the scenarios. Parents' comments drew on discourses of abuse that position men as a potential threat to children's innocence which requires the proactive management of public–private boundaries. Their responses illustrate that the presence of a man in close (intimate) proximity with a child almost invariably raises particular concerns. Simply stated, men were seen as representing a risk that could not be ignored, however unfair this may be to those whose intentions and feelings are wholly innocent.

The discourses of risk and male sexual predation were not the only frameworks around which parents wrapped their responses. Using vignettes and photographs allowed me to explore the significance afforded to the discursive and everyday (lived) *context* of intimacy. Where a scenario took place typically shaped whether an activity was deemed appropriate or inappropriate. What is acceptable in the privacy of an individual's home becomes risky or unacceptable when taken outside. Discussing the vignette of the young boy who begins to play with his genitals in the park, Jocelyn tried hard to cover all possibilities and get the 'right' answer. Her response sought to avoid introducing unnecessary inhibition for the child or causing offence to others (especially children), and also to protect the child from harm. The boundaries between public–private that Jocelyn asserted are materialised in spatial terms: public = outside, private = home. But as discussed in chapter 4, the boundaries of the home are not impermeable (Johnston and Valentine 1995). This is illustrated most clearly by Jocelyn's subsequent description of how an event affected her own family practices of intimacy. She referred to a case that hit the media headlines as a direct reason why she and her husband have changed their affective behaviour.

> *Jocelyn* (F9): a woman newsreader [Julia Somerville], some years ago she took some photographs, or her husband took some photos, very innocently and the child took it to [the photo lab] and it all kicked off. So I think from that point on we already had Charlotte [daughter] and we were very careful about it after that. We thought it was ridiculous, but we were a bit more careful.

The case that Jocelyn cites involves the private actions of a public figure which were sensationally reported in the press. In 1996 the partner of the former BBC newsreader Julia Somerville took a roll of film containing family snapshots into a local chemist to be processed. An employee handed the photographs to the police when they became 'suspicious' about some naked bath-time pictures. The story was leaked to the press even though police investigations established there was no case to answer. Notwithstanding the distress this sequence of events had on the Somerville family, Jocelyn's memory of this scenario is interesting because it illustrates the cyclic reworking of stories: the interrelationship of the public and the private. The private pictures of a naked child sharing a bath with their parent became a public story, which affected another family's private practices. Jocelyn and her family changed how they interacted at home for fear that information about physical intimacy between father and child could be similarly misconceived. This situation was heightened further for Jocelyn because she perceives her family to be highly visible in the local community.

Vignettes and photo interview data are good at reaching opinions where public–private factors intersect. In *Behind Closed Doors* parents' responses to scenarios were typically constituted through normative values that comprise the prevailing codes of sexual conduct. Their unacknowledged understanding of affective and sexuality boundaries drew on shared social meanings. Families measured themselves against a template of 'good parenthood'; a model mediated through advice and parenting handbooks. This advice and media hyperbole around 'stories' of child abuse coalesce to generate risk-knowledge, which serves to shape and/or consolidate parents' own stance on what is/what is not appropriate behaviour. However, opinions are not only fashioned through external factors they are also shaped through individual circumstances.

Responses highlighted that while guidelines may structure parents' sense of right and wrong there are many *sets of action* that may proceed from these. Emotions are individually comprehended and mediated through particular circumstances, life histories and social conditions, including race, gender, age, and so on. We do not all share a single ideological stance. There may be many legitimate responses – sets of feeling – which simultaneously remain within 'the rules' but which may significantly differ (Hochschild 2003). This illustrates how parenting and family practices are reflexive processes. There is no singular affective template. Normative behaviour and values accommodate the particularities of individual socio-cultural circumstance. This reflexivity allows parents to be secure in their differences – as long as these differences come within the normative range and judgements on propriety and sexuality conduct. Within this reflexive framework, the public–private stories of relationships that emerged through vignettes and photo interviews data materialised ideas of intimate citizenship. Participants' accounts illustrated the enmeshing of the public and private in understandings and experiences of intimacy and the dynamic of everyday living.

7
Conclusion

In this book I have explored the sociology of family intimacy through analysis of conceptual frameworks and methodological approaches that have shaped this field of study. In chapter 1 I set out the scope of my inquiry and introduced the empirical research through which I developed my analysis. In chapter 2 I sketched an outline of families and childhood research, highlighting how these interconnected areas have developed. Two main factors characterise these developments; first, the shift in emphasis from ideas of 'the family' as a structuring unitary social unit, towards diverse relational networks that are constituted through everyday practices of intimacy; and second, the repositioning of children as agentic subjects rather than adults-in-waiting, passing through the transitional phase of childhood. I examined how these changes affected the scope and framing of research. These issues and ideas were unpacked under the rubric of 'sensitive topic' research and the ethical debates around researching families and childhood. Following from this in chapter 3, I detailed research approaches that characterise and have shaped these fields of study. I outlined the qualitative methods and analytical strategies that are typically used to examine familial relationships and the everyday lives of parents and children.

In a similar vein in chapter 4 I provided a comprehensive overview of the conceptual and theoretical frameworks of intimacy in the context of sociological analysis of family relationships. This chapter is structured around critical junctures in the field of intimacy research, through which I traced shifts in experience and the theoretical framing of relationality in the domain of public–private family life. In chapter 5 I built on some of the key ideas in these frameworks. Through analysis of data from *Behind Closed Doors* I examined lived experiences of contemporary intimacy and parent–child relationships. I demonstrated how relational experience resists uniform interpretation and requires a fresh look at the boundaries of intimacy. In so doing I aimed to extend the conceptual and theoretical research imagination. In chapter 6 I returned to the research approaches that were outlined in chapters 2 and 3. Using examples from my research, I examined the kinds of data which different qualitative methods produce, focusing attention on how these frame and make sense of intimacy and family relationships.

Future research

In the course of these chapters I have raised questions around research approaches and conceptual frameworks and this has identified areas where more research could be done and/or where we need to push harder at the parameters of existing work. Here I want to pull together a few of these areas. It should be noted, however, that these are mostly headlines and do not claim to be the most pressing and/or significant gaps in research. The points arise as incidental findings from *Behind Closed Doors* and from my own research interests. I hope that the material presented in this book connects with readers' own interests and raises many other questions in the fields of families and childhood research and beyond.

Identifying where further research could be done is not simply an academic enterprise. For example, I highlighted in chapter 4 a study by the psychologists Marjorie Smith and Margaret Grocke (1995), who found that the boundaries between abusive and non-abusive parenting are hard to define. Behaviours typically acknowledged as indicators of abuse, such as over-sexualised behaviour and genital touching, were common among their sample of 'ordinary families'. This begins to unravel understandings of what constitutes 'normal family sexuality'. Decisions on family intervention and child custody rely on agreed understandings of normative behaviour. It is therefore important that we find out more about what ordinarily goes on in families so that we can establish where boundaries are drawn. If abusive practices are measured against what is normally taking place, then it is imperative that the pictures of everyday family relationships are neither partial nor rose-tinted. Sociological studies of intimate relationships and family practices should not shy away from the responsibilities of this task.

Most of the areas identified for further research push at the boundaries of intimacy and the framing of relationality in families research. For example, I have suggested that work on child-centred families and parents' investment in their children typically foregrounds the emotional rewards for mothers and fathers (Beck-Gernsheim 1999). Data from *Behind Closed Doors* indicate that more attention needs to be paid to the consequences for children of these instrumental affective strategies, requiring significant longitudinal research on child-centred relationships. So far we do not know how children will manage parents' emotional needs across the lifecourse. Will parents' neediness be experienced as an emotional burden or form the basis of an affirming and reliable relationship that holds firm while others fail? Will children live up to their parents' expectations or affectively let them down? Conversely, more research is needed on how parents will affectively manage as their children grow up and away from them. What will be the consequences for the individual adult and for the couple relationship? Will parents continue with their strategic affective practices when their children reach adulthood? Everyday parenthood and the practices of intimacy through which families operate are not necessarily altruistic. It is unrealistic to expect that family relationships and routine interactions can be uniformly harmonious. Thus I suggest that we need more research which muddies the waters around ideas of child-centred families in order to add clarity to our understandings of these complex and multidimensional experiences of parent–child relationships.

Data from *Behind Closed Doors* also suggest that it may be pertinent to look again at the academic boundaries which delimit intimate life, to reflect the diversity of families' affective experience. This requires that we reconsider what constitutes an intimate and the parameters around understandings of intimacy. In *Behind Closed Doors* pets were often identified as emotionally significant, integral to families' relational networks. Focusing attention on animal–human relationships may seem trivial, especially given the seriousness of points raised earlier. However, in many cases pets were an important part of the composite picture of family intimacy. To omit them overrides what many people say and feel. Moreover, pets serve as a valuable case in point above and beyond the animal–human relationship. If sociological understandings of family relationships and family intimacy are constituted through participants' accounts of relationality, pets need to be included. Their exclusion raises questions about boundary settings around intimacy and 'significant others' research. Why is there a delimiting focus on *interpersonal* relationships? This suggests that more attention should be focused on what and/or who defines intimacy and relationships.

The final area I would like to highlight raises further questions about limitations of scope in relationships research. In chapter 5 I examined differences that affected the patterning of intimacy and family relationships. This queried the significance traditionally afforded to sexual orientation and the association of different 'types' of family with particular formations of affective behaviour. I suggested that suppositions about kinds of families, forms of intimacy and which differences shape behaviour should be resisted. The focus on non-traditional and/or radical forms of kinship as exempla of contemporary patterns and transformations of intimacy may be unduly narrow. There is no easy correlation between differences among families and sets of affective practice. Attempts to map particular forms of family onto particular kinds of intimate practice serve to obscure rather than elucidate diversity in experience. Future research could usefully trace the patterning of intimate practices and affective behaviour among different groups. This should include groups which ordinarily fall outside the research gaze and do not reside within those typically associated with 'hard to reach communities' and/or from the social–sexual margins. This extends the range of the wide-angle research lens. The ideas presented here are areas for future inquiry are just the beginning. The emerging scope and methodological complexity of intimacy research will necessarily continue to expand, adding depth and breadth to understandings of family relationships and intimate life.

Mixing methods: a family portrait

For the remainder of this final chapter I focus on a family case study in order to demonstrate the benefits of an extended and extending approach in research of the conceptual and empirical boundaries of family intimacy. This will pull together some of the methodological and conceptual dimensions detailed in previous chapters and offer indicative findings in some of the areas cited under future research. I examine data from one family to demonstrate the breadth of data produced through a mixed-methods approach. Through this case study analysis I explore the management and experience of relationships and intimacy in everyday family life and the emotion exchanges through which feelings are communicated. I show how the combination of layer upon layer of mixed-methods data captures the complexity of everyday family relationships.

I have selected this family (F5) because data were collected from both parents and their co-resident child. All research methods were completed by all members of the family and so the household affective portrait is comprehensive. Moreover, while all families have interesting stories to tell and cross-sectional analysis of any family would be engaging, this family stood out as a notably interesting case study. At the time of data collection they were in the middle of a significant transition which meant that all parties were already thinking about the dynamic process of family and interpersonal relationships. At times the accounts presented are disarmingly honest and make uncomfortable reading, but this reflects the family's degree of reflexivity. Overall the picture painted of this family's everyday intimate practices and emotional world does not present an unproblematic, 'happy family', but such a two-dimensional picture would be undoubtedly superficial. Instead the story that gets told is multifaceted. It shows close and at times intense parent–child and adult couple relationships and the processes through which these individuals work at family relationships in the context of their personal circumstances.

The analysis that I present in this chapter highlights the ethical unease that can be generated through close reading of case study data, not least because it unpicks some of the narrative threads that are individually constructed. To be clear, in this instance there appeared to be no disclosures that were previously unknown to the family group. This is important because in drawing together data across methods and individuals confidentiality among the group is impossible. This family was in part selected for case study analysis because of these ethical considerations: because they know themselves so well and are already engaged in a process of self-reflection. When participation in the research project facilitated moments of personal insight these were always warmly welcomed. One final factor was the age of the 'child'. At 17 the daughter is arguably more capable of controlling the degree and parameters of disclosure than younger children might be. As a young adult she is able to provide meaningful informed consent for her involvement in the research process.

Family 5 comprises a married couple (Harriet and Henry) and two children (Harry and Kelly). Harry no longer lives as part of the household and did not take part in the study. The family have a pet dog, Scott, who features heavily in their account of family life. Harriet is in full-time professional employment; Henry is a semi-retired skilled tradesman who now identifies himself as a 'house-husband'. The family describe themselves as white British although Harriet has a different cultural background (not specified for reasons of anonymity). Harriet is an observant Catholic; Henry and Kelly express no religious affiliation. They live near the centre of a northern town in a large, well-presented, semi-detached Victorian house.

The researcher's field notes sketch a pen portrait of the family. These describe the house as 'very traditional and homely, well organised and

busy, full of 'projects on the go' – most of which seemed to be Harriet's ...
the kitchen/dining room was large and obviously the centre of the home
and a hive of activity'. Harriet is depicted as 'a very confident and
self-assured person'. 'She has no difficulties whatsoever in talking and
expressing her self. She was very interested in the project and me', asking many questions. Henry is described as 'a warm, friendly person', but
the researcher comments that he appears 'less dynamic than his wife'.

> [Henry] appeared to be somewhat in [Harriet's] shadow. Harriet did
> all the talking for him and he eventually excused himself leaving the
> room to dry the dog that was very wet and muddy from the walk ...
> [Harriet] directs everyone [in her family] and appears to want to know
> exactly what they are doing at any one time. Henry seems to act in
> accordance with her wishes and directions but there are indications
> that Kelly has very different ideas and does not necessarily accede to
> her mother's wishes.

In the analysis that follows I flesh out this family portrait, exploring how the group individually and collectively experience personal
relationships and manage intimate family life.

The boundaries of intimacy

Material from across the dataset, from different methods, in different
forms, illustrate that this family work hard to extend the boundaries
around whom and what constitutes intimacy and an intimate. The pet
dog, Scott, is perceived as a member of the family whom everyone
equally loves (see chapter 5, 'Significant others', for a detailed analysis of the animal–human relationship) Friends are included as part
of their extended kin network. The doors of the household are figuratively and literally open, welcoming outsiders in, embracing them
as part of the family's intimate circle. Harriet was particularly keen to
present the openness of affective boundaries both within and beyond
'the family'. The dinner party that was observed (described as a 'typical family event') included immediate kin, Kelly's boyfriend and several
'close family friends'. Dinner parties were characterised as exempla of
this family's 'the more the merrier' philosophy, providing occasions that
brought everyone together to spend quality time as extended family. In
observation data the researcher noted how Harriet and Henry adeptly
performed the role of hosts. There was an abundance of food, far in
excess of what the guests could reasonably eat. Overall the image was
one of open and free-flowing conversation among friends and family.

The conscious crafting of family and relationships in evidence at the dinner party revealed how the family – or more accurately stated the parents – wanted to be seen to affectively operate. However, this idealised picture had leaky edges. Intergenerational tensions bubbled just beneath the surface as Harriet and Henry's constructed portrait of 'happy family life' began to unravel. For example, at one point Kelly dropped into the conversation a significant disclosure. She flippantly recounted a recent experience where she put herself at considerable risk, an event that was previously unknown to her parents. As conversations progressed it became apparent that parent–child negotiations on 'sensitive topics' such as the risky event were conducted almost entirely through jokes and sarcasm. All three used affective humour as a means to dissipate negative or emotionally charged debate.

The parents were clearly anxious about their daughter's safety and well-being. Kelly's attributed untidiness, and her sometimes risky and/or 'unmanageable behaviour', however were approached through jokes and fond teasing rather than by serious dialogue. This form of communication provided a linguistic buffer for parents and child alike, a way of making particularly difficult subjects such as social drug-taking and sex among young adult children less threatening. Kelly made purposeful use of this device to control the boundaries of parent–child talk, using sarcasm and humour to keep her parents at arm's length and/or to point out to them when they had overstepped personal boundaries. This strategy avoided any public airing of direct conflict, sidestepping battles that could not be won given the daughter's age and growing independence. In this extended family context humour was used to negotiate an uneasy truce, keeping channels of communication open rather than affording any long-term conflict resolution.

One of the merits of video observation is that it records dialogue and other forms of *visual communication* which can add another dimension to the verbal picture. This is important because embodied encounters are characteristically multifaceted. An exchange of glances, a stiffening of posture, raised eyebrows – all these visual clues signify meaning and are part of interpersonal interaction. Over dinner Kelly may have closed down conversation with a quip, but this did not end the exchange. Her verbal closure was reinforced by visual clues. Confrontational stares between parents and child dared the 'opponent' to push the matter further. Body language denoted when it was time to move on. Video observation data such as these illustrated how Kelly and her parents used their bodies to add gravitas to their statements and/or shield themselves from banter; how the balance of power shifted from person to person as positions were set out along generational lines.

While Harriet was keen to celebrate the openness of her family and worked hard to present a democratic model of family relationships, analysis of material from across the dataset revealed a far more contradictory account. Rather than talk through problems the family data suggest that there was a tendency to withhold opinions that might cause upset or distress. When detailing how the family are managing to come to terms with their new roles now that Henry is the 'house-husband', Harriet acknowledged that she refrains from saying what she really thinks because 'he'd be hurt'. She then changed this to 'well, he'd be annoyed'. This suggests that in order to avoid an argument she censured what was said, an approach that is at odds with the dialogic ethos she is keen to present. When data such as these are combined with data from observations, it suggests that the family typically navigates their way *around* areas of conflict and disagreement rather than talking them through. The setting of boundaries around communication and intimacy were not agreed upon, but had to be constantly worked and reworked in order for them to be individually secured.

In the *Behind Closed Doors* project while the process of affective boundary management arose incidentally on many occasions in data from different methods, the subject was addressed head on in vignettes and photo interviews. One of the vignettes presented was a scenario in which a close friendship has developed between a woman and a male colleague, someone the woman identifies as her closest friend. This intimate relationship fulfils an emotional area of her life that her husband does not. While she has no intention of starting a sexual relationship with this friend she is described as feeling excited and guilty about the situation. Harriet responded to this scenario by saying that she could not understand why the female character should feel guilty. In contrast Henry was far more circumspect.

Henry (vignettes interview): I thought her husband would be her closest friend, actually. I'm not sure what the area in life is that he's not filling ... It sounds a bit dodgy that. I don't think she's really happy in her relationship ... There's nothing wrong with having a close friend ... It depends how the friendship is limited. Has it got its limitations? ... It's all to do with trust at the end of the day. If the trust is broken down, then really I'd have thought that that would be it ... There's nothing wrong with having good fun with people at work and

that's part of the fun in going to work I suppose, and coming home
again at night and being with your partner, but I think she's got to
be a bit careful... once [boundaries are] established I think everything
will be fine ... I rattled on a bit there didn't I, my God!

Harriet and Henry's responses emphasise their need for clarity in setting boundaries around intimate experience – albeit that where these
boundaries should be was not agreed upon. In other contexts (notably
biographical narrative interviews and observations) they both went to
considerable length to present their 'open house' philosophy. Here they
moved to categorise kinds of relationships through constitutive differences marked by the absence/presence of sexual desire. This reinforces
the idea that sex and the conjugal relationship are paramount to the
management of boundaries around intimacy and relationships. As long
as trust is secured, there may be intimacy and affective reciprocity among
any number or constellation of intimates. Once there is sexual desire this
makes a relationship something else, more than *just* intimacy. This contradicts contemporary ideas on the 'fluidity of sexuality' (Giddens 1992)
in which sex and sexuality are part of a wider narrative of self that is
refashioned along the lifecourse. In this family, as in many others, parents identified sex and sexual desire as critical, a turning point, shaping
the boundaries of intimacy and understandings of what constitutes an
intimate.

The vignette data from Harriet and Henry also showed that notwithstanding couples' shared perspective on the overriding rules of their
relationship there also may be internal dissent around the detail. Henry
believes that a husband and wife should be *the* best friends while Harriet expressed no such certainty. Henry's assertion may be indicative
of his general insecurity and emotional uncertainty. Alternatively, it
could be that it reflects real differences between him and his wife in
the setting of boundaries. Harriet's extended network of friends may be
experienced as quite threatening, challenging Henry's need for a central
position in her intimate network. There are some hints that this may be
the case. The emotional rewards of collegial friendship facilitated in the
workplace is a moot point for Henry who no longer has access to this
affective resource, a point that is frequently returned to across the family
dataset. In contrast Harriet both invests in and gets emotional reward
from several social contexts beyond the home from which Henry is
excluded. Thus it may be that Henry 'rattled on' because he was emotionally rattled by this line of thought. Data from Harriet substantiate this
supposition.

Empirical complexities and conflicting narratives

Most individuals' stories of past and present relationships will at times be contradictory, contingent on the vagaries of memory and conflicting emotions. After all the families we live by (ideal) and the families we live with (experience) may intersect, but they are not identical (Gillis 1996). I do not want to suggest that Harriet, Henry and Kelly were any different in this respect from any other family. In fact, it is likely that the contradictions between individual accounts were as much a consequence of the richness of the data as indicative of any deliberate or unintentional concealment of self. Notwithstanding this, here and in the previous two chapters, several contradictions have come to light in how this family present themselves and their emotion exchanges. In particular, I have drawn attention to the way that Harriet talks about her family living by a democratic ethos whereas in practice intergenerational power relations are in place.

Parental engagement with the daughter was often fact-finding rather than typifying a mutually respecting, disclosing relationship. Protected mother–child time afforded an opportunity to inculcate codes of conduct as much as it represented quality relational time together. Harriet talked about wanting to give Kelly a degree of freedom, and both mother and daughter acknowledged that the teenager is often out; however, this is a source of parental anxiety. In her diary Harriet included several descriptions of the hours she spent lying awake before her daughter returned home and she gave in to restful sleep, confident in the knowledge that Kelly was home safe. Harriet's concerns about Kelly's well-being were heightened through any increase in the physical distance between mother and child. As a result she uses her daughter's mobile phone as a means to check on her well-being, or in Kelly's terms, to 'keep tabs' on her. The overriding story that emerged was a familiar one: a mother wanting to keep hold of her daughter while simultaneously knowing that she needs to let her grow up and become independent.

When discussing their emotion maps and the affective geography of the home both Harriet and Henry talked with regret and fondness of past, emotionally demonstrative times when Kelly was much younger, a period that both parents seemed to miss. During this period of transition from childhood to young adulthood, it is perhaps unsurprising that contradictions characterise parent–child interactions and pepper these family data. Moreover, the contradictions within and between individual accounts were not unknown to Henry, Harriet and Kelly.

In fact negotiating these areas of difference appeared to bring this family together, albeit that in the heat of the encounter this may not have been the immediate perception.

In Kelly's diary there was a sense of a young woman struggling to gain independence while wanting to retain the benefits of being a child. For example, she talked about liking the regular phone calls she receives from her parents as these provide emotional security and reassurance, making her feel loved. Yet she also resented this intrusion into her friendship time.

> *Kelly* (diary): Mum rang me later that evening asking if I was OK. Sometimes I like her ringing me to check up on me, as it shows that she is thinking about me. But sometimes it can be annoying as I just want to have a night with my friends.

Despite her desire to retain links with her parents Kelly is evidently starting to focus her world away from family. Her data illustrate shifting patterns of intimacy as she begins to envelop friends within her circle of intimates, corresponding with, and in some instances supplanting, her parents' role as the primary source of intimacy. In emotion map data she was keen to demarcate a privacy of space and in interview talked about using internet 'chat rooms' as a means to get away from her family when they were annoying her, to be with friends. In the subsequent biographical narrative interview she described her first holiday away from her parents as a significant event, saying that during this time she felt extremely positive about herself. In contrast, in her father's corresponding interview, Henry fondly recalled family holidays and said that Kelly recently spoke about wanting to go camping with friends in Europe. Rather than seeing this as a sign of his daughter's independence Henry conjoined it with happy childhood memories: 'She obviously thinks back to her camping experience . . . This closeness of all being in a tent at night with the lovely sunshine and the swimming pools and the wine and the family barbecues obviously has stuck with her as being a really happy time of her life'.

It is highly likely that the motivation behind Kelly's newly discovered affinity for camping with friends stems from both father's and daughter's reasoning. Holidays, like so many other areas of shared experience, have become a site of conflicting emotions, epitomising shifts and differences in levels of understanding and meaning within the family. For example, Kelly's pleasure and satisfaction in the autonomy that she experienced during her holiday is tempered with recognition that being away from home can be a cause of anxiety.

Kelly (BNIM interview): I was excited, but I was sad to leave them behind, but at the same time it was like going independently. But when my mum and dad went away... I was left alone for the weekend and I felt really lonely. I was really worried about them and I was calling them up saying 'Be safe' and stuff like that, and making a fuss.

Interestingly, Kelly seems to have taken on some of her parents' anxieties around separation and travel. The tensions in her account characterise the sometimes emotionally fraught period of young adulthood. During this time of heightened emotions, parents and child alike appeared to be struggling as they adjust to their new position. For example, Kelly's displacement of the family from the centre of her physical and emotional world is challenging Harriet's central role by taking away her absolute right to knowledge. Kelly no longer believes that she can tell her mother everything and is far more selective in what she says. This undermines Harriet's expressed 'need to know everything'. Data from the mother's vignettes and photo interview reinforced her belief that it is the parents' responsibility to set boundaries for children, something that requires intimate knowledge of their lives. Other sources, such as friendships, school and popular culture, must be carefully managed so that their influence does not detract from the codes of conduct advocated by parents.

In her biographical narrative interview Harriet acknowledged that both Harry (son) and to a lesser extent Kelly retain areas of their private life and keep her at a physical and emotional distance. She appears to find this very difficult as she senses she is missing out on important aspects and experiences in their lives. In particular, what she describes as Harry's strategy of 'not talking' is taken as a rejection of the openness that she extols. By carefully choosing which events he wants to talk about with his mother and refusing to give in to her desire to know everything, he is rejecting her. She works hard to claim this as a parental achievement – as a mother she has given him the sense of security which has allowed him to become separate – but this is a positive spin on a painful emotion. At other times she acknowledged that she feels resentful about this purposeful and, in her eyes, unnecessary exclusion.

Notwithstanding Harriet's investment in her children's life, it was changes in the father–daughter relationship that were identified as something new and which were singled out by Kelly as especially difficult. She talked about the growing distance between her and her father and recognised that she is no longer daddy's little girl. Both she and Henry realised that things have irrevocably changed but neither knows how to bridge the affective gap. In her diary Kelly talked about her father being in a bad mood most of the time and/or being frequently annoyed with her. She later tried to draw the sting from this comment and in interview suggested that she finds his outbursts a source of amusement. However, there was little indication that either finds the current situation funny. Her explanation is more likely to be indicative of how difficult she is finding their new relationship than any genuine sense of amusement.

Henry is indeed having a hard time at the moment and as a result he is frequently losing his temper which is putting a strain on all members of the family. Henry talked about how completing his emotion map, charting patterns of emotion exchange in the household, made him realise the extent of the current breakdown in communication between him and his daughter. He attributed this to his own 'faults', putting his 'foot in it', 'saying the wrong thing'. When detailing these negative interactions he talked in a reflective, melancholy tone and apparently saw few positives in the changes to his work–family circumstances.

Henry has recently retired and is making a very difficult adjustment from a highly structured working life with many colleagues working alongside him to being a house-husband, 'stuck in the house' without a routine. These changes have made him physically and affectively isolated as he has lost touch with many of his former workmates. Henry spoke about his retirement several times and his descriptions and tone were tinged with regret. There were pertinent times in the biographical narrative interview when Henry began to talk about his unhappiness with his present situation, but he then fell silent and paused for thought. When he reconnected he did not resume where he left off, either changing the subject himself or waiting for the researcher to interject.

The psycho-social (BNIM and FANI) approach requires the interviewer to be an active listener, to facilitate and be non-directive. As such Henry's deliberate closing down of his train of thought was tricky for the researcher to manage. The pauses were not natural breaks in the narrative but deliberate ruptures, orchestrated by Henry in order to pull back from painful or emotionally charged thoughts. As far as she could, the researcher resisted the temptation to fill these socially awkward pauses and/or change the course of the interview to make it less painful. But her role was more directive than in other interviews as it was often left to her to pick up the pensive threads, selecting which to pursue and which to leave. On several occasions Henry's discomfort was such that the most difficult option was not selected, and it is true to say that this was probably for the emotional comfort of Henry and the researcher alike.

In contrast to the ebullient character he portrays in public, a persona that was on show in observation data, in the private context of the interview Henry appeared to be full of self-doubt in many areas of his life. Henry's role as a house-husband was foisted on him after taking early retirement. In his diary he detailed the routine of his day. In contrast to most parents' data, it was often a matter of finding activities to productively fill his day rather than managing any time shortage.

> *Henry* (diary): Monday evening after tea had a moody moment with Kelly while watching her trying to do her art work … I should have been more helpful instead of interfering and let her do the work. Later I said sorry, but I don't think Kelly thought I was with her on this one (sad emoticon).
>
> …perhaps I should be thinking of going down that road [to the allotment] to get out of the house. I think Harriett would be quite happy for this to happen. I must admit, the best thing about work is your workmates, that's what I miss (sad emoticon). But who knows what's around the corner, time will tell!

In his diary Henry reflected on his current situation and was extremely self-critical. His diary, post-diary interview and biographical narrative interview all presented a similar account – a man struggling to come to terms with changed circumstances that have left him uncertain and insecure. He spoke about patterns across the course of parenthood that were characterised as mistakes or errors of judgement. Henry's biographical narrative interview began with him recounting an occasion when he had 'done the wrong thing' by his son. He deeply regretted the event which, he suggested, has been the cause of enduring disillusionment and upset for his son. Henry believes that he is repeating past father–child mistakes with his daughter. Despite the increased time he has available to him, he is giving less time and consideration to his daughter and their previously close relationship is being undermined. He talked about this with apparent regret, especially his perceived lack of emotional capacity.

Henry used the process of research participation to reflect on his parenting strategies and more broadly on changes in the father–child relationship. He found it difficult to express his feelings yet they preoccupied him. In response to the vignettes and images he quickly moved from talking in the third party to talking about events in his own family – what he would or should do. Across the methods he talked of his struggle to adapt to his new circumstances and the exigencies of parenthood.

Henry (post-diary interview): . . . It's quite interesting, because you start to look at yourself as if you're like in a cocoon and you're looking in at yourself [in] close-up which you don't normally do . . . and that actually is quite enlightening . . . You realise that there are much more aspects to your behaviour that should be important towards other people and you're not doing it; you're too involved in . . . With Kelly, basically at the moment I tend to put my foot in it and say the wrong thing and do the wrong thing at the wrong time.

Henry's perception that there is growing distance between him and his daughter is corroborated by Kelly, who noted that 'I don't really interact with my dad as much as my mum'. Henry's awkwardness around sustaining a connection with his daughter and their increasing physical and emotional separation figure throughout the data. Analysis of their respective emotion maps adds another dimension to this story. Through this method father and daughter document how they experience and utilise household space in different ways. Kelly's map revealed her creation of private space and a distinct individual identity. The PC, located in the office, afforded her the chance to be (virtually) with her friends, away from family. Her bedroom is a space for her and her friends/boyfriend. The entrance (bedroom door) is identified as the place where angry exchanges occur as parents intrude on her physical and emotional territory. In contrast Henry's emotion map data graphically charted his loss of a separate identity beyond family. It illustrated his 'angry' self-perception, especially around father–daughter exchanges, compared to the characteristically happy exchanges between husband and wife and loving/affectionate exchanges between Henry and Scott (the pet dog).

Activities identified as 'happy' take place inside and outside the home. Taking the dog for a walk and going to the allotment, an activity that was frequently mentioned in both Henry and Harriet's interview data, are jointly characterised as a source of considerable pleasure for Henry. The couple identify Henry's need for something apart from family and household, and both invest in the potential of rebuilding this through time spent on the allotment. This place may be public and is in fact a family plot, but it is becoming a space that is something individual for Henry, about him and his needs. It is an environment where he can establish new friendships and invest in the nurturing process of gardening. Henry, albeit involuntarily, is having to recreate himself and his identity, and the research process further facilitated this constitutive reflexivity. Having time on his hands, a theme that preoccupied him, affords Henry an opportunity to think about family relationships and this led him to

179

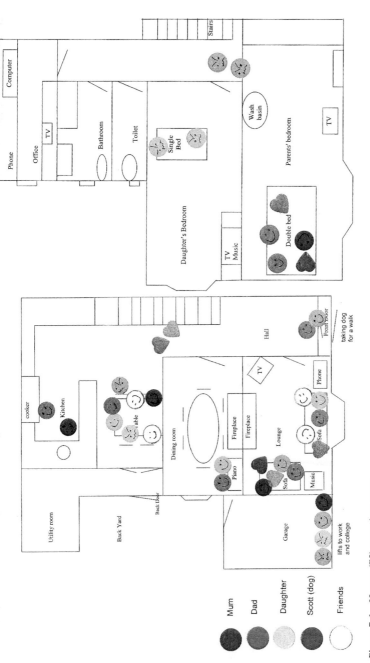

Figure 7.1 Henry (F5) emotion map

question his role in the family and his achievements (and failings) as a father.

> *Henry* (BNIM interview): ... There's things that I've achieved with my children especially in storytelling. I hope it's stuck in their minds forever. You know, I've made up stories, various stories about things, and they really enjoyed that ... I feel as though I've achieved something in life. It's like anything you do in life, you look back and think, 'Well why did I do that?' and 'I could have done that so much better at the time', made mistakes and done things that I shouldn't have done and upset people and what was that all about? If you could turn the clock back – but you can't, of course. You can't forget.

Henry began by talking about scenarios from when his children were young that are a source of pride for him. He works to position this quality experience as something that is quantifiable; his parenting skills amount to something that can be measured as success. Given his current situation Henry's investment in his former parental achievements is hardly surprising. He no longer has a career and appears to be looking for an alternative sense of purpose. However self-doubt follows and he immediately takes away any parental credit, focusing on his 'mistakes', how he should have done a better job and avoided causing distress. In the emotional space afforded by the biographical narrative interview Henry sought an explanation for why things have changed. Answers did not readily emerge, but Henry valued the thought process. 'I hope I've sort of said things that are really important and I'd like to read it again'.

Henry's participation in the research did not raise anxieties that were not already there, but it did focus his thoughts on the subject of parent–child relationships. Talking through some of the issues may have been a painful experience, but it provided a framework through which Henry could express his self-doubts, and, perhaps more importantly, acknowledge credit where it was due. For example, while he may have withdrawn from the father–child relationship in previous times, he was keen to detail how he is currently working hard to re-establish these connections. He has recently started spending time with Harry, developing a mutually disclosing adult–adult relationship. His retirement has given him the affective time previously unavailable to him and in this transitional stage of his life he is developing his emotional capacity, albeit in troubled and testing circumstances.

Henry's new role as a house-husband is requiring a major period of adjustment, not just for Henry but for Harriet also. She has had to relinquish control of the home, which was previously perceived as her domain, handing over responsibility for household, domestic and primary child care tasks to Henry. These changes have not been accomplished smoothly. When Harriet and Henry do domestic chores together these times were described by both as fraught, with tempers becoming frayed. The issue seems to rest on the fact that Henry does not do things the way that Harriet prefers and/or used to do them when she was at home full-time. She attributes her quarrel to differences in personality or to gendered differences: 'Men do not have the multi-tasking skills'. Men do things differently – that is to say, not as well as she would have done.

> *Harriet* (BNIM interview): ... The mundane jobs like hanging the washing on the line or popping something in [the washing machine] doesn't get done as readily as it used to when I was in sole charge of the house ... At the moment with Henry being retired he doesn't do what I did when I was at home and that's a bit of a sore point and I do tell him, but I probably hold back on how much I tell him ... It's personal expectations. I would sort of calculate what he could do in the time that he has and when he doesn't achieve that I'm not happy with that, but that's a personal expectation of how I would react in the same situation and again he's a different person and he's more laid back than I am ... I suppose it's just two different people and the way people work and organise their time. He's not as organised as I am about the time. So it's time management, basically.

When completed chores do not measure up to Harriet's standards, the couple have what Harriet referred to in her diary as 'a discussion', until the 'air is cleared'. What is interesting is that while Harriet thoroughly documented most events in her diary, she simply brushed aside the content of these exchanges. This could be because she did not want to air private disagreements in public; alternatively, she may have preferred to pretend they did not happen. Whatever Harriet's motivation, it is telling that it was Henry who added detail to these combative exchanges, which might suggest that they are more significant to him than to his wife. In many ways Henry appears to be in an unenviable position. Whatever he does fails to match up to the expectations and standards set by Harriet, but because domestic responsibilities are now his, he has no choice but to do them.

In Henry's diary data there is a sense that he is both disillusioned and bored with his life as a house-husband and the domestic chores that now fall to him, including what he describes as providing a 'taxi service' for his daughter and at times his wife. He acknowledged being angry about what he sees as unimportant time-keeping things and also finds being at home every day very isolating. However his 'escape' strategies (walking the dog and going to the allotment) represent another source of conflicting emotions for Harriet. She acknowledged that she is pleased he is beginning to meet new friends at the allotment and find interests outside the home. However, she also is resentful that these activities take him away from the domestic chores which, she would devote a lot of time to when she was a 'housewife' irrespective of whether they were rewarding. Housework is done because it needs doing, and for no other reason.

Harriet presented a positive and confident picture of herself, a portrait that was corroborated by Henry, who described her as his 'role model' for affective conduct; the person who has taught him how to be emotionally expressive. In her biographical narrative interview Harriet described a memorable occasion when all family members got together for a festive meal. She spoke about enjoying the fact that everyone was there sharing the experience – with her situated at the centre. Another reason why this event may have been recalled as particularly enjoyable was because current tensions in the household did not surface. In the heavily scheduled and busy dinner preparations 'everyone knew what they were doing', that is to say they knew where they stood in terms of roles and pecking order in relation to the tasks assigned to them. Arguments did not arise at least in part because categorical structuring of the family was temporarily in place.

In Harriet's presentation of self there were, however, many contradictions around this ordering of family with her at the top. While she did appear to hold the family together, and certainly seems to do most of the emotion work, in observation data there were indications that Harriet may have ambivalent feelings about her matriarchal position. At times her emotional centrality and incumbent motivating role appeared to be experienced as a burden. Harriet's perception that she must present a unified front (of self and family) to the world meant that she was unable or unwilling to acknowledge problematic and/or distressing feelings and memories.

Whereas Henry and Kelly spoke openly about difficult and sometimes painful emotions, Harriet did not speak as candidly about her feelings. For example, in her diary Kelly wrote about the tensions and conflicts that she perceived as characterising her relationship with her parents. Likewise Henry acknowledged the changing relationship that he has with his daughter and questioned his emotional capacity to deal effectively with the conflicts that are arising with ever greater frequency. In contrast, across the methods, Harriet described a comfortable, traditional family life, with very few instances of conflict. 'Discussions' were either glossed over or framed as a consequence of someone else's failings.

Cross-referencing data between family members illustrated the partiality of her account and called into question the confident and self-assured public face that she presented. Family data suggest that her fulsome account and her invocation of the rhetoric of openness may be utilised to obscure her feelings of uncertainty and at times resentment towards both her daughter and husband. These feelings came close to the surface on several occasions during the course of the research, but she continually reworked them into her version of 'happy family life'.

> *Harriet* (diary): Head for church. What a beautiful morning, the fields covered in white frost, sun shining. It really is the best time of the day (if you can get up early). Buy a paper on the way home. Henry up when I get home. We make breakfast; Scott [pet dog] shares a taste of toast with us. Cup of tea and retire to the living room to enjoy a read of the paper.

In her diary, Harriet focused her thoughts on her self. The diary data of Harriet's weekend routine illustrated how she makes time for the different aspects of her life, some of which are shared, while others remain individually enjoyed pleasures. While the diary serves to document her weekly itinerary, revealing a heavily scheduled life, it also detailed moments of relaxation time – time spent lounging in the bedroom, chatting, sharing a cup of tea and watching Saturday morning television with those she loves before enjoying a leisurely breakfast. Here and elsewhere food and mealtimes emerged as extremely important, whether watching cookery programmes, sharing meals or the 'gift exchange' of a cup of tea. As discussed in detail in chapter 5, food performed a symbolic role, providing a material scenario and an affective metaphor through which emotions could be exchanged.

While Harriet portrayed herself as very oriented around the needs of others, in her diary data she detailed her enjoyment of more solitary pleasures, apart from her family: 'I do enjoy this time on my own in the morning (wouldn't admit to the family of course)'. Harriet's Catholicism is not shared by other family members. As a consequence, her church attendance may be part of her weekly routine and was evidently an important part of her life, but it appeared to be squeezed to the margins of her time to avoid encroachment into family activities. For example, she said that she goes to early morning service because this means that her church attendance does not interfere with her family's needs and not because of any personal preference.

Through careful strategies of time management she has found a way to achieve what she wants without inconveniencing anyone else. Friendships and church-related activities are kept outside the family and are fitted in around the primary needs of her daughter and husband: 'By going to the early service allows the family to organize the day without my obligations interfering with their plans'. However, diary data indicate that she is not unaware of her selflessness. Her bracketed comment 'if you can get up early' when placed alongside other comments, such as 'Leave them both to it!' hint at underlying resentments. These feelings are directed towards her daughter who refuses to get up in the mornings and her husband who is no longer tied into the exigencies of employment schedules. In this way Harriet, like Henry and Kelly, presented a somewhat conflicting account, as she negotiates extra- and intra-family intimacies. Looking at some of the data, Harriet could be characterised as a 'controlling mother' and 'bossy wife', but across the range of mixed-methods material the complexity of her character and the family dynamic emerges.

Through a case study analysis of one family I have tried to demonstrate how different data combine to build up a picture of the ways that relationships are experienced and managed in everyday life. Analysis of the mixed-methods data illustrates the utility of this approach in producing dynamic accounts of family relationships. The multilayered, richly textured data broaden understandings of family intimacy and relationality by revealing empirical complexities and conflicting narratives across the dataset. In this way a picture of how family members interrelate begins to come together that challenges a cohesive account of family. This can artificially foreground areas of contestation and difference within and between individuals and it is important to recognise this in the analytical process; the same is true of differences between the kinds of data collected through different methods.

In *Behind Closed Doors* it was possible to discern both distinctive patterns between methods and among the data they produced. Emotion maps did clearly situate family intimacy, that is to say locating *where* intimate encounters occurred. Diaries illustrated affective routines, producing data on *when* intimacy happens and *how* participants framed these emotion exchanges – conceptually and literally. These methods documented particular emotional events or intimate practices based in the here-and-now. In contrast, biographical narrative interviews elicited in-depth stories, reflective accounts that spanned participants' lifecourse.

Family members and affective exchanges were unpicked and remade by participants as they navigated their way through accounts of emotional events in their life. These connections often revealed the story behind the story. Notwithstanding how interesting these methodological differences may be, it is the *richness of data,* the different layers of material that surface through the process of mixing methods, that is most illuminating. Combining methods in families research accords insight into *where, when, how* and *why* intimacy is experienced in certain ways in families. It generates a holistic picture of interpersonal relationships and family life. The portrait of Harriet, Henry and Kelly that emerged through their mixed-methods data is grounded in the materiality of everyday life, but it is not a static portrait. The different stories of self and emotional connections with others are woven together through past and present experiences into a narrative that reflects the dynamic process of families.

Mixed-methods produce comprehensive data on family life which capture different emotional dimensions and the interiority of affective experience. The approach enables researchers to piece together the empirical contradictions and narrative connections of lives. This integrative approach highlights complementarity among data more than discrepancies between them. Intimacies are not simply about our close relationships with others – friends, family, children, lovers, other species and beyond – but are also about 'the deep and important experiences we have with the self ... with our feelings, our bodies, our emotion, our identities' (Plummer 2003: 13). The different layers of meaning and understandings that come to the fore through a mixed-methods approach demonstrate the significant potentialities of this research strategy in addressing multidimensional intimacies. I am not positioning mixed-methods research as a panacea for studies of family, childhood and relationships analysis, but I do want to suggest that it could be one of the key approaches within these fields of inquiry. Just as the conceptual and material networks of intimacy have extended, so too must the methodological approaches that interrogate and shape the patterning of intimate life and our emotional capacities to love and care. Mixing methods extends the scope and field of vision through which we can explore everyday relational experience. The approach provides a wide angle lens through which we can capture the expansive networks that comprise contemporary experiences and understandings of intimacy.

References

Adam, B. D. (2004) Care, Intimacy and Same-Sex Partnership in the 21st Century. *Current Sociology* **52**(2): 265–279.

Adler, P. A. and P. Adler (1993) Ethical Issues in Self Censorship Ethnographic Research on Sensitive Topics. *Researching Sensitive Issues*. C. M. Renzetti and R. M. Lee. London, Sage: 249–266.

Alaszewski, A. (2005) *Using Diaries in Social Research*. London, Sage Publications.

Alderson, P. (1995) *Listening to Children: Children, Ethics and Social Research*. Essex, Barnardos.

Alexander, K. J. et al. (2001) Young Children's Emotional Attachments to Stories. *Social Development* **10**(3): 374–398.

Allan, G. and G. Crow (1989) Insiders and Outsiders: Boundaries around the Home. *Home and Family*. Basingstoke, Macmillan.

Allatt, P. (1993) Becoming Privileged: The Role of Family Processes. I. Bates and G. Riseboroug. *Youth and Inequality*. Buckingham, Open University Press: 139–159.

Allen, L. (2004) 'Getting Off' and 'Going Out': Young People's Conceptions of (Hetero)sexual Relationships. *Culture, Health & Sexuality* **6**(6): 463–481.

Altman, D. (1982) *The Homosexualization of America, the Americanization of the Homosexual*. New York, St. Martin's Press.

Altmann, L. and D. Taylor (1973) *Social Penetration: The Development of Interpersonal Relationships*. New York, Holt, Rinehart & Winston.

Armstrong, J. (2006) Beyond 'Juggling' and 'Flexibility': Classed and Gendered Experiences of Combining Employment and Motherhood. *Sociological Research Online* **11**(2): http://www.socresonline.org.uk/11/11/armstrong.html.

Aubry, T. D. et al. (1995) Public Attitudes and Intentions Regarding Tenants of Community Mental Health Residences who are Neighbors. *Community Mental Health Journal* **31**: 39–52.

Bailey, J. (2000) Some Meanings of 'the Private' in Sociological Thought. *Sociology* **34**(3): 381–401.

Baker, L. G. (1983) 'In My Opinion: The Sexual Revolution in Perspective'. *Family Relations* **32**(2): 297–300.

Balen, R. et al. (2001) Giving Children a Voice: Methodological and Practical Implications of Research Involving Children. *Pediatric Nursing* **12**(10): 24–30.

Barrett, M. and M. McIntosh (1982) *The Anti-Social Family*. London, Verso.

Barter, C. and E. Renold (1999) The Use of Vignettes in Qualitative Research. *Social Research Update 25* Accessed 14 February 2006, http://www.soc.surrey.ac.uk/sru/SRU25.html.

Barter, C. and E. Renold (2000) 'I Wanna Tell You a Story': Exploring the Application of Vignettes in Qualitative Research with Children and Young People. *International Journal of Social Research Methodology* **3**(4): 307–323.

Bauman, Z. (2000) *Liquid Modernity*. Cambridge, Polity Press.

Bauman, Z. (2001) *The Individualized Society*. Cambridge, Polity Press.

Bauman, Z. (2003) *Liquid Love: On the Frailty of Human Bonds*. Cambridge, Polity Press.

Baumeister, R. F. (1986) *Identity: Cultural Change and the Struggle for the Self.* New York and Oxford, Oxford University Press.

Beardsworth, A. and T. Keil (1997) *Sociology on the Menu: Invitation to the Study of Food and Society.* London, Routledge.

Beck-Gernsheim, E. (1999) On the Way to a Post-Familial Family. M. Featherstone, *Love & Eroticism.* London, Sage: 53–70.

Beck, U. and E. Beck-Gersheim (1995) *The Normal Chaos of Love.* Cambridge, Polity Press.

Becker, H. S. (1978) Do Photographs Tell the Truth? *Afterimage* 5: 9–13.

Beishon, S. et al. (1998) *Ethnic Minority Families.* York, Policy Studies Institute, Joseph Rowntree Foundation.

Bell, D. (1991) Insignificant Others: Lesbian and Gay Geographies. *Area* 23: 323–329.

Bell, D. and G. Valentine (1997) *Consuming Geographies: We Are Where We Eat.* London, Routledge.

Bell, L. (1998) Public and Private Meanings in Diaries: Researching Family and Childcare. J. R. McCarthy and R. Edwards, *Feminist Dilemmas in Qualitative Research: Public Knowledge and Private Lives.* London, Sage: 72–86.

Bendelow, G. (1993) Using Visual Imagery to Explore Gendered Notions of Pain. C. M. Renzetti and R. M. Lee, *Researching Sensitive Topics.* London, Sage: 213–228.

Benhabib, S. (1992) *Situating the Self: Gender, Community and Postmodernism in Contemporary Ethics.* Cambridge, Polity Press.

Bergen, R. K. (1993) Interviewing Survivors of Marital Rape: Doing Feminist Research on Sensitive Topics. C. M. Renzetti and R. M. Lee, *Researching Sensitive Topics.* London, Sage: 197–211.

Berger, C. and R. Calabrese (1975) Some Explorations in Initial Attraction and Beyond. *Human Communication Research* 1: 99–112.

Berlant, L. and M. Warner (2000) Sex in Public. L. Berlant, *Intimacy.* Chicago, IL, Chicago University Press.

Bernstein, B. (1971) *Class, Codes and Control. Volume 1.* London, Routledge & Kegan Paul.

Berthoud, R. (2000) Introduction. R. Berthoud and J. Gershuny, *Seven Years in the Lives of British Families.* London, Policy Press.

Blaikie, N. (1993) *Approaches to Social Enquiry.* London, Polity Press.

Blatner, A. (1973) *Acting-in: Practical Applications of Psychodramatic Methods.* New York, Springer.

Blyth, S. and G. Straker (1996) Intimacy, Fusion and Frequency of Sexual Contact in Lesbian Couples. *South African Journal of Psychology* 26(4): 253.

Blyton, P. (1987) Continuing Debate: The Image of Work. Documentary Photography and the Production of 'Reality'. *International Social Science Journal* 113: 415–424.

Bolton, A. et al. (2001) Picture This: Researching Child Workers. *Sociology* 35(2): 501–518.

Bordo, S. (1993) *Unbearable Weight.* Berkeley, CA, University of California Press.

Bott, E. (1971) *Family and Social Network: Roles, Norms, and External Roles in Ordinary Urban Families.* London, Tavistock.

Bowlby, J. (1969) *Attachment and Loss.* Harmondsworth, Penguin Books.

Bramwell, K. (1998) Supporting Families. A Consultation Document. London, HMSO.

Brannen, J. (1988) The Study of Sensitive Subjects. *Sociological Review* **36**: 552–563.

Brannen, J. (ed.) (1992) *Mixing Methods: Qualitative and Quantitative Research*. Aldershot and Brookfield, VT, Avebury.

Brannen, J. et al. (1994) *Young People, Health and Family Life*. Buckingham, Open University Press.

Brannen, J. and A. Nilsen (2006) From Fatherhood to Fathering. *Sociology* **40**(2): 335–352.

Brannen, J. and M. O'Brien (1995) *Childhood and Parenthood*. ISA Committee for Family Research, London, Institute of Education, University of London.

Brannen, J. and M. O'Brien (eds.) (1996) *Children in Families: Research and Policy*. London, Falmer Press.

Bray, S. (2003) *Safer Caring*. London, National Foster Care Association.

Brewer, J. and A. Hunter (1989) *Multimethod Research. A Synthesis of Styles*. Newbury Park, CA, Sage.

Brewer, J. D. (2000) *Ethnography*. Buckingham, Open University Press.

Brilleslijper-Kater, S. N. and H. E. M. Baartman (2000) What do Young Children Know About Sex? Research on the Sexual Knowledge of Children between the Ages of 2 and 6 Years. *Child Abuse Review* **9**: 116–182.

Brown, M. (1995) Ironies of Distance: An Ongoing Critique of the Geographies of AIDS. *Environment and Planning D: Society and Space* **13**: 159–183.

Bryant, K. and C. Zick (1996) An Examination of Parent–Child Shared Time. *Journal of Marriage and the Family* **58**: 227–237.

Bryman, A. (2001) *Social Research Methods*. Oxford, Oxford University Press.

Bryman, A. (2006) 'Editorial'. *Qualitative Research* **6**(1): 5–7.

Bryman, A. et al. (eds.) (1985) *Rethinking the Life Cycle*. Basingstoke, Macmillan.

Buchanan, A. (1995) Young People's Views on Being Looked after in Out-of-Home-Care under the Children Act 1989. *Children and Youth Services Review* **17**(5/6): 681–696.

Buchanan, E. (2000) 'Ethics, Qualitative Research and Ethnography in Virtual Space'. *Journal of Information Ethics* Fall: 82–87.

Budgeon, S. and S. Roseneil (2004) Editors' Introduction: Beyond the Conventional Family. *Current Sociology* **52**(2): 127–134.

Burgess, R. G. (1984) *In the Field: Introduction to Field Research*. London, Harper-Collins.

Burghes, L. et al. (1997) *Fathers and Fatherhood in Britain*. London, Family Policy Studies Centre.

Cade, B. W. (1982) Some Uses of Metaphor. *Australian Journal of Family Therapy* **3**(3): 135–140.

Carsten, J. (2004) *After Kinship*. Cambridge, Cambridge University Press.

Caskey, J. D. and S. Rosenthal (2005) 'Conducting Research on Sensitive Topics with Adolescents: Ethical and Developmental Considerations'. *Journal of Developmental and Behavioural Pediatrics* **26**(1): 61–67.

Castells, M. (1997) *The Power of Identity*. Malden, MA., Blackwell.

Chamberlain, M. (1999) Brothers and Sisters, Uncles and Aunts: A Lateral Perspective on Caribbean Families. E. B. Silva and C. Smart, *The New Family?* London, Sage: 129–142.

Chamberlayne, P. and A. King (1997) The Biographical Challenge of Caring. *Sociology of Health and Illness* **19**(5): 601–621.

Chambers, R. (1998) *Facing It: AIDS Diaries and the Death of the Author.* Ann Abor, MI, University of Michigan Press.

Chandler, J. et al. (2004) 'Living Alone: Its Place in Household Formation and Change'. *Sociological Research Online* **9**(3): http://www.socresonline.org.uk/9/3/chandler.html.

Chase, S. E. (2005) Narrative Enquiry. Multiple Lenses, Approaches, Voices. N. K. Denzin and Y. S. Lincoln. *Handbook of Qualitative Research.* Thousand Oaks, CA, Sage: 651–679.

Cherlin, A. (1992) *Marriage, Divorce, Remarriage.* Cambridge, MA, Harvard University Press.

Cicirelli, V. (1994) Sibling Relationships in Cross-cultural Perspective. *Journal of Marriage and the Family* **56**: 7–20.

Clark, A. and P. Moss (2001) *Listening to Young Children: The Mosaic Approach.* Trowbridge, National Children's Bureau.

Clark, L. (1996) Demographic Change and the Family Situation of Children. J. Brannen and M. O'Brien, *Children in Families: Research and Policy.* London, Falmer Press: 66–83.

Collins, P. H. (1994) Shifting the Center: Race, Class, and Feminist Theorising about Motherhood. E. N. Glenn, G. Chang and L. R. Forcey, *Mothering. Ideology, Experience and Agency.* New York, Routledge: 45–66.

Comfort, M. et al. (2005) 'You Can't Do Nothing in This Damn Place': Sex and Intimacy among Couples with an Incarcerated Male Partner. *Journal of Sex Research* **42**(1): 3–12.

Constantine, L. L. (1978) Family Sculpture and Relationship Mapping Techniques. *Journal of Marriage and Family Counselling* **4**: 13–23.

Cottam, R. (2001) Diaries and Journals: General Survey. M. Jolly, *The Encyclopaedia of Life Writing.* London and Chicago, Fitzroy Dearborn. **1**: 267–269.

Coxon, A. P. M. (1996) *Between the Sheets: Sexual Diaries and Gay Men's Sex in the Era of AIDS.* London, Cassell.

Crichton, S. and E. Childs (2005) Clipping and Coding Audio Files: A Research Method to Enable Participant Voice. *International Journal of Qualitative Methods* **4**(3): 2–9.

Crossley, N. (2006) *Reflexions in the Flesh: The Body in Late Modern Society.* Buckingham, Open University Press.

Crow, G. (2002) *Social Solidarities: Theories, Identities and Social Change.* Buckingham, Open University Press.

Curtis, G. C. (1963) Violence Breeds Violence Perhaps? *American Journal of Psychiatry* **120**: 386–387.

Daly, K. J. (1992) The Fit between Qualitative Research and Characteristics of Families. J. F. Gilgun, K. J. Daly and G. Handel, *Qualitative Methods in Family Research.* Beverly Hill, CA, Sage: 3–11.

Daly, K. J. (2007) *Qualitative Methods for Family Studies & Human Development.* Thousand Oaks, CA, Sage Publications.

Davison, K. P. et al. (2000) Who Talks? The Social Psychology of Illness Support Groups. *American Psychologist* **55**: 205–217.

Deacon, S. A. (2000) Creativity within Qualitative Research on Families: New Ideas for Old Methods. *The Qualitative Report* **4**(3 & 4): http://www.nova. edu/ssss/QR/QR4-3/deacon.html.

Deegan, M. J. and J. A. Kotarba (1980) On Responsibility in Ethnography (Comment on Kotarba, *Qualitative Sociology*, September 1979). *Qualitative Sociology* **3**(4): 323–331.

Delphy, C. (1992) Mothers' Union? *Trouble & Strife* **24**: 12–19.

Delphy, C. and D. Leonard (1992) *Familiar Exploitation: A New Analysis of Marriage in Contemporary Western Societies*. London, Polity Press.

Denzin, N. K. (1988) *Research Act in Sociology: A Theoretical Introduction to Sociological Methods*. Englewood Cliffs, NJ, Prentice Hall.

Denzin, N. K. (1989) *Interpretive Biography*. Newbury Park, CA, Sage.

Dermott, E. (2003) The 'Intimate Father': Defining Paternal Involvement. *Sociological Research Online* **8**(4): http://www.socresonline.org.uk/8/4/dermott.html.

Devault, M. L. (1991) *Feeding the Family: The Social Organization of Caring as Gendered Work*. Chicago, Chicago University Press.

Doucet, A. (1996) Encouraging Voices: Towards More Collective Methods for Collecting Data on Gender and Household Labour. L. Morris and E. S. Lyon, *Gender Relations in Public and Private*. Basingstoke, Macmillan: 156–175.

Doucet, A. (2001) 'You See the Need Perhaps More Clearly than I Have': Exploring Gendered Processes of Domestic Responsibility. *Journal of Family Issues* **22**(3): 328–348.

Doucet, A. (2006) *Do Men Mother? Fatherhood, Care, and Domestic Responsibility* Toronto, University of Toronto Press.

Dowling, R. (1999) 'Classing the Body'. *Environment and Planning D: Society and Space* **17**: 511–514.

Duhl, F. J. (1981) The Use of the Chronological Chart in General Systems Family Therapy. *Journal of Marital and Family Therapy* **7**: 361–373.

Duncombe, J. and J. Jessop (2002) Doing Rapport and the Ethics of Faking Friendship. M. Mauthner, M. Birch, J. Jessop and T. Miller. *Ethics in Qualitative Research*. London, Sage: 107–123.

Duncombe, J. and D. Marsden (1995) 'Workaholics' and 'Whingeing Women': Theorising Intimacy and Emotion Work – The Last Frontier of Gender Inequality? *Sociological Review* **43**(1): 150–169.

Duncombe, J. and D. Marsden (1996) Can We Research the Private Sphere? Methodological and Ethical Problems in the Study of Intimate Emotions in Personal Relationships. L. Morris and E. S. Lyon. *Gender Relations in Public and Private*. Basingstoke, Macmillan: 141–155.

Duncombe, J. and D. Marsden (1996) Whose Orgasm is This Anyway? 'Sex Work' in Long-term Heterosexual Couple Relationships. J. Weeks and J. Holland, *Sexual Cultures: Communities, Values and Intimacy*. Basingstoke, Macmillan: 220–238.

Dunn, J. and K. Deater-Deckard (2001) *Children's Views of their Changing Families*. York, Joseph Rowntree Foundation.

Dunne, G. A. (1998a) Opting into Motherhood: Blurring the Boundaries and Redefining the Meaning of Parenthood. *LSE Gender Institute Discussion Paper*. London, London School of Economics.

Dunne, G. A. (1998b) 'Pioneers Behind Our Own Front Doors'. New Models for the Organization of Work in Partnerships'. *Work, Employment and Society* **12**(2): 273–295.

Dunne, G. A. (1999) A Passion for 'Sameness'? Sexuality and Gender Accountability. E. B. Silva and C. Smart, *The New Family?* London, Sage: 66–82.

Edholm, F. (1982) The Unnatural Family. E. Whitelegg et al., *The Changing Experience of Women*. Oxford, Martin Robertson: 166–177.

Edwards, R. (1993) An Education in Interviewing: Placing the Researcher and the Researched. C. M. Renzetti and R. M. Lee, *Researching Sensitive Topics*. London, Sage: 181–196.

Edwards, R. et al. (2006) *Sisters and Brothers: Sibling Identities and Relationships*. London, Routledge.

Edwards, R. and M. Mauthner (2002) Ethics and Feminist Research: Theory and Practice. M. Mauthner, M. Birch, J. Jessop and T. Millier, *Ethics in Qualitative Research*. London, Sage: 14–31.

Elam, G. and K. A. Fenton (2003) Researching Sensitive Issues and Ethnicity: Lessons from Sexual Health. *Ethnicity and Health* **8**(1): 15–27.

Elliott, H. (1997) The Use of Diaries in Sociological Research on Health Experience. *Sociological Research Online* **2**(2): http://www.socresonline.org.uk/2/2/7.html.

Ennew, J. (1986) *The Sexual Exploitation of Children*. Cambridge, Polity.

Epstein, D. (1994) *Challenging Lesbian and Gay Inequalities in Education*. Buckingham, Open University Press.

Ermisch, J. F. and R. E. Wright (1995) Lone Parenthood and Employment: Male–Female Differences in Great Britain. *Labour Economics* **2**(3): 299–319.

Estep, R. E. et al. (1977) The Socialization of Sexual Identity. *Journal of Marriage & the Family* **39**: 99–112.

Evans, D. (1993) *Sexual Citizenship: The Material Construction of Sexualities*. London, Routledge.

Farley, R. et al. (1980) Barriers to the Racial Integration of Neighbourhoods – The Detroit Case. *Annals of the American Academy of Political and Social Science* **444**: 97–113.

Farrington, J. (2000) Can People be Intimate without Sex? *Current Health 2; Supplement Human Sexuality* **26**(6): 2.

Feldman, S. S. et al. (1998) Family Relationships and Gender as Predictors of Romantic Intimacy in Young Adults: A Longitudinal Study. *Journal of Research on Adolescence* **8**(2): 263–286.

Ferri, E. and K. Smith (1998) *Step-Parenting in the 1990s*. York, Family Policy Studies Centre, Joseph Rowntree Foundation.

Field, J. et al. (1994) *Sexual Behaviour in Britain*. London, Penguin Books.

Finch, J. (1984) 'It's Great to Have Someone to Talk to'. The Ethics and Politics of Interviewing Women. C. Bell and H. Roberts, *Social Researching*. London, Sage: 181–196.

Finch, J. (1987) The Vignette Technique in Survey Research. *Sociology* **21**: 105–114.

Finch, J. (1990) *Family Obligations and Social Change*. Cambridge, Polity Press.

Finch, J. (1997) The State and the Family. S. Cunningham-Burley and L. Jamieson, *Families and the State*. London, Palgrave: 29–44.

Finch, J. and J. Mason (1993) *Negotiating Family Responsibilities*. London, Routledge.

Fineman, M. A. (1995) *The Neutered Mother, The Sexual Family, and Other Twentieth Century Tragedies*. New York, Routledge.

Fletcher, B. (1993) *Not Just a Name: The Views of Young People in Foster and Residential Care*. London, National Consumer Council/Who Cares Trust.

Flewitt, R. (2005) Is Every Child's Voice Heard? Researching the Different Ways 3-Year-Old Children Communicate and Make Meaning at Home and in a Pre-School Playgroup. *Early Years* 25(3): 207–222.

Fontana, A. and J. H. Frey (2005) Interviewing: The Art of Science. N. K. Denzin and Y. S. Lincoln, *Handbook of Qualitative Research*. London, Sage: 695–728.

Fox, J. et al. (2003) Conducting Research Using Web-based Questionnaires: Practical, Methodological and Ethical Considerations. *International Journal of Social Research Methodology* 6(2): 167–180.

Fox, N. et al. (1991) Attachment to Mother/Attachment to Father. *Child Development* 62(210–25).

Francesconi, M. (2004) An Evaluation of the Childhood Family Structure Measures from the Sixth Wave of the British Household Panel Survey. *Royal Statistical Society* 168(3): 539–566.

Friedman, J. (1990) Being in the World: Globalisation and Localisation. *Theory, Culture and Society* 7(3): 11–28.

Frosh, S. et al. (2001) *Young Masculinities: Understanding Boys in Contemporary Society* Basingstoke, Palgrave.

Gabb, J. (2001) Desirous Subjects and Parental Identities: Toward a Radical Theory on (Lesbian) Family Sexuality. *Sexualities* 4(3): 333–352.

Gabb, J. (2002) Perverting Motherhood? Sexuality and Lesbian Parent Families. *Women's Studies*. York, University of York.

Gabb, J. (2004a) 'I Could Eat My Baby to Bits'; Passion and Desire in Lesbian Mother–Children Love. *Gender, Place, Culture* 11(3): 399–415.

Gabb, J. (2004b) Critical Differentials: Querying the Contrarieties between Research on Lesbian Parent Families. *Sexualities* 7(2): 171–187.

Gabb, J. (2005a) Lesbian M/Otherhood: Strategies of Familial-Linguistic Management in Lesbian Parent Families. *Sociology* 39(4): 585–603.

Gabb, J. (2005b) Locating Lesbian Parent Families. *Gender, Place, Culture* 12(4): 419–432.

Geertz, C. (1973) Thick Description: Toward an Interpretive Theory of Culture. C. Geertz, *The Interpretation of Cultures*. New York, Basic Books: 3–30.

Gehring, T. M. and R. B. Schultheiss (1987) Family Measurement Techniques. *American Journal of Family Therapy* 15: 261–264.

Gershuny, J. et al. (2005) Exit, Voice and Suffering: Do Couples Adapt to Changing Employment Patterns? *Journal of Marriage & Family* 67(3): 656–665.

Gershuny, J. and O. Sullivan (1998) The Sociological Uses of Time-use Diary Analysis. *European Sociological Review* 14(1): 69–85.

Giddens, A. (1991) *Modernity and Self-identity: Self and Society in the Late Modern Age*. Cambridge, Polity Press.

Giddens, A. (1992) *The Transformation of Intimacy: Sexuality, Love and Eroticism in Modern Societies*. Cambridge, Polity Press.

Giddens, A. (1999) *Family*. Reith Lecturers 4.

Gillies, V. (2003) *Family and Intimate Relationships: A Review of the Sociological Research*. London, Families & Social Capital ESRC Research Group, South Bank University.

Gillies, V. (2005) Meeting Parents' Needs? Discourses of 'Support' and 'Inclusion' in Family Policy. *Critical Social Policy* **25**(1): 70–90.

Gillies, V. (2006) *Marginalised Mothers. Exploring Working Class Experiences of Parenting*. London, Routledge.

Gillies, V. et al. (2001) *'Pulling Together, Pulling Apart': The Family Lives of Young People*. York, Family Policy Studies Centre, Joseph Rowntree Foundation.

Gillis, J. R. (1996) *A World of Their Own Making. A History of Myth and Ritual in Family Life*. Oxford, Oxford University Press.

Gittins, D. (1993) *The Family in Question*. Basingstoke, Macmillan.

Glenn, E. N. et al. (eds.) (1994) *Mothering. Ideology, Experience, and Agency*. New York, Routledge.

Goffman, E. (1969) *The Presentation of Self in Everyday Life*. London, Allen Lane.

Golombok, S. (2000) *Parenting – What Really Counts?* London, Routledge.

Gordon, T. and E. Lahelma (2003) From Ethnography to Life History: Tracing Transitions of School Students. *International Journal of Social Research Methodology* **6**(3): 245–254.

Gorell-Barnes, G. et al. (1997) *Growing up in Stepfamilies*. Oxford, Oxford University Press.

Graham, H. (1983) Do Her Answers Fit His Questions? Women and the Survey Method. E. Gamarnikow, D. Morgan, J. Purvis and D. Taylorson, *The Public and the Private*. London, Heinemann: 181–196.

Graham, H. (1984) Surveying through Stories. C. Bell and H. Roberts, *Social Researching*. London, Kegan Paul: 181–196.

Grant, L. (1997) Moyenda: *Black Families Talking – Family Survival Strategies, Exploring Parenthood*. York, Social Policy Research, Joseph Rowntree Foundation.

Gray, A. (2005) The Changing Availability of Grandparents as Carers and its Implications for Childcare Policy in the UK. *Journal of Social Policy* **34**(4): 557–577.

Greenberg, I. A. (1974) *Psychodrama: Theory and Therapy*. New York, Behavior Publications.

Greenhalg, G. et al. (1998) Health Beliefs and Folk Models of Diabetes in British Bangladeshis: A Qualitative Study. *British Medical Journal* **316**: 978–983.

Greenstein, T. N. (2006) *Methods in Family Research*. Thousand Oaks, CA, Sage.

Greenwood, D. and D. Lowenthal (2005) Case Study Research as a Means of Researching Social Work and Improving Practitioner Education. *Journal of Social Work Practice* **19**(2): 181–193.

Gross, E. (1992) Bodies–Cites. B. Colomina, *Sexuality and Space*. New York, Princeton Architectural Press: 241–254.

Gross, J. and H. Hayne (1998) Drawing Facilitates Children's Verbal Reports of Emotionally Laden Events. *Journal of Experimental Psychology: Applied* **4**(2): 163–174.

Gross, N. (2005) The Detraditionalisation of Intimacy Reconsidered. *Sociological Theory* **23**(3): 286–311.

Hadfield, L. et al. (2007) 'Making of Modern Motherhoods'. Accessed 5 June 2007, http://www.open.ac.uk/hsc/MoMM/index.htm.

Halford, W. K. et al. (1992) Towards a Behavioural Ecology of Stressful Marital Interactions. *Behavioral Assessment* **14**: 199–217.

Halley, J. O. M. (2007) *Boundaries of Touch. Parenting and Adult-Child Intimacy.* Champaign, IL, University of Illinois Press.

Hanscombe, G. and J. Forster (1981) *Rocking the Cradle: Lesbian Mothers, A Challenge to Family Living.* London, Sheba.

Hansen, H. T. et al. (2006) Poverty among Households with Children: A Comparative Study of Norway and Germany. *International Journal of Social Welfare* 15(4): 269–279.

Hantrais, L. (1995) Comparative Research Methods. *Social Research Update 13* Accessed 1 September 2006, http://www.soc.surrey.ac.uk/sru/SRU13.html.

Haraway, D. J. (2003) *Companion Species Manifesto: Dogs, People, and Significant Otherness.* Chicago, Prickly Paradigm Press.

Harden, J. et al. (2000) Can't Talk, Won't Talk? Methodological Issues in Researching Children. *Sociological Research Online* 5(2): http://www. socresonline.org.uk/5/2/harden.html.

Harocopos, A. and D. Dennis (2003) Maintaining Contact with Drug Users over an 18-month Period. *International Journal of Social Research Methodology* 6(3): 261–266.

Harris, M. B. and P. H. Turner (1985) Gay and Lesbian Parents. *Journal of Homosexuality* 12(2): 101–113.

Hazel, N. (1995) Elicitation Techniques with Young People. *Social Research Update 12.* Accessed 4 January 2006, http://www.soc.surrey.ac.uk/sru/SRU12.html.

Heath, S. (2004) Peer-Shared Households, Quasi-Communes and Neo-Tribes. *Current Sociology* 52(2): 161–179.

Heilbrun Jr., A. B. (1984) Identification with the Father and Peer Intimacy of the Daughter. *Family Relations.* 33: 597.

Henderson, S. et al. (2006) *Inventing Adulthoods: A Biographical Approach to Youth Transitions.* London, Sage.

Herdt, G. (1981) *Guardians of the Flutes.* New York, McGraw-Hill.

Herzberger, S. D. (1993) The Cyclical Pattern of Child Abuse. C. M. Renzetti and R. M. Lee, *Researching Sensitive Topics.* London, Sage: 33–51.

Hewson, C. (2003) Conducting Research on the Internet. *The Psychologist* 16(6): 290–293.

Hey, V. (1997) *The Company She Keeps: An Ethnography of Girls' Friendships.* Buckingham, Open University Press.

Hill, M. (1987) *Sharing Child Care in Early Parenthood.* London, Routledge & Kegan Paul.

Hill, M. (1997) Research Review, Participatory Research with Children. *Child and Family Social Work* 2: 171–183.

Hill, M. et al. (1996) Engaging with Primary-aged Children about their Emotions and Well-being: Methodological Considerations. *Children & Society* 10(1): 129–144.

Hochschild, A. R. (1979) Emotion Work, Feeling Rules and Social Structure. *American Journal of Sociology* 85: 551–575.

Hochschild, A. R. (1983) *The Managed Heart: Commercialization of Human Feeling.* Berkeley, CA, University of California Press.

Hochschild, A. R. (1989) *The Second Shift: Working Parents and the Revolution at Home.* New York, Viking.

Hochschild, A. R. (1995) The Culture of Politics: Traditional, Postmodern, Cold-Modern, and Warm-Modern Ideas of Care. *Social Politics* 2: 331–346.

Hochschild, A. R. (2003) *The Commercialization of Intimate Life: Notes from Home and Work*. Berkeley, CA, University of California Press

Holland, J. et al. (1998) *The Male in the Head: Young People, Heterosexuality and Power*. London, Tufnell Press.

Holland, J. et al. (1994) Methodological Issues in Researching Young Women's Sexuality. M. Boulton, *Challenge and Innovation: Methodological Advances in Social Research on HIV/AIDS*. Basingstoke, Falmer: 219–240.

Holland, J. et al. (2003) Families, Intimacy and Social Capital. *Social Policy and Society* 2(4): 339–348.

Hollway, W. (2001) The Psycho-Social Subject in 'Evidence-Based Practice'. *Journal of Social Work Practice* 15(1): 9–21.

Hollway, W. (2006) *The Capacity to Care: Gender and Ethical Subjectivity*. London, Routledge.

Hollway, W. (2006) Family Figures in 20th-Century British 'Psy' Discourses. *Theory & Psychology* 16(4): 443–464.

Hollway, W. and T. Jefferson (2000) *Doing Qualitative Research Differently: Free Association, Narrative and the Interview Method*. London, Sage.

Holstein, J. A. and J. F. Gubrium (2005) Interpretive Practice and Social Action. N. K. Denzin and Y. S. Lincoln, *Handbook of Qualitative Research*. California, Sage: 483–505.

Hook, M. K. et al. (2003) How Close Are We? Measuring Intimacy and Examining Gender Differences. *Journal of Counselling & Development* 81(4): 462–472.

Hughes, R. (1998) Considering the Vignette Technique and its Application to a Study of Drug Injecting and HIV Risk and Safer Behavior. *Sociology of Health and Illness* 20(3): 381–400.

Hughes, R. and M. Huby (2001) The Application of Vignettes in Social and Nursing Research. *Journal of Advanced Nursing* 37(4): 382–386.

Hurworth, R. (2003) Photo-Interviewing for Research. *Social Research Update 40* Accessed 6 April 2006, http://www.soc.surrey.ac.uk/sru/SRU40.html.

Huston, T. L. and R. I. Burgess (eds.) (1979) *Social Exchange in Developing Relationships*. New York, Academic Press.

Illouz, E. (1997) *Consuming the Romantic Utopia: Love and the Cultural Contradictions of Capitalism*. Berkeley, CA, University of California Press.

Ingraham, C. (1996) The Heterosexual Imaginary. Feminist Sociology and Theories of Gender. S. Seidman, *Queer Theory/Sociology*. Cambridge MA, Blackwell: 168–193.

Ingram, G. B. et al. (1997) *Queers in Space. Communities, Public Places, Sites of Resistance*. Seattle, WA, Bay Press.

Irigaray, L. (1974) *Speculum of the Other Woman*. Ithaca, NY, Cornell University Press.

Itzen, C. (2000) Child Sexual Abuse and the Radical Feminist Endeavour. C. Itzen, *Home Truths about Child Sexual Abuse*. London, Routledge: 1–25.

Jackson, S. (1982) *Childhood and Sexuality*. Oxford, Basil Blackwell.

Jackson, S. (1993) Even Sociologists Fall in Love: An Exploration in the Sociology of Emotions. *Sociology* 27(2): 201–220.

Jackson, S. (1997) Women, Marriage and Family Relationships. V. Robinson and D. Richardson, *Introducing Women's Studies*. Basingstoke, Macmillan: 323–348.

Jackson, S. and S. Scott (2004) Sexual Antinomies in Late Modernity. *Sexualities* 7(2): 233–248.

James, A. et al. (1998) *Theorizing Childhood*. Cambridge, Polity Press.

James, A. and A. Prout (eds.) (1990) *Constructing and Reconstructing Childhood: Contemporary Issues in the Sociological Study of Childhood*. London, Falmer Press.

Jamieson, L. (1998) *Intimacy: Personal Relationships in Modern Societies*. Cambridge, Polity Press.

Jamieson, L. (1999) Intimacy Transformed? A Critical Look at the 'Pure' Relationship. *Sociology* 33(3): 477–494.

Jamieson, L. (2005) Boundaries of Intimacy. L. McKie and S. Cunningham-Burley, *Families in Society. Boundaries and Relationships*. Bristol, Policy Press: 189–206.

Jamieson, L. and C. Tonybee (1990) Shifting Patterns of Parental Control. H. Corr and L. Jamieson. *Politics of Everyday Life: Continuity and Change in Work and the Family*. London, Macmillan: 86–113.

Janoski, T. (1998) *Citizenship and Civil Society: A Framework of Rights and Obligations in Liberal, Traditional, and Social Democratic Regimes*. Cambridge, Cambridge University Press.

Jenkins, S. P. et al. (2003) The Dynamics of Child Poverty: Britain and Germany Compared. *Journal of Comparative Family Studies* 34(3): 336–355.

Johnson, V. et al. (1995) *Listening to Smaller Voices: Children in an Environment of Change*. London, ActionAid.

Johnston, L. and G. Valentine (1995) Wherever I Lay My Girlfriend: That's My Home. The Performance and Surveillance of Lesbian Identities in Domestic Environments. D. Bell and G. Valentine, *Mapping Desires. Geographies of Sexuality*. London, Routledge: 99–113.

Jones, G. P. (1990) The Study of Intergenerational Intimacy in North America. *Journal of Homosexuality* 20(1/2): 275–295.

Kakabadase, A. and N. Kakabadse (2004) *Intimacy: An International Survey of the Sex Lives of People at work*. Basingstoke, Palgrave Macmillan.

Kaufman, G. (1997) Men's Attitudes towards Parenthood. *Population Research and Policy Review* 16(5): 435–446.

Kazi, M. and J. Wilson (1996) Applying Single Case Evaluation in Social Work. *British Journal of Social Work* 26: 699–717.

Kelly, L. (1992) Journeying in Reverse: Possibilities and Problems in Feminist Research on Sexual Violence. A. Morris, *Feminist Perspectives in Criminology*. Milton Keynes, Open University Press: 107–114.

Kelly, L. et al. (1998)*Legacies of Abuse – 'It's More Complicated than That': A Qualitative Study of the Meaning and Impacts of Sexual Abuse in Childhood*. London, University of North London.

Kerr, D. and R. Beaujot (2003) Child Poverty and Family Structure in Canada, 1981–1997. *Journal of Comparative Family Studies* 34(3): 321–335.

King, C. E. and A. Christensen (1983) The Relationship Events Scale: A Guttman Scaling of Progress in Courtship. *Journal of Marriage & Family* 45(3): 671.

Kinkaid, J. (1998) *Erotic Innocence*. Durham, NC, Duke University Press.

Kinsey, A. et al. (1948) *Sexual Behaviour in the Human Male*. Philadelphia, W. B. Saunders.

Kinsey, A. et al. (1953) *Sexual Behaviour in the Human Female*. Philadelphia, W. B. Saunders.

Kirkman, M. et al. (2001) Freeing up the Subject: Tension between Traditional Masculinity and Involved Fatherhood through Communication about Sexuality with Adolescents. *Culture, Health & Sexuality*, 3: 391–411.

Kitzinger, J. (1988) Defending Innocence: Ideologies of Childhood. *Feminist Review* 28: 77–86.

Kitzinger, S. (1978) *Women as Mothers*. Glasgow, Fontana Books.

Kopp, R. R. (1995) *Metaphor Therapy*. New York, Brunner/Mazel.

Kotarba, J. A. (1979) The Accomplishment of Intimacy in a Jail Visiting Room. *Qualitative Sociology* 2(2): 80–103.

L'Abate, L. and S. Sloan (1984) A Workshop Format to Facilitate Intimacy in Married Couples. *Family Relations*, 33: 245.

Langford, W. (1999) *Revolutions of the Heart. Gender, Power and the Delusions of Love*. London, Routledge.

Langstead, O. (1994) Looking at Quality from the Child's Perspective. P. Moss and A. Pence, *Valuing Quality in Early Childhood Services*. London, Paul Chapmen: 28–42.

Lansdown, G. (1994) Children's Rights. B. Mayall, *Children's Childhoods Observed and Experienced*. London, Falmer Press.

Larossa, R. et al. (1981) Ethical Dilemmas in Qualitative Family Research. *Journal of Marriage and the Family* 43: 303–313.

Larson, J. H. and S. M. Allgood (1987) A Comparison of Intimacy in First-Married and Remarried Couples. *Journal of Family Issues* 8(3): 319–331.

Larson, R. W. and D. M. Almeida (1999) Emotional Transmission in the Daily Lives of Families: A New Paradigm for Studying Family Process. *Journal of Marriage & Family* 61(1): 5–20.

Laslett, B. and R. Rapport (1975) Collaborative Interviewing and Interactive Research. *Journal of Marriage and the Family* 37: 968–977.

Laurenceau, J.-P. and N. Bolger (2005) Using Diary Methods to Study Marital and Family Processes. *Journal of Family Psychology* 19(1): 86–97.

Lee, R. M. (1993) *Doing Research on Sensitive Topics*. London, Sage.

Leonardo, M. D. (1987) The Female World of Cards and Holidays: Women, Families, and the Work of Kinship. *Signs* 12: 440–453.

Leveton, E. (1992) *A Clinician's Guide to Psychodrama*. New York, Springer.

Levin, I. (2004) Living Apart Together: A New Family Form *Current Sociology* 52(2): 223–240.

Levinas, E. (1981) *Otherwise than Being Or Beyond Essence*. The Hague and Boston, MA, Martinus Nijhoff.

Levinger, G. and J. Snoek (1972) *Attraction in Relationship: A New Look at Interpersonal Attraction*. Morristown, NJ, General Learning.

Lewin, E. (1993) *Lesbian Mothers. Accounts of Gender in American Culture*. Ithaca, NJ, Cornell University Press.

Lewin, E. (2002) You'll Never Walk Alone: Lesbian and Gay Weddings and the Authenticity of the Same-Sex Couple. M. Yalom, L. Carstensen, E. Freedman and B. Gelpi. *Inside the American Couple: New Thinking/New Challenges*. Berkeley, CA, University of California Press: 87–107.

Longhurst, R. (1995) The Body and Geography. *Gender, Place, Culture* 2(1): 97–106.

Longhurst, R. (1997) (Dis)embodied Geographies. *Progress in Human Geography* 21(4): 486–501.

Lupton, D. (1996) *Food, Body and the Self.* London, Sage.

Lupton, D. and L. Barclay (1997) *Constructing Fatherhood.* London, Sage.

MacKnee, C. M. (2002) Profound Sexual and Spiritual Encounters among Practising Christians: A Phenomenological Analysis. *Journal of Psychology & Theology* 30(3): 234–245.

Malinowski, B. (1992) *Argonauts of the Western Pacific.* London, Routledge & Kegan Paul.

Mandell, N. (1991) The Least Adult Role in Studying Children. F. C. Waksler, *Studying the Social Worlds of Children.* Basingstoke, Falmer: 433–487.

Mansfield, P. and J. Collard (1988) *The Beginning of the Rest of Your Life?* London, Macmillan.

Markham, A. (2005) The Methods, Politics, and Ethics of Representation in Online Ethnography. N. K. Denzin and Y. S. Lincoln, *Handbook of Qualitative Research.* Thousand Oaks, CA, Sage: 793–820.

Marks, S. (1994) Intimacy in the Public Realm: The Case of Co-workers. *Social Forces* 72: 845–858.

Mason, J. (1996) *Qualitative Researching.* London, Sage.

Mason, J. (2006) Mixing Methods in a Qualitatively-driven Way. *Qualitative Research* 6(1): 9–25.

Mason, J. (2008) Tangible Affinities and the Real Life Fascination of Kinship. *Sociology* 42(1): 24–46.

Mason, J. and B. Tipper. (2006) Children, Kinship and Creativity. Accessed 22 September 2006, http://www.socialsciences.manchester.ac.uk/morgancentre/research/childrens-kinship/2006-07-morgan-children-kinship.pdf.

Masters, W. H. and V. E. Johnson (1966) *Human Sexual Response.* Boston, MA, Little, Brown.

Masters, W. H. and V. E. Johnson (1970) *Human Sexual Inadequacy.* Boston, MA, Little, Brown.

Mauthner, M. (1997) Methodological Aspects of Collecting Data from Children: Lessons from Three Research Projects. *Children and Society* 11(1): 16–28.

Mauthner, M. (1998) Bringing Silent Voices into a Public Discourse: Researching Accounts of Sister Relationships. J. Ribbens and R. Edwards, *Dilemmas of Feminist Research: Public Knowledge and Private Lives.* London, Sage: 39–57.

Mauthner, M. (2000) Snippets and Silences: Ethics and Reflexivity in Narratives of Sistering. *International Journal of Social Research Methodology* 3(4): 287–306.

Mauthner, M. et al. (eds.) (2002) *Ethics in Qualitative Research.* London, Sage.

Mauthner, M. et al. (2005) *Sisters and Brothers: Under Their Skins.* London, Routledge, Taylor & Francis.

Mauthner, M. et al. (1993) *Children and Food at Primary School.* London, SSRU/Science Education, Institute of Education.

Mayall, B., Ed. (1994) *Children's Childhoods Observed and Experienced.* London, Falmer Press.

Mayall, B. (2002) *Towards a Sociology for Childhood: Thinking from Children's Lives.* Buckingham, Open University Press.

Maynard, M. and J. Purvis (eds.) (1994) *Researching Women's Lives from a Feminist Perspective.* London, Taylor and Francis.

Mazur, R. (1973) *The New Intimacy. Open-Ended Marriage and Alternative Lifestyles.* Boston, MA, Beacon Press.

McCabe, M. P. (1999) The Interrelationships between Intimacy, Relationship Functioning, and Sexuality among Men and Women in Committed Relationships. *Canadian Journal of Human Sexuality* **8**(1): 31–38.

McCarthy, J. R. and R. Edwards (2001) Illuminating Meanings of 'the Private' in Sociological Thought: A Response to Joe Bailey. *Sociology* **35**(3): 765–777.

McCarthy, J. R. et al. (2003) *Making Families. Moral Tales of Parenting and Step-parenting*. Durham, NC, Sociology Press.

McDowell, L. (1993) Space, Place and Gender Relations. Part II. Identity, Difference, Feminist Geometries and Geographies. *Progress in Human Geography* **17**: 305–318.

McKenna, K. Y. A. and J. A. Bargh (1998) Coming Out in the Age of the Internet: Identity 'Demarginalization' Through Virtual Group Participation'. *Journal of Personality and Social Psychology* **75**(3): 681–694.

McLeod, J. (2003) Why We Interview Now – Reflexivity and Perspective in a Longitudinal Study. *International Journal of Social Research Methodology* **6**(3): 201–212.

Measor, L. (2004) Young People's Views of Sex Education: Gender, Information and Knowledge. *Sex Education* **4**(2): 153–166.

Meth, P. (2003) Entries and Omissions: Using Solicited Diaries in Geographical Research. *Area* **35**(2): 195–205.

Miles, M. B. and A. M. Huberman (1994) *Qualitative Data Analysis: An Expanded Sourcebook*. London, Sage.

Miller, B. C. (1986) *Family Research Methods*. Beverly Hill, CA, Sage.

Miller, C. L. et al. (1990) Sexually Abused and Non-abused Children's Conceptions of Personal and Body Safety. *Child Abuse and Neglect* **14**: 99–112.

Miller, J. and B. Glassner (1997) 'The "Inside" and "Outside": Finding Realities in Interviews'. D. Silverman, *Qualitative Research: Theory, Method and Practice*. London, Sage: 99–112.

Mitchell, B. A. (2006) Changing Courses: The Pendulum of Family Transitions in Comparative Perspective. *Journal of Comparative Family Studies* **37**(3): 325–343.

Moran-Ellis, J. et al. (2006) Triangulation and Integration: Processes, Claims and Implications. *Qualitative Research* **6**(1): 45–59.

Morgan, D. H. J. (1996) *Family Connections: An Introduction to Family Studies*. Cambridge, Polity Press.

Morgan, D. L. (1997) *Focus Groups as Qualitative Research*. Thousand Oaks, CA, Sage.

Morrow, V. (1998a) My Animals and Other Family: Children's Perspectives on Their Relationships with Companion Animals. *Anthrozoos* **11**(4): 218–226.

Morrow, V. (1998b) *Understanding Families: Children's Perspectives*. London, National Children's Bureau.

Murray, C. D. and J. Sixsmith (1998) Email: A Qualitative Research Medium for Interviewing? *International Journal of Research Methodology* **1**(2): 103–121.

Musil, C. M. and T. Standing (2005) Grandmothers' Diaries: A Glimpse at Daily Lives. *International Journal of Aging & Human Development* **60**(4): 317–329.

Nardi, P. M. (1992) That's What Friends Are for: Friends as Family in the Gay and Lesbian Community. K. Plummer, *Modern Homosexualities: Fragments of Lesbian and Gay Experience*. London, Routledge: 108–120.

Neale, B. et al. (2007) Young Lives and Times: the Dynamics of Young People's Relationships. Accessed 21 June 2007, http://www.reallifemethods. ac.uk/research/young/.

Neale, B. and J. Flowerdew (2003) Time, Texture and Childhood: The Contours of Longitudinal Research. *International Journal of Social Research Methodology* 6(3): 189–200.

Nelson, J. A. (1998) One Sphere or Two? *American Behavioural Scientist* **41**: 1467–1471.

Newton, E. (1995) *Cherry Grove, Fire Island: Sixty Years in America's First Gay and Lesbian Town*. Boston, MA, Beacon Press.

Nobes, G. and M. Smith (1997) Physical Punishment of Children in Two-Parent Families. *Clinical Child Psychology and Psychiatry* 2(2): 271–281.

Noland, C. M. (2006) Auto-Photography as Research Practice: Identity and Self-esteem Research. *Journal of Research Practice 2*. Accessed 11 April 2006, http://jrp.icaap.org/content/v2.1/noland.html.

O'Brien, M. et al. (1996) Children's Constructions of Family and Kinship. J. Brannen and B. O'Brien, *Children in Families: Research and Policy*. London, Falmer Press: 84–100.

O'Connor, P., et al. (2004) Relational Discourses: Social Ties with Family and Friends. *Childhood: A Global Journal of Child Research* 11(3): 361–382.

Oakley, A. (1981) Interviewing Women: A Contradiction in Terms. H. Roberts, *Doing Feminist Research*. London, Routledge & Kegan Paul: 30–61.

Ochiltree, G. (2006) *Grandparents, Grandchildren and the Generation Inbetween*. Camberwell, Victoria, Acer Press.

Okely, J. (1996) *Own or Other Culture*. London, Routledge.

Pahl, J. (1989) *Money and Marriage*. Basingstoke, Macmillan.

Pahl, R. and D. Pevalin (2005) Between Family and Friends: A Longitudinal Study of Friendship Choice. *British Journal of Sociology* 56(3): 433–450.

Pahl, R. and L. Spencer (1997) The Politics of Friendship. *Renewal* 5(34): 100–107.

Pahl, R. and L. Spencer (2004) Personal Communities: Not Simply Families of 'Fate' or 'Choice'. *Current Sociology* 52(2): 199–221.

Parsons, T. (1959) *The Social Structure of the Family*. Oxford, Blackwell.

Parsons, T. and R. Bales (1955) *Family, Socialisation and Interaction Process*. Glencoe, IL, Free Press.

Passmore, B. (1998) Less Freedom but More Intimacy. *Times Educational Supplement*.

Perlesz, A. and J. Lindsay (2003) Methodological Triangulation in Researching Families: Making Sense of Dissonant Data. *International Journal of Social Research Methodology* 6(1): 25–40.

Personal-Narratives-Group (ed.) (1989) *Interpreting Women's Lives: Feminist Theory and Personal Narratives*. Bloomington, IN, Indiana University Press.

Pfau-Effinger, B. (2004) Socio-historical Paths of the Male Breadwinner Model: An Explanation of Cross-National Differences. *British Journal of Sociology* 55(3): 377–399.

PFMA (2003) Pet Ownership, Pet Population Trends, Facts and Figures. Accessed 5 October 2003, http://www.pfma.com/petownershipstats.htm.

Platt, L. (2005) The Intergenerational Social Mobility of Minority Ethnic Groups. *Sociology* 39(3): 445–461.

Plummer, K. (1983) *Documents of Life*. London, George Allen & Unwin.

Plummer, K. (1990) Understanding Childhood Sexualities. *Journal of Homosexuality* 20(1/2): 231–249.

Plummer, K. (1995) *Telling Sexual Stories: Power, Change and Social Worlds*. London, Routledge.

Plummer, K. (1999) *Inventing Intimate Citizenship: An Agenda for Diversity and Rights?* Sexual Diversity and Human Rights: IASSCS, Manchester Metropolitan University.

Plummer, K. (2001) *Documents of Life 2. An Invitation to Critical Humanism*. London, Sage.

Plummer, K. (2003) *Intimate Citizenship: Private Decisions and Public Dialogues*. Seattle, WA and London, University of Washington Press.

Plumridge, L. and R. Thomson (2003) Longitudinal Qualitative Studies and the Reflexive Self. *International Journal of Social Research Methodology* 6(3): 213–223.

Portrie, T. and N. R. Hill (2005) Blended Families: A Critical Review of the Current Research. *Family Journal* 13(4): 445–451.

Prosser, J., Ed. (1998) *Image Based Research: A Sourcebook for Qualitative Researchers*. London, Falmer Press.

Punch, S. (2002) Research with Children: The Same or Different from Research with Adults? *Childhood* 9: 321–343.

Qvortrup, J. (1994) Childhood Matters: An Introduction. J. Qvortrup et al., *Childhood Matters: Social Theory, Practice and Politics*. Aldershot, Avebury: 1–24.

Race, K. E. et al. (1994) Rehabilitation Programme Evaluation: Use of Focus Groups to Empower Clients. *Evaluation Review* 18: 730–740.

Rahman, N. (1996) Caregivers' Sensitivity to Conflict: The Use of the Vignette Methodology. *Journal of Elder Abuse and Neglect* 8(1): 35–48.

Reay, D. (2000) A Useful Extension of Bourdieu's Conceptual Framework? Emotional Capital as a Way of Understanding Mothers' Involvement in Their Children's Education. *Sociological Review* 48(4): 568–585.

Renzetti, C. M. and R. M. Lee (1993) *Researching Sensitive Topics*. London, Sage.

Richardson, D. (1993) *Women, Motherhood and Childrearing*. Basingstoke, Macmillan.

Richardson, D. (1998) 'Sexuality and Citizenship'. *Sociology* 32(1): 83–100.

Rifkin, J. (2000) *Age of Access: The Culture of Hypercapitalism Where All Life is a Paid-up Experience*. New York, Jeremy P. Tarcher.

Robinson, V. et al. (2004) 'What I Used to Do ...On My Mother's Settee': Spatial and Emotional Aspects of Heterosexuality in England. *Gender, Place, Culture* 11(3): 417–435.

Rose, G. (1993) *Feminism and the Limits of Geographical Knowledge*. Cambridge, Polity Press.

Rose, G. (1995) Geography and Gender, Cartographies and Corporealities. *Progress in Human Geography* 19: 544–548.

Rose, G. (2000) *Visual Methodologies: An Introduction to Interpreting Visual Objects*. London, Sage.

Rose, G. (2003) Family Photographs and Domestic Spacings: A Case Study. *Transaction of the Institute of British Geographers* 28(1): 5–8.

Roseneil, S. (2000) Queer Frameworks and Queer Tendencies: Towards an Understanding of Postmodern Transformations of Sexuality. *Sociological Research Online* 5(3): www.socresonline.org.uk/5/3/roseneil.html.

Roseneil, S. and S. Budgeon (2004b) Cultures of Intimacy and Care Beyond 'the Family': Personal Life and Social Change in the Early 21st Century. *Current Sociology* 52(2): 135–159.

Roy, R. and J. F. Benenson (2000) Beyond Intimacy: Conceptualizing Sex Differences in Same-Sex Friendships. *Journal of Psychology* 134(1): 93.

Russell, D. (1990) *Rape in Marriage*. New York, Macmillan.

Sanders, G. S. and J. Suls (1982) Social Comparison, Competition and Marriage. *Journal of Marriage & Family* 44(3): 721.

Sandfort, T. (1987) *Boys on Their Contacts with Men*. Elmhurst, NY, Global Academic Publishers.

Sandfort, T. and J. Rademakers (2000) Childhood and Sexuality. *Journal of Psychology & Human Sexuality* 12(1/2).

Saunders, J. M. and J. N. Edwards (1984) Extramarital Sexuality: A Predictive Model of Permissive Attitudes. *Journal of Marriage & the Family*, 46: 825.

Schoenberg, N. E. and H. Ravdal (2000) Using Vignettes in Awareness and Attitudinal Research *International Journal of Social Research Methodology* 3(1): 63–75.

Schreurs, K. M. G. and B. P. Buunk (1996) Closeness, Autonomy, Equity and Relationship Satisfaction in Lesbian Couples. *Psychology of Women Quarterly* 20(4): 577.

Schwartz, D. (1989) Visual Ethnography: Using Photography in Qualitative Research. *Qualitative Sociology* 12(2): 267–300.

Scott, J. (2000) 'Is it a Different World to when You Were Growing up?' Generational Effects on Social Representations and Child-rearing Values. *British Journal of Sociology* 51(2): 355–376.

Scott, S. et al. (1998) Swings and Roundabouts: Risk Anxiety and the Everyday Worlds of Children. *Sociology* 32(4): 689–705.

Scott, S. and D. Morgan (eds.) (1993) *Body Matters: On the Sociology of the Body*. London, Routledge & Kegan Paul.

Seale, C. (1999) *The Quality of Qualitative Research*. London, Sage.

Seery, B. L. and M. S. Crowley (2000) Women's Emotion Work in the Family. Relationship Management and the Process of Building Father–Child Relationships. *Journal of Family Issues* 21(1): 100–127.

Seymour, J. (1992) Women's Time as a Household Resource. *Women's Studies International Forum* 15(2).

Sharpe, S. and R. Thomson (2005) *All You Need Is Love? Sexual Morality through the Eyes of Young People*. London, National Children's Bureau.

Sheehey, G. (1995) *New Passages: Mapping Your Life across Time*. New York, Ballantine.

Sieber, J. E. and B. Stanley (1988) Ethical and Professional Dimensions of Socially Sensitive Research. *American Psychologist* 43(1): 49–55.

Silva, E. B. (1996) *Good Enough Mothering? Feminist Perspectives on Lone Motherhood*. London, Routledge.

Silva, E. B. and C. Smart (1999) *The New Family?* London, Sage.

Silverman, D. (1993) *Interpreting Qualitative Data*. London, Sage.

Simonsen, K. (2000) Editorial: The Body as Battlefield. *Transactions of the Institute of British Geographers* 25(1): 7–9.

Sin, C. H. (2006) The Feasibility of Using National Surveys to Derive Samples of Older People from Different Ethnic Groups in Britain: Lessons from

'Piggy-Backing' on the Family Resources Survey. *International Journal of Social Research Methodology* 9(1): 15–28.

Sinclair, I. and I. Gibbs (1996) Quality of Care in Children's Homes. York, University of York/Department of Health.

Skeggs, B. (1997) *Formations of Class and Gender. Becoming Respectable*. London, Sage.

Skolnick, A. and J. Skolnick (eds.) (1974) *Intimacy, Family and Society*. Boston, MA, Little, Brown.

Smart, C. (2004a) Equal Shares: Rights for Fathers or Recognition for Children. *Critical Social Policy* 24(4): 484–503.

Smart, C. (2004b) Retheorizing Families. *Sociology* 38(5): 1043–1048.

Smart, C. (2007) *Personal Life*. Cambridge, Polity Press.

Smart, C. et al. (2001) *The Changing Experience of Childhood. Families and Divorce*. Cambridge, Polity.

Smart, C. and B. Shipman (2004) Visions in Monochrome: Families, Marriage and the Individualization Thesis. *British Journal of Sociology* 55(4): 491–509.

Smith, M. et al. (eds.) (1995) *Parental Control with the Family: The Nature and Extent of Parental Violence to Children*. Child Protection. Messages from Research. London, HMSO.

Smith, M. and M. Grocke (1995) Normal Family Sexuality and Sexual Knowledge in Children. *Child Protection. Messages from Research*. London, HMSO: 81–83.

Smith, N. (2003) Cross-sectional Profiling and Longitudinal Analysis. *International Journal of Social Research Methodology* 6(3): 273–278.

Smithson, J. (2000) *Using and Analysing Focus Groups: Limitations and Possibilities.*, Taylor & Francis.

Sobolewski, J. M. and V. King (2005) The Importance of the Coparental Relationship for Nonresident Fathers' Ties to Children. *Journal of Marriage and Family* 67(5): 1196–1212.

Solomon, Y. et al. (2002) Intimate Talk between Parents and their Teenage Children. Democratic Openness or Covert Control? *Sociology* 36(4): 965–983.

Spinetta, J. J. and D. Ringler (1972) The Child-Abusing Parent: A Psychological Review. *Psychological Bulletin* 77: 296–304.

Stacey, J. (1996) *In the Name of the Family. Rethinking Family Values in the Postmodern Age*. Boston, MA, Beacon Press.

Stacey, J. (2004) Cruising to Familyland: Gay Hypergamy and Rainbow Kinship. *Current Sociology* 52(2): 181–197.

Stake, R. E. (2005) Qualitative Case Studies. N. K. Denzin and Y. S. Lincoln. *Handbook of Qualitative Research*. London, Sage: 443–466.

Stanley, L. (ed.) (1990) *Feminist Research Praxis: Research, Theory and Epistemology in Feminist Sociology*. London, Routledge.

Stanley, L. (1995) *The Auto/Biographical I*. London, Manchester University Press.

Stone, L. D. and J. W. Pennebaker (2002) Trauma in Real Time: Talking and Avoiding Online Conversations about the Death of Princess Diana. *Basic and Applied Social Psychology* 24(3): 173–183.

Sturges, J. E. and K. J. Hanrahan (2004) Comparing Telephone and Face-to-Face Qualitative Interviewing: A Research Note. *Qualitative Research* 4(1): 107–118.

Sullivan, O. (2000) The Division of Domestic Labour: Twenty Years of Change. *Sociology* 34(3): 437–456.

Swindells, J. (1995) *The Uses of Autobiography: Feminist Perspectives on the Past and the Present*. London, Taylor & Francis.

Symon, G. (1998) Qualitative Research Diaries. G. Symon and C. Cassell, *Qualitative Methods and Analysis in Organizational Research: A Practical Guide*. London, Sage: 94–117.

Teachman, J. (2003) Premarital Sex, Premarital Cohabitation, and the Risk of Subsequent Marital Dissolution among Women. *Journal of Marriage & Family* 65(2): 444–455.

Temple, B. (1994) Combining Methods: Epistemological Considerations in the Study of Families and Households. *Journal of Family Issues* 15(4): 562–573.

Thomas, N. and C. O'Kane (1998) The Ethics of Participatory Research with Children. *Children And Society* 22: 336–348.

Thompson, L. et al. (1985) Developmental Stage and Perceptions of Intergenerational Continuity. *Journal of Marriage & Family* 47(4): 913.

Thompson, P. (2004) Researching Family and Social Mobility with Two Eyes. *International Journal of Social Research Methodology* 7(3): 237–257.

Thomson, E. S. and A. W. Laing (2003) 'The Net Generation': Children and Young People, the Internet and Online Shopping. *Journal of Marketing and Management* 19: 491–512.

Thomson, R. and J. Holland (2003) Hindsight, Foresight and Insight: The Challenges of Longitudinal Qualitative Research. *International Journal of Social Research Methodology* 6(3): 233–244.

Thomson, R. et al. (2003) Editorial. Longitudinal Qualitative Research: A Developing Methodology. *International Journal of Social Research Methodology*: 185–188.

Throop, E. A. (1999) *Net Curtains and Closed Doors: Intimacy, Family and Public Life in Dublin*. New York, Bergin & Garvey.

Tizard, B. and A. Phoenix (2003) *Black, White or Mixed Race: Race and Racism in the Lives of Young People of Mixed Parentage*. London, Routledge.

Tomanovic, S. (2003) Capturing Change: Doing Research in a Society Undergoing Transformation. *International Journal of Social Research Methodology* 6(3): 267–272.

Turner, B. (1984) *The Body and Society*. Oxford, Blackwell.

Turney, L. and C. Pocknee. (2005) Virtual Focus Groups: New Frontiers in Research. *International Journal of Qualitative Methods 4(2)* Accessed 6 August 2006, http://www.ualberta.ca/~ijqm/english/engframeset.htm.

Twigg, J. (2000) *Bathing. The Body and Community Care*. London, Routledge.

Valentine, G. (1999) Doing Household Research: Interviewing Couples Together and Apart. *Area* 31(1): 67–74.

Valentine, G. and S. L. Holloway (2002) Exploring Children's Identities and Social Networks in On-line and Off-line Worlds. *Annals of the Association of American Geographers* 92: 296–315.

Van den Hoonaard, W. C. (1997) *Working with Sensitising Concepts: Analytical Field Research*. London, Sage.

VanEvery, J. (1995) *Heterosexual Women Changing the Family: Refusing to be a 'Wife'!* London, Taylor & Francis.

Vincent, C. and S. J. Ball (2006) *Childcare, Choice and Class Practices*. London, Taylor & Francis.

Waddington, K. (2005) Using Diaries to Explore the Characteristics of Work-related Gossip. *Journal of Occupational & Organizational Psychology* **78**(2): 221–236.

Walby, S. (1997) *Gender Transformations*. London, Routledge.

Walker, A. (2004) The ESRC Growing Older Research Programme, 1999–2004. *Ageing & Society* **24**(5): 657–674

Walker, A. and L. Thompson (1983) Intimacy and Intergenerational Aid and Contact among Mothers and Daughters. *Journal of Marriage & Family* **45**: 841–848.

Walkerdine, V. (2001) Safety and Danger. Childhood, Sexuality and Space at the End of the Millennium. K. Hultqvist and G. Dahlberg, *Governing the Child in the New Millennium*. New York, Routledge Falmer: 15–34.

Walkerdine, V. and H. Lucey (1989) *Democracy in the Kitchen: Regulating Mothers and Socialising Daughters*. London, Virago.

Wang, C. and M. A. Burris (1997) Photovoice; Concept, Methodology and Use for Participatory Needs Assessment. *Health and Behaviour* **24**(3): 369–387.

Ward, J. and Z. Henderson (2003) Some Practical and Ethical Issues Encountered while Conducting Tracking Research with Young People Leaving the 'Care' System. *International Journal of Social Research Methodology* **6**(3): 255–260.

Warren, T. (2003) Class- and Gender-based Working Time? Time Poverty and the Division of Domestic Labour. *Sociology* **37**(4): 733–752.

Warren, T. (2004) Working Part-time: Achieving a Successful 'Work–Life' Balance? *British Journal of Sociology* **55**(1): 99–122.

Wasoff, F. et al. (2005) Solo Living, Individual and Family Boundaries. L. McKie and S. Cunningham-Burley, *Families in Society. Boundaries and Relationships*. Bristol, Policy Press: 207–226.

Weeks, J. (1986) *Sexuality*. London, Routledge.

Weeks, J. (1998) 'The Sexual Citizen'. *Theory, Culture, Society* **15**(3/4): 35–52.

Weeks, J. et al. (1999) Everyday Experiments: Narratives of Non-heterosexual Relationships. E. B. Silva and C. Smart, *The New Family?* London, Sage: 83–99.

Weeks, J. et al. (2001) *Same Sex Intimacies: Families of Choice and Other Life Experiments*. New York, Routledge.

Wengraf, T. (2001) *Qualitative Research Interviewing: Biographic Narrative and Semi-structured Method*. London, Sage.

Wesson, M. and K. Salmon (2001) Drawing and Showing: Helping Children to Report Emotionally Laden Events. *Applied Cognitive Psychology* **15**: 301–320.

Weston, K. (1997) *Families We Chose. Lesbians, Gays, Kinship*. New York, Columbia University Press.

Wheelock, J. and K. Jones (2002) 'Grandparents Are the Next Best Thing': Informal Childcare for Working Parents in Urban Britain. *Journal of Social Policy* **31**(3): 441–464.

Wiederman, M. W. (2000) Women's Body Image. Self-Consciousness during Physical Intimacy with a Partner. *Journal of Sex Research* **37**(1): 60–68.

Wiles, R. et al. (2006) Researching Researchers: Lessons from Research. *Qualitative Research* **6**(3): 283–299.

Wilkinson, S. (1998) Focus Group Methodology: A Review. *Social Research Methodology* **1**(3): 181–203.

Williams, F. (2004) *Rethinking Families. Moral Tales of Parenting and Step-Parenting*. London, Calouste Gulbenkian Foundation.

Williams, L. M. and D. Finkelhor (1995) Paternal Care-Giving and Incest. *American Journal of Orthopsychiatry* **65**(1): 101–113.

Winnicott, D. W. (1965) *The Family and Individual Development*. London, Tavistock.

Woodhead, M. et al. (eds.) (1991) *Growing up in a Changing Society*, Buckingham, Open University.

Wyre, R. and T. Tate (1995) *The Murder of Childhood*. Harmondsworth, Penguin Books.

Yan, Y. (2003) *Private Life under Socialism: Love, Intimacy and Family Change in a Chinese Village, 1949–1999*. Palo Alto, CA, Stanford University Press.

Yaughn, E. and S. Nowicki Jr. (1999) Close Relationships and Complementary Interpersonal Styles among Men and Women. *Journal of Social Psychology* **139**(4): 473–478.

Young, I. M. (1990) *Throwing Like a Girl and Other Essays in Feminist Philosophy and Social Theory*. Bloomington and Indianapolis, IN, Indiana University Press.

Young, I. M. (1997) Asymmetrical Reciprocity: On Moral Respect, Wonder, and Enlarged Thought. *Constellations* **3**(3): 340–363.

Zelizer, V. A. (2005) *The Purchase of Intimacy*. Princeton, NJ, Princeton University Press.

Ziller, R. C. (1990) *Photographing the Self: Methods for Observing Personal Orientations*. Newbury Park, CA, Sage.

Zimmerman, D. H. and L. Wieder (1977) The Diary-Interview Method. *Urban Life* **5**(4): 479–497.

Index

advice
  'good parenting', 85–6, 107–8, 163
  'simulations of intimacy', 86
age/generation
  children's age/maturity, 5, 69, 74,
    83, 100–2, 107, 156–7, 170
  retirement, 176–7, 180–1
  see also lifecourse

Bailey, J., 88–9
Beck, U., 71–2
Beck-Gernsheim, E., 71–2
Berlant, L., 77, 89, 130
BNIM (biographical narrative
    interview method), 9, 24, 51–4,
    150–4, 176–7, 180, 184
  see also interviews; Wengraf
body language, 126–7, 170–1
  see also embodiment
boundaries of intimacy, 77, 93,
    115–18, 165–6, 169–73
  setting/management, 100, 106–8,
    159–62, 170–2, 175
  public/private, 88–9, 92–3, 106,
    161–3
  self/other, 106, 126–8
  see also risk; rules

case studies, 58–60, 153, 167–8, 184–5
child abuse
  impacts of, 86, 105, 107, 139, 163
  perceptions of, 106, 158–61
  research, 22–4, 55, 82–4
  see also risk
child-centredness, 108–10, 130, 165–6
  investment in child/family, 103,
    108–10, 122, 129–30, 140–1,
    153, 165–6, 175
childhood
  research approaches, 18–21, 26,
    32–4, 39–41, 43–5, 49–51, 54–5,
    133–5, 144, 150, 156–7, 168

  sexuality, 68–9, 159–61
citizenship
  intimate, 88–96, 163
  sexual, 78, 85, 93–4
class, 73, 75, 109–10, 122, 128
  social/cultural capital, 21, 148
'coming-out', 39, 128
companionate marriage, 113
conflict
  avoidance, 118, 154–6, 170–1
  management, 40, 100, 118, 182–3
  spaces/places of, 136–8
couples, 14, 16–17
  'couple time', 118, 123, 161
  friendship/companionship, 77–8,
    112–14
  intimate relationship, 67–8, 71–2,
    124, 142–3, 161, 183
  research techniques, 27, 44, 142–4
cross-sectional analysis, 60–2

Daly, K., 31
Deegan, M. J., 67
democracy
  communication, 74–5, 99–100
  gender/generation, 74–5
  parenting practices, 73–5, 100–1,
    173–4
  rhetoric, 99–102, 171, 173–4
democratisation thesis, 70, 71–5,
    97–8, 113, 115
diaries, 8, 41–3, 140–4, 173–6, 181,
    183–4
divorce, 15, 17, 75–6, 112, 151
Doucet, A., 44
Dunne, G., 41, 44, 70, 128

economy
  and intimacy, 90–3, 120–1
  see also 'gift exchange'
Edwards, R., 22, 23, 88–9

'transformation of intimacy', 16, 65, 70–1, 99–100, 167
trust, 11, 16, 81, 123, 171–2
Twigg, J., 67–8

vignettes, 9, 54–5, 63, 154, 157–63, 171–2
visual methods, 43–8, 133–40, 159–63, 170–1
  see also emotion maps; interviews; observation methods; participatory methods

Warner, M., 77, 89, 130
Weeks, J., 70, 72, 76, 79, 93–4
Wengraf, T., 24, 51–2, 150
  see also BNIM
women
  sex and intimacy, 67, 143, 171–2
  friendships, 103–4, 113, 171–2
  see also gender; mothers

Young, I. M., 79–80, 99

Zelizer, V., 90–3, 122–3